Teachers' Professional Lives

New Prospects Series

General Editors: Professor Ivor Goodson. Faculty of
                   Education. University of Western
                   Ontario. Canada and
                   Professor Andy Hargreaves. Ontario
                   Institute for Studies in Education.
                   Canada.

Teachers' Professional Lives

Edited by

Ivor F. Goodson

and

Andy Hargreaves

 Falmer Press

(A member of the Taylor & Francis Group)
London • Washington, D.C.

UK   Falmer Press, 1 Gunpowder Square, London, EC4A 3DE
USA Falmer Press, Taylor & Francis Inc., 1900 Frost Road, Suite 101, Bristol, PA 19007

First published in 1996

A catalogue record for this book is available from the British Library

Library of Congress Cataloging-in-Publication Data are available on request

ISBN 0 7507 0513 2 cased
ISBN 0 7507 0514 0 paper

Jacket design by Caroline Archer

Typeset in 10/12pt Times by
Graphicraft Typesetters Ltd., Hong Kong.

Printed in Great Britain by Biddles Ltd., Guildford and King's Lynn on paper which has a specified pH value on final paper manufacture of not less than 7.5 and is therefore 'acid free'.

Contents

Contents

Editorial Preface

Setting professional standards and redefining what it means to be professional in teaching are at the forefront of educational reform. Universities and unions, governments and business all have aspirations to raise the professional status of teaching and establish professional standards for their work. Professional development and training are experiencing sweeping changes, professional standards are being created, self-regulating, professional bodies for teachers are being set up.

Yet while the aspirations for greater professionalism in teaching are admirable, what such professionalism might mean is often vague, unclear or contested. Moreover, what teachers themselves think about professionalism or what they experience under its name are addressed too rarely. This international book examines just what's behind the push for professionalism. A key opening chapter sets out the field and distinguishes between six different models of meanings of professionalism. With others, it disentangles altruistic visions of professionalism from ones that are nakedly self-serving, or that disguise and excuse the imposition of even greater bureaucratic control. Other chapters portray what teacher professionalism and teachers' professional lives look like in practice, in the daily working lives of teachers themselves.

The movement for teacher professionalism, professional standards and professional self-regulation has become a bandwagon for academic and bureaucratic cheerleaders who presume to know what is best for teachers. This timely book takes discussion off the bandwagon and lodges it firmly within the working lives and realities of teachers themselves.

The chapters in this book have all been written specially for it. They come from experienced researchers across the world in North America, England, Australia, Israel and Scandinavia, who have been stimulated by our own professional network of inquiry and dialogue that has helped push our thinking in international and interdisciplinary ways on what teacher professionalism is, what it means, and whether it is always a good thing.

Building collaborative communities of critical colleagues is as difficult in educational research as it is in schoolteaching, and we are grateful for the various funding bodies who have believed in the value of professional dialogue, and supported our efforts to interact electronically and in person in pursuit of greater knowledge and understanding of these important challenges that confront teaching and education.

Among the groups and individuals we would like to thank for supporting our network, Professional Actions and Cultures of Teaching (PACT), and this book which has sprung from it are our financial supporters: the Ontario Public School Teachers' Federation of Canada who provided the seed funding for our first meeting in San Francisco; the Social Science and Humanities Research Council of Canada who have funded the secretariat for the International and Canadian networks; and several bodies in England who financed PACT members to organize and present at an important national conference on teacher education reform. Supporters for this event included the Roehampton Institute, the Association of Teachers and Lecturers, the National Association of Headteachers, the Association of University Teachers and the *Times Educational Supplement*.

The production of this book would not have been possible without the brilliant organizational skills and editorial attentiveness of Alicia Fernandez, PACT's Administrator. Bob Macmillan, Alicia's predecessor, was vital in making PACT an effective collaborative force in its early days. Leo Santos and Odilla Van Delinder have provided their usual invaluable secretarial assistance in making elegant tableaux of the chaotic fragments which we academics put before them. Many thanks to all of you.

We also would like to thank Malcolm Clarkson at Falmer Press for his financial and intellectual support of the conference at Spencer Hall, London Ontario at which many of these papers were first presented. We would also like to thank Odilla Van Delinder for her substantial help in organizing this conference and the workers and management at Spencer Hall for their splendid, nay lavish, hospitality.

We believe that effective professional collaboration among teachers works best when it is directed by members of the professional community themselves, within facilitating structures and on the basis of enabling resources that others who believe in their vision, and trust them to bring it to fruition, are prepared to risk making available. Our own professional community, embodied in PACT, has been built on a similarly risky vision. Our colleagues in PACT and external supporters of it deserve our most heartfelt gratitude for committing to it with us. What we advocate for others, we should try and practise ourselves. In this sense, PACT has represented our own joyful struggle to establish and develop the kind of postmodern professional community we would like to see more educators seeking for themselves. *Teachers' Professional Lives* is PACT's first concrete product; the first published 'fruit' of its labour. We hope our readers will find much of value in it to inform all our individual searches and collective struggles for better professional lives.

Ivor Goodson
Andy Hargreaves

Chapter 1

Teachers' Professional Lives: Aspirations and Actualities

Andy Hargreaves and Ivor Goodson

Introduction

The struggle of teachers for professional recognition and for the associated working conditions and rewards that might bring it about has a long and chequered history. More pay, higher status, greater autonomy, increased self-regulation and improved standards of training — these recurrent themes have underscored the individual and collective struggles of teachers for many decades. Yet, notwithstanding a few historical and geographical exceptions such as the substantial salaries achieved by Canadian teachers in the 1970s, the high degree of autonomy over curriculum development and decision-making enjoyed by British teachers in the 1960s and early 1970s (Grace, 1987) and the conversion of teaching to an all-graduate profession during the same period almost everywhere, the project of professionalization has been steadfastly resisted by cost-conscious, and control-centred governments and bureaucracies. Collectively and individually, teachers themselves have also often seemed ambivalent about whether their identity is that of professionals or cultural workers. They have therefore been uncertain and inconsistent about whether they should pursue middle class status in 'acceptable professional' ways, or use the collective strategies of union bargaining to defend their interests (Ginsburg *et al.*, 1980; Carlson, 1992; Bascia, 1994).

For these reasons and others, teacher professionalization has been a historically precarious project: resisted by governments, bureaucracies and business interests without, and undermined by ambiguities of loyalty, strategy and identity within. Recent years have seen an intriguing twist in this familiar tale, however. Across many parts of the world, teacher professionalization is now being sponsored with exceptional vigour by governments, bureaucracies and big business. There seems to be an enormous interest, politically and administratively in identifying, codifying and applying professional standards of practice to the teaching force. A National Board of Professional Teaching Standards has been established in the United States, which teachers can choose to join by having their knowledge and skills inspected and certified by their peers. In England and Wales, the creation of a General Teaching Council has been proclaimed as a policy priority by the opposition Labour Party. In Australia, several states have created career ladder structures for newly designated 'advanced skills teachers', who receive modest increments of pay for excellence in classroom teaching and teacher leadership, as attested to by their peers. Nationally, Australian teacher unions and state employers have also jointly established a standard-certifying Council of Teachers, with voluntary member-ship, much on the lines of the National Board of Professional Teaching Standards in the USA. The Canadian province of Ontario has gone further than this and fol-lowed the recommendations of a Royal Commission on Learning by legislating a self-regulating Teachers' Council or College of Teachers as it is known, which all teachers will be required to join if they are to be granted certificates to practise. This self-regulating college or council, will draw up and maintain an official regis-ter of teachers, define standards of practice, establish a province-wide framework for professional learning and leadership training, and accredit all programmes of teacher education (including postgraduate programmes of teacher preparation that have been legislatively lengthened to two-years).

Alongside these initiatives which might seem to support the project of teacher professionalization are ones in other jurisdictions which appear categorically bent on achieving just the opposite effect. In a number of American states, for example, teachers have been compelled to take written tests of basic competency in order to retain their qualifications to teach. Moreover, continuing conditions of low pay where US teachers earn 20 per cent to 30 per cent less than other similarly educated workers, more competition for the skills of able women from fields of employ-ment outside teaching, the creation of alternate certification arrangements to recruit teachers for the inner cities, and difficulties of finding qualified teachers in a number of shortage subject areas, have led to a position where, in 1991, one in four new entrants to teaching held a substandard certificate or none at all (Darling-Hammond, 1994, p. 8). Indeed the number of bachelor's degrees conferred in education actu-ally declined by over 50 per cent between 1972 and 1987 (p. 6).

The Government of England and Wales, meanwhile, has started to dig up and destroy some of the traditional paths to professionalization by making postgraduate courses of preparation for secondary teachers predominantly school-based, by estab-lishing schemes to allocate funds directly to schools rather than universities as centres of teacher training, and by attenuating the links between teacher training and universities in general (A. Hargreaves, 1995; Barton *et al.*, 1994). More broadly, while movements towards site-based management in schools may have involved teachers more in school development planning and collective decision-making, this has often been in a context where overall budgets have been reduced ('we give you less; you allocate it'); where many of the major areas of decision-making in terms of curriculum outcomes and testing requirements have been arrogated to the centre ('we set the ends: you deliver the means'); and where what schools and teachers are required to manage is downloaded administrivia rather than issues of fun-damental purpose and direction ('we control; you manage') (Robertson, 1993). As Darling-Hammond (1993) has noted, 'we see states passing laws that pay lip service to teacher professionalism while, with the other hand, they erect greater restraints on curricula, textbooks, tests and teaching methods' (p. 60). Paradoxically, some of the jurisdictions that have been most proactive on teacher professionalization issues are the selfsame ones that have capped teachers' salaries (e.g., Ontario, Canada), made sweeping job cuts (e.g., Victoria, Australia) or reduced resourcing for education in general. Persuasive rhetorics of professionalization all too often seem to be accompanied by conditions where professionalization is actually being dismantled.

Contemporary projects of teacher professionalization therefore seem paradoxical, confused and contradictory. Teacher professionalization appears to be advancing in some respects; retreating in others. In part, this may come down to a simple distinction between rhetoric and reality. In some ways, the title of our book, *Teachers' Professional Lives*, perhaps speaks more to aspirations than actualities. Teachers deserve and demand professional lives but some of the new directions and developments may mean that this historic aspiration is being seriously threatened. Somehow, *Teachers' Proletarianized Lives* does not have the same ring to it (not, we thought, the optimistic, motivational stuff of a best selling book!). But to some extent, economic and policy forces are indeed pushing the life and work of the teacher in disturbing directions. As 'fast capitalism' is eroding workers' lives generally, these forces are also beginning to attack the professional lives of teachers through reduced resources, wage restraints and the restructuring of what teachers are expected to do. For this reason, we have adopted the title of our book knowingly: cognizant of the fact that while the aspiration is legitimate, the possibilities are perilous. Hence the title of this book provides a benchmark, a desirable aspirational plateau, from which to scrutinize new developments and directions in the teacher's life and work.

A second way to interpret the seeming paradoxes of teacher professionalization is to see that some parts of the teacher's work are becoming *reprofessionalized* in ways that involve broader tasks, greater complexity, more sophisticated judgment, and collective decision-making among colleagues, while other parts of the work are becoming *deprofessionalized* in terms of more pragmatic training, reduced discretion over goals and purposes, and increased dependence on detailed learning outcomes prescribed by others (e.g., Barton *et al.*, 1994). We will say more about these processes of *deprofessionalization* and *reprofessionalization* a little later.

Thirdly, governmental and administrative sponsorship of teacher professionalization may also signal a shift in the *steering mechanisms* the State uses to regulate education. As states in fiscal crisis find they are unable to sustain large educational bureaucracies and their more direct forms of administrative control, the tasks and costs of licensing and registering teachers, monitoring standards of conduct and practice, handling promotions and securing dismissals can be handed over to teachers themselves as matters for self-regulation (paid for by member subscription!), as can the detailed delivery of centrally defined outcomes through school development planning, site-based decision-making and the like. Yet self-regulation and collegial decision-making are not simply cynical in their origins and consequences. The empowering effects of these professionalizing tendencies for building strong senses of professional competence and community among teachers should not be underestimated (Talbert and McLaughlin, 1994). Teacher professionalization may well mark a shift in the mechanisms of state steering (through self-regulation of means) *and* in opportunities for empowerment as well. How these twin tendencies play out in practice is an important subject for investigation and analysis.

The aspiration for teachers to have professional lives is not a given phenomenon but a contested one, then. It marks a struggle to redefine the work of teaching by governments, administrators, business and teachers themselves. Achieving the actuality of professional lives in teaching is not easy. Nor is it totally clear what this aspiration for professional lives might mean, or entail, even if it could be realized.

What it means to be professional, to show professionalism or to pursue professionalization is not universally agreed or understood. Some writers, including several in this volume, do draw an important distinction between *professionalization* as a social and political project or mission designed to enhance the interests of an occupational group, and *professionalism* as something which defines and articulates the quality and character of people's actions within that group. But beyond this, what counts as professional knowledge and professional action in teaching is open to many different interpretations. Current debates about teacher professionalism and professionalization reveal at least five different often overlapping discourses which carry different connotations of what it means for teachers to be professionals. These discourses are ones that we call classical professionalism, flexible professionalism, practical professionalism, extended professionalism and complex professionalism. We then want to sketch out a preliminary agenda for a sixth form of teacher professionalism — which we call postmodern professionalism.

In the remainder of this opening chapter, we want to describe and analyse these discourses, along with their claims and assumptions regarding teacher professionalism and professionalization. We will examine to what extent and in what ways these discourses advance the cause of *professionalization* (and whether that is altogether a good thing). We will also investigate whether conversely and perversely, the discourses foster contrary processes of *deprofessionalization* too. Moreover, we will pose questions as to whether projects of *professionalization* and commitments to *professionalism* seem to work together in tandem or in contrary directions. As we undertake this analysis, we will draw on the chapters published in this collection. These chapters have been solicited to highlight the ordinary conceptions of professionalism and professional knowledge that are now pervasive in teaching, and to illuminate the paths which the project of teacher professionalization appears to be following.

Forms of Professionalism

Classical Professionalism

Classical professionalism has historically rested on the exemplary claims to professional status of law and medicine. In seeking professional status and recognition, it is the claims of these highly ranked, publicly recognizable and largely masculine professions that teachers have usually tried to emulate — not the less recognizable professions like architecture or dentistry, and certainly not the more female (and arguably more closely related) 'semi-professions' (Etzioni, 1969) of nursing, social work or librarianship (Soder, 1990).

What Lindblad (1993) has called a *naive* view of professionalism has tended to endorse and celebrate high status professionals' views of themselves (e.g., Parsons, 1954).

> By and large, it was assumed that those in professions were benign and altruistic beings serving society by combining the virtues of rationality, technique, control and codes of ethics, and only incidentally (albeit deservedly) reaping pecuniary and other rewards. (Soder, 1990, pp. 38–9)

Within this naive or benign view, 'professions' (modelled after law and medicine) have been characterized as having a specialized knowledge base or *shared technical culture*; a strong *service ethic* with a commitment to meeting clients' needs; and *self-regulated*, collegial control rather than external bureaucratic control over recruitment and training, codes of ethics and standards of practice. Much of the literature on teacher professionalism and professionalization has measured teachers' work and occupational status against these criteria, and found them largely wanting. In his classic study of school teachers, Lortie (1975, p. 23) argued that teaching was only 'partially professionalized' at best. 'Although teachers have managed to dull the edges of administrative power, they continue to be employed subordinates' (p. 22).

Let's look at just one of the characteristics of a profession in the classical sense, that of a shared technical culture, and see how well teaching fares in relation to it. In an occupation where teachers gave high primacy to personal experience, Lortie found little evidence of a 'shared technical culture of teaching' (pp. 69–70). Indeed, workplace conditions of classroom isolation discouraged teachers from sharing and developing the technical aspects of their work (also Little, 1984; Rosenholtz, 1989; Flinders, 1988). David Hargreaves (1980) argued that secondary school teachers might claim some semblance of technical expertise in the knowledge base of their subject matter (although school subject knowledge often lagged seriously behind the university disciplines themselves), but primary or elementary teachers, stripped of any subject pretensions, had few shared technical conceptions and little specialized language concerning child development or pedagogy. On most matters, Philip Jackson (1968) argued, teachers' language was quite indistinguishable from ordinary language. Practical experience, not scientific theory was what teachers found most useful in their work (A. Hargreaves, 1984). Teaching was neither technical nor shared. It did not measure up to this professional mark.

One response to this problem of professional definition has been to categorize and codify the practical and experiential knowledge that teachers already have in more technical and scientific terms. In this neo-classical or neo-technical attempt to reinvent teacher professionalism, the central project has become one of redefining a knowledge base for teaching. The knowledge base of teaching, it is argued, should consist of 'a codified or codifiable aggregation of knowledge, skill, understanding and technology, of ethics and disposition, of collective responsibility — as well as a means of representing it' (Shulman, 1987, p. 4). One important part of this knowledge base is what Shulman (1986) calls 'pedagogical content knowledge': 'that amalgam of content and pedagogy that is uniquely the province of teachers, their own special form of professional understanding' (Shulman, 1987, p. 8). Pedagogical content knowledge is the knowledge of how to teach one's subject or subject matter. Its possession, it is claimed, is one key factor that distinguishes experts from novices in the classroom. By explicating this knowledge, it is argued, one can make teachers' intuitive, practical know-how and technique into visible, codifiable, professional knowledge. Indeed, Shulman's outline of the new knowledge base for teaching has been explicitly incorporated into definitions of standards of practice in the National Board of Professional Teaching Standards in the USA, and in similar efforts in Australia and elsewhere.

This academic quest to develop and clarify a knowledge base for teaching tries to build an edifice of teacher professionalism and professionalization on a foundation of *scientific certainty*. But it seems to us to be problematic. Indeed, in important ways, this strategy of *professionalization* may actually undermine *teachers' professionalism*: the ethics and purposes that guide teachers' actions, and the extent to which teachers are able to pursue these purposes with fidelity and integrity. How is this so?

After a systematic comparison of teaching and medicine, Soder (1990, p. 68) concludes that 'teaching cannot achieve the high status of medicine by following the medical model of professionalization'. Principally, this is because 'the probability of teachers . . . developing a new technology' as medicine did, 'is very low' (p. 67). For all their virtues, pedagogical content knowledge, cooperative learning strategies and the like scarcely constitute the kinds of scientific and technological breakthroughs achieved by medicine. Claims for professionalization predicated on the medical model of scientific certainty and novelty can therefore seem transparently inauthentic. Even arguments for lengthening the period of postgraduate teacher preparation to two years can stretch public credibility to the limits, given that the existence of a new technology for teaching which might demand more training, is not demonstrable.

Over sixty years ago, Willard Waller observed that:

> It is sometimes proposed to remedy the low standing of the teaching profession by making teaching a real profession. Let it be known that teaching is a difficult art, and one that requires years of expensive training, say those who argue for this remedy, and the people will esteem their teachers accordingly. As a part of this program, it is usually proposed to increase the amount of teacher training necessary for obtaining a teaching position. (Waller, 1932, p. 64)

Such strategies can seem manifestly self-serving: more suited to the career interests of teachers and teacher educators themselves than to the quality of service they can provide to those who teach. Furthermore, while the medical model is often emulated as the prototype of successful *professionalization* (as a strategy), it is by no means a paragon of *professionalism* (as quality of judgment and action). Doctors and lawyers are notoriously self-protective in the face of public complaint and criticism. Their monopoly over service creates dependency among their clients. They have been cynically systematic in the ways they have discredited other occupations who impinged on their professional territory and their claims to exclusivity: for instance, with regard to holistic and chiropractic medicine. And, behind closed doors, doctors are also deeply divided among themselves, with subspecialisms like obstetrics, paediatrics, neurological and geriatric medicine engaged in scrambles for higher status, reward and recognition (Bucher and Strauss, 1961) — just as school subject communities compete for status in the world of education (Goodson, 1993; 1995).

It may not be true that, as Adam Smith said, 'every profession is a conspiracy against the people'. It is, however, certainly true that professional groups construct their 'missions' in terms of the pursuit of status and resources (i.e., professionalization projects), as well as broader ideals (including these groups' representations of their own 'professionalism'). Our worry is that the self-interested pursuit of *professionalization* (along the lines of the medical model) may actually undercut the very *professionalism* (commitment to quality of service) and wider ideals which teachers claim to embrace. A good illustration of our point here is the case of teacher education.

Some years ago, Veblen (1962, p. 15) said that 'the difference between the modern university and the lower schools (such as education) is broad and simple; not so much a difference of degree as of kind'. This distinctiveness of purpose and mission 'unavoidably leads them to court a specious appearance of scholarship and so to invest their technological discipline with a degree of pedantry and sophistication whereby it is hoped to give these schools and their work some scientific and scholarly prestige (p. 23). More recently, Clifford and Guthrie have argued that:

> schools of education, particularly those located on the campuses of prestigious research universities, have become ensnared improvidently in the academic and political cultures of their institutions and have neglected their professional allegiances. They are like marginal men, aliens in their own worlds. They have seldom succeeded in satisfying the scholarly norms of their campus letters and science colleagues, and they are simultaneously estranged from their practicing professional peers. The more forcefully they have rowed toward the shores of scholarly research, the more distant they have become from the public schools they are duty bound to serve. Conversely, systematic efforts at addressing the applied problems of public schools have placed schools of education at risk on their own campuses. (Clifford and Guthrie, 1988, pp. 3–4)

In short, the schools of education may have entered into a *devil's bargain* when they entered the university milieu. Marginalized by status and geography from the rest of the university and from the schools beyond, they turned towards the university for identity and recognition (A. Hargreaves, 1995). Their mission changed from being primarily concerned with matters central to the practice of schooling, towards issues of status passage through more conventional university scholarship. Hence, faculties of education codified and created bodies of knowledge to maximize the terms of the *devil's bargain*. Bodies of knowledge were created with two major functions: the creation of a corpus of 'expert knowledge with which to instruct trainee teachers; secondly, and closely allied to this, bodies of knowledge were designed to maximize status and esteem within the university milieu. Disciplinary theory served both purposes and symbolically enshrined the essentially academic and scholarly purposes of the faculties of education. Labaree (1992) has noted that the first two Holmes Group reports in the United States which sought to increase the academic respectability of teacher education, met the professionalization needs of teacher education faculties much more than those of teachers. Similarly, the most recent attempts of Shulman and others to classify a knowledge base for teaching can be seen as one more attempt to professionalize teaching and teacher education by providing a seemingly scientific basis for their practice (Goodson, 1995).

The devil's bargain in education can be seen as an especially pernicious form of a more general displacement of discourse and debate within the development of university knowledge and its production. University knowledge evolved as separate and distinct from public knowledge, for as Mills (1979) noted: 'Men of knowledge (sic) do not orient themselves exclusively toward the total society, but to special segments (i.e., élite and scholastic ones — eds) of that society with special demands, criteria of validity, of significant knowledge, of pertinent problems, etc.'

Mills worried that knowledge produced in this way did not have public relevance, and was not related to public and practical concerns:

> Only where publics and leaders are responsive and responsible, are human affairs in democratic order, and only when knowledge has public relevance is this order possible. Only when mind has an autonomous basis, independent of power, but powerfully related to it, can it exert its force in the shaping of human affairs. Such a position is democratically possible only when there exists a free and knowledgeable public, to which men of knowledge may address themselves, and to which men of power are truly responsible. Such a public and such men — either of power or of knowledge, do not now prevail, and accordingly, knowledge does not now have democratic relevance in America. (Mills, 1979, p. 613)

The problems Mills describes are particularly acute when the knowledge that is produced relates to schooling. The kinds of knowledge valued by secondary school teachers in particular as well as those who train them — academic, abstract and rooted in the structures and traditions of university disciplines — is precisely the knowledge which children who are poor, working-class or members of racial minorities find irrelevant and hard to achieve at. A science of teaching based on classifications of content knowledge, pedagogical knowledge, pedagogical content knowledge and so on, also privileges knowledge and cognition above care as the foundation of schoolteaching — yet it is the absence of being cared for much more than the absence of being cognitively challenged that mainly leads young people to drop out of secondary school (Noddings, 1992; Hargreaves, Earl and Ryan, 1996). Care as well as cognition should be at the heart of the teaching profession and for many teachers is so. Yet, Sockett (1987) argues that Shulman's elaboration of pedagogical content knowledge as part of a new, scientific knowledge base for teaching, ignores almost everything that is specifically moral, emotional and contextual about teaching. The proper comparisons, in terms of teaching wider missions of caring and social justice, are probably those of nursing, social work and other 'caring' professions rather than the 'higher status' (and mainly masculine) professions of medicine and law. Yet the status aspiration to be like lawyers and doctors (for teachers), or 'real' university professors (for teacher educators), puts the pursuit of professionalization as a self-interested status strategy before the wider social and educational purposes of teacher professionalism in terms of providing service and social justice for the community as a whole. The cart of professionalization is repeatedly put before professionalism's horse.

As Lasch (1995) has recently inveighed, American democracy is threatened precisely because of the 'revolt of élites': of professional communities which evolved as self-serving professionalization projects. Many worthwhile social movements have stumbled into this fissure. Our fear is that teaching and teacher education will fall among them. In this volume, Englund captures the dangers that lurk here, when he cites Burbules and Densmore (1986):

> Rather than relying on an undemocratic concept that connotes privilege, special status, and the superiority of mental over manual labor, teachers should look to other bases for organization. A progressive strategy would emphasize the common purposes and commitments to education that we must build in a democracy and place these squarely in the public domain, not within the professional associations of an occupational elite. (Burbules and Densmore, 1986)

If pursuing professionalization through claims to *scientific certainty*, along the lines of the medical model will always have its problems, it is also true that the conditions in which professionalization is now being pursued are currently ones of profound social change. Harvey has provided a particularly valuable summary of this new 'condition of postmodernity' — a world of globalization in business and professions, where new divisions of labour are being defined and where flexible economies or what he calls 'flexible accumulation regimes' are leading to fundamental changes in people's working lives (Harvey, 1989). Elsewhere we have described the general implications for teachers of these new postmodern conditions (A. Hargreaves, 1994; Goodson, 1996). Here we wish to focus specifically on the new definitions of teacher professionalism which are emerging in the postmodern age. We define these as flexible professionalism, practical professionalism, extended professionalism and complex professionalism.

Flexible Professionalism

If scientific certainty has provided one route to remedying the supposed weaknesses in teachers' shared technical cultures, by redefining the technical aspects of teachers' work, another strategy has been to develop senses of shared professional community and cultures of collaboration. One such remedy has been to develop cultures of collaboration or senses of shared professional community among particular groups of teachers in particular schools or subject areas so that sharing can take place and dialogue about teaching and its improvement can begin (Talbert and McLaughlin, 1994; Nias, Southworth and Yeomans, 1989; Lieberman, 1988). Here it is the shared aspects of teachers' technical cultures that are the focus for change. Of course, these cultures of collaboration have sometimes turned out to be rather weak, with teachers exchanging resources and 'tricks of the trade' rather than scrutinizing practice together (Little, 1990). Such cultures have also often been colonized and controlled by educational bureaucracies, locking teachers into stilted, mandated forms of *contrived collegiality* in the shape of compulsory peer coaching or labyrinthine procedures of school development planning that are the very antithesis of self-directed professionalism (Hargreaves and Dawe, 1990; A. Hargreaves, 1994). But as Talbert and McLaughlin show in their carefully researched chapter in this volume, it is nonetheless possible for local professional communities which are strongly collaborative in nature, to build shared technical cultures piece-by-piece, community-by-community. In this respect, the authors claim, 'the challenge of enhancing teacher professionalism is . . . significantly a local matter . . . Local communities of teachers are the vehicle for enhanced professionalism in teaching.'

Embedding professionalism and professionalization in *local* teacher communities replaces principles of *scientific certainty* with ones of *situated certainty* (Hargreaves, 1994) as the basis for teacher professionalism. These situated certainties among local professional communities of teachers are made up of common agreements and certainties about professional knowledge and standards of practice that teachers seem able to achieve department-by-department, or school-by-school.

Building local professional communities which can set standards of practice suited to the immediate context is an important issue and Talbert and McLaughlin's chapter delineates the possibilities worth exploring here. Professional needs and professional standards will not be absolutely the same for kindergarten teachers and secondary teachers, for teachers in inner city schools and teachers in élite private ones, for teachers of drama and teachers of mathematics, or for subject teachers who need to know their disciplines and teachers in more flexible school settings who need to see the relationships among them. Local professional communities do matter. Indeed, Wideen, Mayer-Smith and Moon's chapter shows how a strong and vigorous professional community *within* the school can mediate, give life to and interact critically with ideas and initiatives coming into the school from the outside.

However, pursuing professionalization solely through the *situated certainties* of local professional communities at school or department level poses significant problems. Our fears here concern what Gitlin and Labaree call the problem of 'fragmented community'. To see professional communities as predominantly local communities is to treat them in essentially internalized ways as communities grouped in a specific physical location (like a department or a school) around a specific set of interests (e.g., those of the subject or of a private school). Where all or most aspirations to heightened professionalism are invested in the local, we run the risk of fragmenting teachers; of fracturing them in ways that make the possibility of commitment to broader professional goals more elusive.

An additional danger is the frequent insulation of these local professional communities from wider communities that surround them and extend beyond them. It should already be clear from our critique of scientific certainty that professional élites do not constitute community in any broad-based sense. There is a great need to push our notions of community and connectedness further, beyond our schools, to the neighbourhood community and the wider society, and not leave them locked within the local institutional preoccupations of teachers themselves (Hargreaves and Fullan, forthcoming). Indeed, placing an exclusive or excessive emphasis on issues of professional community at the local level may amount to giving teachers a local anaesthetic; numbing them against their capacity to feel committed and to actively engage with bigger social missions of justice, equity and community beyond their own workplaces. Fragmentations of these kinds, it is worth noting, may not be entirely accidental.

Drawing on, but to some extent also redefining a suggestive term used by Giddens (1995), we want to argue that our present world is characterized by *manufactured uncertainty* where postmodern chaos, complexity and uncertainty are not merely contingent or unintended, but also to some extent the result of wilful acts by governmental, corporate and financial powers which seek to maximize their own interests by keeping everything flexible, interest groups fragmented and everyone off-balance (see also Jameson, 1991). Treating professionalism as a predominantly local matter and making professional development a predominantly school-based priority will only add to this insularity and fragmentation — creating stronger situational certainty at the local level, at the cost of manufactured uncertainty across the wider system. Such risks of fragmentation are also rife in a third discourse of professionalism and professionalization — that of *practical professionalism*.

Practical Professionalism

Practical professionalism tries to accord dignity and status to the practical knowledge and judgment that people have of their own work. Research on teachers' *personal practical knowledge*, for example, points to 'the existence of teacher knowledge which is practical, experiential and shaped by a teacher's purposes and values' (Clandinin, 1986, p. 4). This approach is 'designed to capture the idea of experience in a way that allows us to talk about teachers as knowledgeable and knowing persons' (Connelly and Clandinin, 1988, p. 25). The reliance on experience that was once seen as a failing of teachers is here regarded as central to their expertise and in its own way, a source of valid theory, rather than theory's opposite or enemy. The routine and situated knowledge that teachers have of curriculum materials and development, subject matter, teaching strategies, the classroom milieu, parents, and so forth — these are the sorts of phenomena that make up the substance of teachers' personal practical knowledge or craft knowledge (Brown and McIntyre, 1993). Such knowledge can also be captured and communicated in particular forms — especially through the images (Elbaz, 1983), metaphors and stories (Connelly and Clandinin, 1988) which teachers routinely use to represent their work to themselves and others.

A particularly powerful extension of the discourse of practical professionalism is the notion of *reflective practice*. The concept of the 'reflective practitioner' has been pioneered and developed by Donald Schön (1983) as a way of describing and developing skilled and thoughtful judgment in professions like teaching. Reflection here means thinking that is not just ivory-towered contemplation, but that is linked directly to practice (Grimmett and Erickson, 1988; Grimmett and Mackinnon, 1993). The heart of professionalism in this perspective is the capacity to exercise discretionary judgment in situations of unavoidable uncertainty (Schön, 1983).

Teacher educators have not been slow to pick up the implications of Schön's work. They have shown how all teaching embodies reflection or thoughtful judgment, within the actual practice of teaching itself (Pollard and Tann, 1987). They have tried to investigate how teachers might best represent and explain their practice reflectively to one another, especially between more and less experienced peers. Some have moved beyond the more technical aspects of reflection regarding the details of classroom judgment — beyond *reflection-in-action* and *reflection-on-action*, that is — to argue for more critical *reflection about action*, and about the social conditions and consequences of one's actions as a teacher (e.g., Elliot, 1991; Fullan and Hargreaves, 1991, pp. 67–9; Carr and Kemmis, 1983; Liston and Zeichner, 1991). Clearly, there are many purposes and ways of reflecting, not just one (Louden, 1991). But what matters throughout this literature are the emphases that all teachers reflect in some way, that teachers can articulate and share their reflections more explicitly, that reflection is at the heart of what it means to be professional, and that teacher education, supervision and development should be constructed in ways that make such explicit reflection more feasible and more thorough.

At its best, the discourse of practical and reflective professionalism superbly deconstructs the intellectual pretensions of university-based, scientific knowledge as a basis for teacher professionalization. At its most critical, it also connects the practical reflection of teachers to broader social agendas of equity and emancipation — making practical reflection social and critical, as well as personal and local. But when it assumes extremely personalized and romantic forms, we believe that the discourse of practical professionalism is open to a damaging dual criticism.

First, not all teachers' practical knowledge is educationally beneficial or socially worthwhile. Sugrue's chapter, describing the perceptions and experiences of beginning teachers, shows how those teachers' images of what they should do and how they should be as teachers, were heavily framed by the practical knowledge they retained of teaching from when they themselves were students, and by the practical knowledge of teaching they culled from prevailing archetypes of teaching within the wider culture. Weber and Mitchell's chapter intriguingly reveals how such traditional archetypal images of teaching influence how children and student teachers represent teachers in their drawings of them. The persistence from child-hood of unexamined practical knowledge of what teaching is, is one of the most serious barriers to improvement in teaching.

Other kinds of practical knowledge are also problematic. Some teachers' prac-tical knowledge 'tells' them that mixed ability teaching isn't workable or appropri-ate (A. Hargreaves, 1996), that children can't be trusted to evaluate their own work, or that sciences are more suitable for boys than girls. If teacher professionalism is to be understood as exercising reflective judgment, and developing and drawing on a wide repertoire of knowledge and skill, to meet goals of excellence and equity within relationships of caring then whether practical knowledge can provide a proper foundation for it depends on what that knowledge is, in what kinds of contexts it has been acquired, the purposes to which it is put, and the extent to which teachers review, renew and reflect on it.

A second critique of the discourse of practical professionalism is that over-zealous promotion of teachers' everyday, practical craft knowledge (albeit for the best intended reasons) may actually redirect teachers' work away from broader moral and social projects and commitments. In this sort of scenario, right-of-centre governments can restructure teachers' work and teacher education in ways that narrow such work to pedagogical skills and technical competences, remove from teachers any moral responsibility over or professional judgment concerning cur-ricular matters, and cut teachers off from university knowledge with the access it can give to independent inquiry, intellectual critique and understanding of other teachers in other contexts. This can turn practical knowledge into parochial know-ledge. Some of the more excessive swings towards school-based training and pro-fessional development schools threaten just this sort of turn.

Martin Lawn (1990) has written powerfully about how teachers' work in England and Wales has been restructured along just these lines:

In the biographies of many teachers is an experience of, and an expecta-tion of, curriculum responsibility not as part of a job description, a task, but as part of the moral craft of teaching, the real duty. The post-war tradition of gradual involvement in curriculum responsibility at primary and second level (in England and Wales) was the result of the wartime breakdown of education, the welfare aspects of schooling and the post-war reconstruction in which teachers played a pivotal, democratic role. The role of teaching expanded as the teachers expanded the role. In its ideo-logical form within this period, professional autonomy was created as an idea. As the post-war consensus finally collapsed and corporatism was demolished by Thatcherism, teaching was again to be reduced, shorn of its involvement in policy and managed more tightly. Teaching is to be reduced to 'skills', attending planning meetings, supervising others, pre-paring courses and reviewing the curriculum. It is to be 'managed' to be more 'effective'. In effect the intention is to depoliticize teaching and to turn the teacher into an educational worker. Curriculum responsibility now means supervising competencies. (Lawn, 1990, p. 389)

Lawn's analysis points to the need for macro-level understanding of the implications of initiatives which, advertently or inadvertently, may redirect teacher professionalization into dark corners or cul-de-sacs. In many places, teacher professionalism is being redefined in terms of workplace competencies and standards of pedagogical practice, while teachers are having moral responsibility for curriculum goals and purposes taken away from them, while financial resources are being withdrawn from them, and while market ideologies of choice, competition and self-management are restructuring school systems and students' lives inequitably all around them.

The promise of practical professionalism, then, is that it can usefully invert and subvert the élitism and esotericism of university-based knowledge as a basis for teacher professionalization. Practical wisdom, developed in suitable contexts, for worthwhile purposes, in appropriately reflective ways, can and should form an important part of what it means to be professional as a teacher. But embraced exclusively and to excess, practical professionalism is easily hijacked in the service of dubious policy projects, which restructure education inequitably and narrow the teachers' task and the teacher's professionalism to delivering the goals of that restructured system technically, competently but unquestioningly. In this sense, we feel, the rise of practical professionalism may threaten to move us into a period of *deprofessionalizing professionalism* where more narrow, technical definitions of professionalism, emptied of critical voice or moral purpose, seriously damage teachers' long-term aspirations for greater professional status and recognition.

Extended Professionalism

A fourth discourse of teacher professionalism distinguishes between different *kinds* of teacher professionalism. It refers to 'new' or 'extended' professionalism as something bigger and better than 'older', more restricted predecessors. Hoyle (1974), for instance, draws a distinction between *restricted* and *extended* forms of professionality. In *restricted professionality*, skills are derived from experience; the teacher's perspective is limited to the here-and-now; classroom events are perceived in isolation; teachers are introspective about their methodology; individual autonomy is valued; there is limited involvement in non-teaching professional activities, in reading professional literature or in attending in-service education sessions (other than 'practical' courses); and teaching is seen as largely intuitive in nature. In *extended professionality*, teachers derive their skills from a mediation between experience and theory; the teacher's perspective extends beyond the classroom to embrace the broader social context of education; classroom events are perceived in relation to other aspects of school; teachers develop their teaching methodology by comparing it to others; high value is placed on professional activities, reading of professional literature, and theoretical as well as practical in-service education experiences; and teaching is seen as a rational rather than an intuitive activity.

While Hoyle's distinction is intended to provide analytical tools with which to investigate the characteristics of and possible changes in teacher professionalism, David Hargreaves (1994) describes what he terms 'the new professionalism' (the successor of 'old professionalism') which, he speculatively suggests (and in some cases, predicts), is actually resulting from government initiated programmes of educational reform in England and Wales.

> At its core, the new professionalism involves a movement away from the teacher's traditional professional authority and autonomy towards new forms of relationships with colleagues, with students and with parents. These relationships are becoming closer as well as more intensive and collaborative, involving more explicit negotiation of roles and responsibilities. The conventional classroom focus of teachers' work is now set within a framework of whole-school policies, and the planning and implementation of agreed priorities. In relation to the curriculum, there is greater concern than in the past with continuity and progression for students, and so far better coordination between teachers. The strong focus on student learning and achievement as well as on institutional improvement leads to more sophisticated models and practices of professional development. Teachers are not merely working more cooperatively; they feel a stronger obligation towards and responsibility for their colleagues. (D. Hargreaves, 1994)

Collaboration, peer coaching, teamwork, partnership, mentoring, professional development, contractual relationships, and a focus on outcomes — these are the hallmarks of the 'new professionalism' for David Hargreaves. Peculiarly, David Hargreaves argues (in a kind of back-handed endorsement of unintended yet purportedly positive effects of Conservative governmental reforms in education), the English and Welsh National Curriculum reform has actually stimulated the growth of the new professionalism; for example, by 'driving primary teachers to rely on colleagues and to coordinate with them to an unusual extent' around prescribed curriculum outcomes. Indeed, Hargreaves continues, 'the National Curriculum will probably reinforce and strengthen existing collaborative cultures.'

In contrast to David Hargreaves' intriguing speculations, Helsby and McCulloch's chapter in this book, based on careful and extensive research of a qualitative and quantitative nature with English secondary teachers, finds that the National Curriculum reforms have made serious dents in teachers' professionalism. Teachers interviewed by Helsby and Murray Saunders felt that the detailed prescriptions of the new National Curriculum placed them 'in a content-based straitjacket', as if they were 'teaching in a box'. The onslaught of initiatives destroyed rather than supported whole-school planning and decision-making, as well as loading teachers up with extra tasks and responsibilities and intensifying their work lives so that there was less and less time to prepare for classroom teaching. As Helsby and McCulloch conclude:

The introduction of a centralized and prescriptive National Curriculum appears to have weakened their professional confidence, lowered morale and left them uncertain both of their ability to cope and of their right to take major curriculum decisions. These findings are consistent with the view of increased State control of the curriculum undermining teacher professionalism. (Helsby and McCulloch, this volume)

Helsby and McCulloch do concede that some 'teachers as individuals and in groups have been able to mediate or even redirect this process', but, they continue, this is a constrained form of resistance, which is only reactive to major redefinitions of curriculum and schooling from above.

It seems to us that research which mainly investigates and emphasizes these minority exceptions and micropolitical resistances, (e.g., Ball and Bowe, 1992) tends to take the restructuring of teacher professionalism at the macro level as a *fait accompli*. Hence in this volume, we have tried to begin by providing a contextual commentary of the broader changes in teachers' professional lives before moving to more micro-political studies later in the book.

Robertson's chapter is one of these more macro-oriented analyses. Her invest-igation into contemporary restructurings of teachers' work in Australia and else-where also makes reference to 'a new professionalism', but her own use of the term is decidedly ironic.

There is little scope in the promise of professionalism to wrest a degree of autonomy because the crucial margin for determination — that is ideo-logical control — has been unceremoniously split from teachers' work and placed in the firm hands of administrators, politicians and transnational capital. The margin of indetermination is now located at the level of de-cisions to meet the system specified outcomes, rather than at the point of judgment about what might constitute an adequate framing of knowledge. Gains to teachers are thus largely illusory. Teachers will be weighed down by the pressure of (self) management, time constraints, larger classes and the management of other workers. What flows from this is a depersonalized authority — an outcome teachers have confused with professionalism. Teachers have not been provided or promised an opportunity to negoti-ate the changing shape of their work. Rather, their work has increasingly been moulded by economic imperative and expediency, and is the out-come of the state's need to establish the new conditions for accumulation. (Robertson, this volume)

Extended professionalism is an admirable aspiration. And Robertson's ana-lysis may underestimate the many initiatives, pilot projects and instances of local school improvement where the aspiration has been converted into actuality. Also, as one of us has argued elsewhere (A. Hargreaves, 1994) it is theoretically pre-sumptuous and demeaning to dismiss all shifts in teachers' practices, perceptions and work roles as misguided or 'confused' professionalism. But overall, in the current context of worldwide educational reform and restructuring, extended professionalism often does turn into a kind of *distended professionalism*, where teachers are stretched so far by their new responsibilities they almost tear apart with the workload and the strain. More than this, what passes for 'new' or extended professionalism, may lead teachers to neglect or short-change their own students as their energies are redirected to working with other teachers in collective planning, staff development, designing instructional interventions and so on. Indeed, paradoxically, the children who often suffer most by having teachers pulled repeatedly from their classes to participate in staff development and team leadership, are the most needy 'at-risk' students, (with the most expendable schedules) for whom the reforms on which the teachers are working have been designed (Richardson, Casanova, Placier and Guilfoyle, 1989). Lastly, whatever increases in skill and collaboration teachers may experience as a result of educational reform, it is still the case that critical engagement with goals and purposes, as well as the curriculum content in which these are embodied and embedded, have largely been excluded from the 'new professionalism' — raising doubts, we feel, about whether what teachers now have amounts to professionalism at all.

Complex Professionalism

Alongside the accelerating changes in global and domestic economies, have teachers' skills and responsibilities changed in real ways that matter? Are the shifts more than cosmetic; more than a gloss for extra administration and busywork? Is teachers' work becoming significantly more difficult and complex or just more extended and overloaded? Issues such as these are central to a fifth discourse of teacher professionalism which rests on the argument that professions should be judged by the complexity of the work tasks which comprise them, and that teaching is characterized by high degrees of complexity.

Devaney and Sykes (1988) argue that schools need professionalism on the part of all teachers, not just among an élite leadership cadre. The reason for this, they propose, is that children are the producers of schoolwork and that schoolwork is highly complex and likely to become more so as problem-solving, cooperative learning strategies and higher order thinking skills are given increasing emphasis. All teachers, say Devaney and Sykes, are leaders of their students, and as such, preside over production processes of great complexity (also Sykes, 1990). Such teachers must be 'knowledgeable, experienced, thoughtful, committed, and energetic workers' (p. 20). To stimulate and support such teachers in being able to handle the complexity of their work, Devaney and Sykes argue that a culture of professionalism must be built in schools and school districts.

Using quantitative indicators to compare the knowledge, skills and tasks of teaching to those employed in other professions, Rowan (1994) concludes that 'teaching is a highly complex form of work' (p. 10). Moreover, given that the data on which he draws were collected in the early 1980s, it is possible that some areas of work which received relatively low ratings then, such as coordination, negoti-ation and collective decision-making, exhibit greater complexity today. At least until the early 1980s, there is no evidence, Rowan suggests, of increased deskilling or proletarianization of teachers' labour over the previous century. These findings are important, Rowan argues, because increases in work complexity appear to help shape increases in professional prestige and occupational earnings.

Rowan goes on to suggest that further attempts to professionalize teaching will likely only come about if teachers' work can be made more complex than it cur-rently is. Many school reforms proposals, he notes, do suggest that teachers' work might become more complex by creating mentor roles for teachers, implementing site-based management and changing school organization to allow teachers to have more personalized relationships with students. But in practice, most of these reform efforts have so far affected the work of teachers only marginally.

What are we to make of these findings given that they appear to run counter to some of our earlier claims about the forces of deprofessionalization that are at work in teaching? First, the finding that teachers' work is highly complex, even by the standards of 1980–1, constitutes significant support for teachers' claims about their professionalism. Second, Rowan's data precede the substantial edu-cational restructurings of the late 1980s and beyond, and so cannot take account of the extent to which standardized testing, detailed learning outcomes and the like may recently have deprofessionalized teachers by reducing their scope of cur-ricular and moral discretion. Nor do the data account for the impact of initiatives like site-based management and school development planning on teachers' work. Whether these initiatives have *deprofessionalized* teachers by burdening them with form-filling and busywork, or *reprofessionalized* them by stimulating dialogue and decision-making about teaching among colleagues, cannot be determined by Rowan's results.

What is clear, though, is that work complexity may be a vital key to improving teacher professionalism. It, rather than scientific claims to esoteric knowledge and specialized technologies, constitutes the strongest case for prolonging the period of professional preparation. There is certainly mounting evidence that very recent educational reforms are making the teacher's work significantly more complex in some areas — not just in terms of collective planning and decision-making, but also in terms of a whole set of new skills in classroom assessment, such as portfolio assessment, peer assessment, self assessment and performance assessment (Pollard, *et al.*, 1994). What matters is the extent to which this increased complexity in some areas of teaching *excludes* other more morally-laden and politicized areas of the teachers' work. Deliberation about curriculum content and purposes and about their relevance to the lives of the students who teachers teach, actually seem to be be-coming *less* complex for many teachers, as these issues are taken out of their hands.

It is also important to investigate what the *cumulative* impact of increased complexity in teachers' work may be for the possibilities of achieving enhanced professionalism. If teachers are simply expected to accommodate greater com-plexity with all the demands this will make on their energy and time, they may only be able to achieve enhanced professionalism in the short term at great long-term cost to their health, their lives and their staying-power. An alternative response might be to reduce the complexity of teaching and make teachers' work more manageable by confining teachers to the classroom and restricting their role in decision-making and contact with the community. But at a time when technological transformation and the shifting cultural and linguistic make-up of communities is presenting significant new challenges to schools, it would be profoundly uncaring and unrealistic to respond in this way. Nor would such a backward step help teachers' claims for greater professional recognition. A third option would be to restructure the work roles of teachers and other educational personnel (Fenstermacher, 1990); for example by creating a group of lower-paid, and lesser-skilled educational personnel (the equivalent of paralegals, dental hygienists or nurse practitioners) who would carry out the less complex tasks of teaching (not just in photocopying, mixing paints or cutting up card, as teachers' aides now do, but in the practice of basic skills and routine drills as well), while releasing highly skilled educators (teachers) to perform more complex work (and to receive the higher levels of status and remuneration that should accrue to it). Such efforts would not be without their problems. They would encounter resistance from penny pinching governments unwilling to reward highly skilled teachers at the levels they deserve. And they might be expected to raise significant boundary disputes among educators and their unions who may not want to acknowledge that other people can readily do some of what had previously been done by teachers (Rowan, 1994). However, unless governments, administrators and teachers together can address and resolve these challenges of restructuring teachers' work with openness, commitment and flexibility, it is likely that complex professionalism — the professionalism that comes with increasing work complexity — will simply become a synonym for teacher exploitation and burnout!

Future Agendas

We believe that our analysis of teacher professionalism and professionalization carries important implications for defining the directions that professionalism and professionalization might productively take, given the challenges that the postmodern age presents to educational policy and practice. There are also other important implications for educational research in terms of how we might best investigate teacher professionalism and professionalization within these changing social conditions.

Towards Postmodern Professionalism

So far we have analysed five different discourses of teacher professionalism and professionalization in a postmodern age that is characterized by increasing organizational complexity, economic flexibility, and scientific and moral uncertainty on a scale of global proportions. Corporate managerial and a number of other organizational theorists, especially those who have colonized the pop management domain, see these postmodern, postindustrial or even postcapitalist developments as positive challenges, even irresistible forces, which organizations will have to meet if they are to be successful (e.g., Drucker, 1993). Some of the current writing in educational leadership, teacher professionalism and teachers' work takes a similar line — proposing and even predicting positive visions of teacher professionalism that are complex, collaborative and competency-based within a 'post-technocratic' world (e.g., D. Hargreaves, 1994). By comparison, as we noted earlier, critics and cynics have argued that appearances of social complexity and government decentralization are wilfully created by finance capital and state power to create social fragmentation, and to diffuse and thereby defuse dissent (Jameson, 1991). In this sense, uncertainty is manufactured; differentiation is deliberate. Professionalism here is viewed as a rhetorical ruse — a way to get teachers to misrecognize their own exploitation and to comply willingly with increased intensification of their labour in the workplace (e.g., Smyth, Robertson, in this volume). Elsewhere, one of us has argued that the nature and future of the postmodern social condition is more complex and contested than either of these portrayals suggest; being shot through with contradictory forces, that make up a struggle which is far from being lost or won (A. Hargreaves, 1994).

The same is true for the agenda of teacher professionalism and professionalization. It is neither universally negative nor positive; pernicious nor benign. We have shown that discourses and practices that we call professionalism and professionalization can empower teachers or exploit them. Our critique of the discourses of teacher professionalism is meant to inform future struggles around the growth and development of teaching as a profession. It is our belief that such struggles should primarily be guided *not* by interests of self-serving status enhancement (as is common within classical professionalism), nor should they be confined to matters of technical competence and personal, practical reflection about how best to deliver the means of an education that others have defined (as in many versions of practical professionalism). The struggle we have in mind, rather, is one which is guided by moral and socio-political visions of the purposes which teacher professionalism should serve within actively caring communities and vigorous social democracies.

Thus alongside all the recent clamour for technical competency and subject knowledge that are widely advocated as being essential to newly defined professional standards of teaching, we believe that what teacher professionalism should also mean in a complex, postmodern age is:

- increased opportunity and responsibility to exercise *discretionary judgment* over the issues of teaching, curriculum and care that affect one's students;
- opportunities and expectations to engage with the *moral and social purposes* and value of what teachers teach, along with major curriculum and assessment matters in which these purposes are embedded;
- commitment to working with colleagues in *collaborative cultures* of help and support as a way of using shared expertise to solve the ongoing problems of professional practice, rather than engaging in joint work as a motivational device to implement the external mandates of others;

- occupational *heteronomy* rather than self-protective *autonomy*, where teachers work authoritatively yet openly and collaboratively with other partners in the wider community (especially parents and students themselves), who have a significant stake in the students' learning;
- a commitment to active *care* and not just anodyne *service* for students. Professionalism must in this sense acknowledge and embrace the emotional as well as the cognitive dimensions of teaching, and also recognize the skills and dispositions that are essential to committed and effective caring;
- a self-directed search and struggle for *continuous learning* related to one's own expertise and standards of practice, rather than compliance with the enervating obligations of *endless change* demanded by others (often under the guise of continuous learning or improvement);
- the creation and recognition of high task *complexity*, with levels of status and reward appropriate to such complexity.

These seven principles of postmodern professionalism are similar to but also extend beyond what Fullan and Hargreaves (1996) have elsewhere called *interactive professionalism.*

Compared to the lofty aspirations of postmodern or interactive professionalism, what passes for teacher professionalism in practice has too often involved delimitation of purpose, downloading of management, dependence on external outcomes and diversion from the classroom. The coming years will see significant and continuing efforts to revive and re-invent teacher professionalism. This revival can use professionalism to justify and mask overextension and deprofessionalization among teachers; or it can re-invent teacher professionalism in ways that maximize discretionary judgment, embrace moral and social purposes, forge cultures of collaboration along with self-directed commitments to continuous improvement, and embody heteronomy, complexity and commitment to care.

Studying Professional Lives

In this opening chapter and throughout this book, we have emphasized the importance of understanding the policy contexts in which agendas of professionalism have arisen — and therefore of investigating the social histories and social geographies of teacher professionalism and professionalization in sensitively contextualized ways. Without such critical and contextual analyses, we believe that rhetorics of professionalism will be hitched all too easily to the wagons of reforms which actually contradict and undermine them.

One area in which educational research and inquiry can be helpful in this respect is in the domain of policy where research can be used to interrogate the meaning and impact of new reform initiatives. In analysing educational policy, though, we must beware of being seduced by professionalization projects in higher education that drive and direct how we practise our own scholarly study. Often, work that helps our own professionalization as researchers and professors (in terms of securing resources for fundable projects by gaining credibility with policy élites) can be complicitous with the powerful groups who seek to restructure and reform schooling in their own interests. There is a scholarly version of Lasch's 'revolt of the élites' here that is and should be a continuing cause for concern in the research community.

So it is important that we develop forms of analysis which critique the 'language of power' that makes up the prevailing discourses of teacher professionalization, rather than allowing our research to accept and work uncritically within those given discourses. As scholars sympathetic to the goal of teacher professionalization and to the enhancement of teachers' professional work, we therefore advocate forms of analysis and social commentary which will seriously engage with the wider rhetorics of reform, restructuring and rationalization, within which agendas for teacher professionalism and professionalization are being defined. Our typology of teacher professionalism is one contribution to that project.

In this book, we have also followed the belief that to confront and critique emerging rhetorics of teacher reform, we shall have to develop distinctive forms of educational study which stay close to the everyday life and work of the teacher. For it is in the details of the everyday working lives of teachers as professionals, that we shall see how the rhetoric actually plays out. We shall, therefore, need modes of analysis which address both the *preactive* framing of policy debate and discourse *and* the *interactive* realization of such policies within the teacher's life and work. Only if we conduct our research at both levels, can meaningful commentary on professionalism and professionalization within a context of restructuring and reform, be attempted.

Fortunately, a strongly developing field of literature on studying teachers' lives is now to hand (Middleton, 1993; Casey, 1993; Goodson and Walker, 1991; Goodson, 1992; Goodson, 1995). In *Studying Teachers' Lives*, one of us has brought together a number of accounts which show how studies of the teacher's life and work throw new light on the 'language of power' which is used within official rhetorics and discourses of educational change (Goodson, 1992). When we look at teaching as lived experience and work, we often find that seductive rhetorics of change pronounced in policy, break down into cynical, contradictory or resistant voices within the lives of teachers themselves. What passes for professionalism and professionalization is very different in the experienced lives and work of teachers, than in the official discourses of policy and change which exalt and advocate it (e.g., Ben-Peretz and Day in this volume). This is why several of the chapters in this book concentrate on understanding teachers' professional lives at this experiential level.

If we wish to enhance teachers' professional lives, we have to direct our inquisitive gaze at teachers' own experienced worlds, and from there, pose demanding questions to those who seek to change and restructure the teacher's work from above. For at the end of the day, teacher professionalism is what teachers and others experience it as being, not what policy makers and others assert it should become. The experience of professionalism and of its denial are to be found by studying the everyday work of teaching. There too, we will start to recognize the social and occupational conditions which support such professionalism or hasten its demise.

As Howard Becker (1970) has cogently argued, the way in which we look at problems is clearly affected by the position from which we take our view. In arguing for life history research, Becker took the phenomenon of delinquency and argued that we would view it totally differently if we saw it through the eyes of delinquents themselves. He describes the case of one such delinquent, to make his point:

> By putting ourselves in Stanley's skin, we can feel and become aware of the deep biases about such people that ordinarily permeate our thinking and shape the kinds of problems we investigate. By truly entering into Stanley's life, we can begin to see what we take for granted (and ought not to) in designing our research — what kinds of assumptions about delinquents, slums, and Poles are embedded in the way we set the questions we study.

> If we take Stanley seriously, as his story must impel us to do, we might well raise a series of questions that have been relatively little studied — questions about the people who deal with delinquents, the tactics they use, their suppositions about the world, and the constraints and pressures they are subject to. (Becker, 1970, p. 71)

The great virtue of studies of everyday life and life history is that they hold the relationship between what C. Wright Mills called private troubles and public issues. If we seek modalities of study which follow this relationship through, it is possible not only to interrogate the rhetorics of educational change, and indeed of professionalization, but also to see the points at which contradiction and ambivalence surface. In looking at the interface between the personal craft knowledge of the teacher and professionalization projects, we have argued that some of the rhetorics of professionalism which focus on personal and practical knowledge, whilst of enormous individual worth in defining teachers' craft knowledge, may actually be antithetical to wider professionalization projects. Hence, as this case, we may be witnessing the sponsorship of *deprofessionalizing professionalisms*. This happens when versions of professionalism are promoted without due regard or sensitivity to the overall professionalization project. The latter project has to relate to the patterns of status and power expected of professional groups.

Likewise, it is possible to think of personal and professional ideologies which may contradict wider democratic, political purposes. This is the central thesis of Christopher Lasch (1995) in his *The Revolt of the Elites*. It argues that we cannot take it for granted that by polishing up our professionalism or promoting our professionalization projects, we are serving a wider human political purpose. Indeed, in the current regimes of governance and emergent patterns of global restructuring, it can be argued that self-serving professionalization is likely to be antithetical to wider democratic aspirations unless the two are closely articulated. By having our inquiry address and bring together the personal, professional, and political, dimensions of teachers' professional lives, we have sought to comment on these potential discontinuities between professionalization processes within education and broader democratic projects beyond it.

In altering our viewpoint in this way, we may capture different representative voices with which to address questions of educational policy. The matter will no longer be framed by those who look down on the system from above, but cogently argued for by those who are so often on the receiving end of policy edicts and system guidelines. After all, it is the teachers who ultimately hold the key to the success of the educational enterprise and it is surely time that we began to see the world of schooling from their viewpoint.

References

BALL, S. and BOWE, R. (1992, March/April) 'Subject departments and the implementation of the national curriculum', *Journal of Curriculum Studies*, **24**, pp. 97–116.

BARTON, L., BARRETT, E., WHITTY, G., MILES, S. and FURLONG, J. (1994) 'Teacher education and teacher professionalism in England: Some emerging issues', *British Journal of Sociology of Education*, **15**, 4, pp. 520–44.

BASCIA, N. (1994) *Unions in Teachers' Professional Lives*, New York, Teachers' College Press.

BECKER, H.S. (1970) *Sociological Work*, Chicago, Aldine Publishing.

BROWN, S. and MCINTYRE, D. (1993) *Making Sense of Teaching*, Milton Keynes, Open University Press.

BUCHER, R. and STRAUSS, A. (1961) 'Professions in process', *American Journal of Sociology*, **66**, pp. 325–46.

BURBULES, N. and DENSMORE, J. (1986) 'The limits of making teaching a profession', *Educational Policy*, **5**, 1.

CARLSON, D. (1992) *Teachers and Crisis: Urban School Reform and Teachers' Work Culture*, New York and London, Routledge.

CARR, W.C. and KEMMIS, S. (1983) *Becoming Critical: Knowing through Action Research*, Lewes, Falmer Press.

CASEY, K. (1993) *I Answer with My Life: Life Histories of Women Teachers Working for Social Change*, New York, Routledge.

CLANDININ, D. (1986) *Classroom Practice: Teacher Images in Action*, Lewes, Falmer Press.

CLIFFORD, G.J. and GUTHRIE, J.W. (1988) *Ed School: A Brief for Professional Education*, Chicago, University of Chicago Press.

CONNELLY, F.M. and CLANDININ, D.J. (1988) *Teachers as Curriculum Planners: Narratives of Experience*, Toronto, OISE Press.

DARLING-HAMMOND, L. (1993) 'Policy and professionalism', in LIEBERMAN, A. (Ed) *Building a Professional Culture in Schools*, New York, Teachers' College Press.

DARLING-HAMMOND, L. (1994) 'The current status of teaching and teacher development in the United States', Background paper prepared for the National Commission of Teaching in America's Future, November.

DEVANEY, K. and SYKES, G. (1988) 'Making the case for professionalism', in LIEBERMAN, A. (Ed) *Building a Professional Culture in Schools*, New York, Teachers' College Press.

DRUCKER, P. (1993) *Post-capitalist Society*, New York, Harper Collins.

ELBAZ, F. (1983) *Teacher Thinking: A Study of Practical Knowledge*, London, Croom Helm.

ELLIOTT, J. (1991) *Action Research for Educational Change*, Milton Keynes, Open University Press.

ETZIONI, A. (1969) *The Semi-professions and their Organization*, New York, Free Press.

FENSTERMACHER, G.D. (1990) 'Some moral considerations on teaching as a profession', in GOODLAD, J., SODER, R. and SIROTNIK, K. (Eds) *The Moral Dimensions of Teaching*, San Francisco, Jossey-Bass.

FLINDERS, D.J. (1988) 'Teachers' isolation and the new reform', *Journal of Curriculum and Supervision*, **4**, 1, pp. 17–29.

FULLAN, M. and HARGREAVES, A. (1991) *What's Worth Fighting for?: Working Together for Your School*, Toronto, Ontario Public School Teachers' Federation, MA; The Network North-East Laboratory, Milton Keynes, Open University Press; Melbourne, Australian Council for Educational Administration.

FULLAN, M. and HARGREAVES, A. (1996) *What's Worth Fighting for?: Working Together for Your School* (2nd ed.), New York, Teachers' College Press.

GIDDENS, A. (1995) *Beyond Left and Right*, Stanford, Stanford University Press.

GINSBURG, M.B., MEYENN, R.J. and MILLER, H.D.R. (1980) 'Teachers' conceptions of professionalism and trades unionism: An ideological analysis', in WOODS, P. (Ed) *Teacher Strategies*, London, Croom Helm.

GOODSON, I.F. (Ed) (1992) *Studying Teachers' Lives*, London, Routledge/New York, Teachers College Press/Toronto, OISE Press.

GOODSON, I.F. (1993) *School Subjects and Curriculum Change*, London, Falmer Press.

GOODSON, I.F. (1995) 'Education as a practical matter: Some issues and concerns', *Cambridge Journal of Education*, **25**, 2, pp. 137–48.

GOODSON, I.F. (forthcoming) *Representing Teachers*, New York, Teachers College Press.

GOODSON, I.F. and WALKER, R. (1991) *Biography, Identity and Schooling*, London, New York and Philadelphia, Falmer Press.

GRACE, G. (1987) 'Teachers and the State in Britain: A changing relationship', in LAWN, M. and GRACE, G. (Eds) *Teachers: The Culture and Politics of Work*, London, Falmer Press.

GRIMMETT, P. and ERICKSON, G.L. (1988) *Reflection in Teacher Education*, New York, Teachers' College Press.

GRIMMETT, P. and MACKINNON, A.M. (1988) 'Craft knowledge and the education of teachers', *Review of Research in Education*, **18**, pp. 385–456.

HARGREAVES, A. (1984) 'Experience counts, theory doesn't: How teachers talk about their work', *Sociology of Education*, pp. 244–54, October.

HARGREAVES, A. (1994) *Changing Teachers, Changing Times: Teachers; Work and Culture in the Postmodern Age*, London, Cassell; New York, Teachers' College Press; Toronto, OISE Press.

HARGREAVES, A. (1995) 'Towards a social geography of teacher education', in SHIMAHARA, N.K. and HOLOWINSKY, I.Z. (Eds) *Teacher Education in Industrialized Nations*, New York, Garland.

HARGREAVES, A. (1996) 'Revisiting voice', *Educational Researcher*.

HARGREAVES, A. and DAWE, R. (1990) 'Paths of professional development: Contrived collegiality, collaborative culture and the case of peer coaching', *Teaching and Teacher Education*, **4**, 2.

HARGREAVES, A., EARL, L. and RYAN, J. (1996) *Schooling for Change*, New York, Falmer Press.

HARGREAVES, A. and FULLAN, M. (forthcoming) *What's Worth Fighting for Out There?*, second edition, Toronto, Ontario Public School Teachers' Federation; New York, Teachers' College Press.

HARGREAVES, D. (1980) 'The occupation culture of teachers', in WOODS, P. (Ed) *Teacher Strategies*, London, Croom Helm.

HARGREAVES, D. (1994) 'The new professionalism: The synthesis of professional and institutional development', *Teaching and Teacher Education*, **10**, 4, pp. 423–38.

HARVEY, D. (1989) *The Condition of Postmodernity*, Cambridge, Polity Press.

HOYLE, E. (1974) 'Professionality, professionalism and control in teaching', *London Educational Review*, **3**, pp. 13–19.

JACKSON, P. (1968) *Life in Classrooms*, Chicago, University of Chicago Press.

JAMESON, F. (1991) *Postmodernism: Or the Cultural Logic of Late Capitalism*, London and New York, Verso.

LABAREE, D. (1992) 'Power, knowledge and the rationalization of teaching: A genealogy of the move to professionalize teaching', *Harvard Educational Review*, **62**, 2, pp. 123–55.

LASCH, C. (1995) *The Revolt of the Elites*, New York and London, W. W. Norton.

LAWN, M. (1990) 'From responsibility to competency: A new context for curriculum studies in England and Wales', *Journal of Curriculum Studies*, **22**, 4, pp. 388–92.

LIEBERMAN, A. (Ed) (1988) *Building a Professional Culture in Schools*, New York, Teachers' College Press.

LINDBLAD, S. (1993) 'On teachers' invisible experience and professional accountability', Paper presented at the PACT Conference, London, Ontario, September 25–27.

LISTON, D.P. and ZEICHNER, K.M. (1991) *Teacher Education and the Social Conditions of Schooling*, New York, Routledge.

LITTLE, J.W. (1984) 'Seductive images and organizational realities in professional development', *Teachers' College Record*, **86**, 1, pp. 84–102.

LITTLE, J.W. (1990) 'The persistance of privacy: Autonomy and initiative in teachers' professional relations', *Teachers' College Record*, **91**, 4, pp. 509–36.

LORTIE, D. (1975) *Schoolteacher*, Chicago, University of Chicago Press.

LOUDEN, W. (1991) *Understanding Teaching*, London, Cassell; New York, Teachers' College Press.

MIDDLETON, S. (1993) *Educating Feminists: Life Histories and Pedagogy*, New York, Teachers' College Press.

MILLS, C.W. (1979) *Power, Politics and People*, New York, Oxford University Press.

NIAS, J., SOUTHWORTH, G. and YEOMANS, R. (1989) *Staff Relationships in the Primary School*, London, Cassells.

NODDINGS, N. (1992) *The Challenge to Care in Schools*, New York, Teachers' College Press.

PARSONS, T. (1954) 'The professions and social structure', in *Essays in Sociological Theory*, New York, Free Press.

POLLARD, A. and TANN, S. (1987) *Reflective Teaching in the Primary School*, London, Cassell.

POLLARD, A., BROADFOOT, P., CROLL, P., OSBORN, M. and ABBOTT, D. (1994) *Changing English Primary Schools: The Impact of the Education Reform Act at Key Stage 1*, London, Cassell.

RICHARDSON, V., CASANOVA, V., PLACIER, P. and GUILFOYLE, K. (1989) *School Children at Risk*, New York, Falmer Press.

ROBERTSON, S. (1993) 'The politics of devolution, self-management and post-Fordism in schools', in SMYTH, J. (Ed) *A Socially Critical View of the Self Merging School*, London and New York, Falmer Press.

ROSENHOLTZ, S. (1989) *Teachers' Workplace*, New York, Longman.

ROWAN, B. (1994) 'Comparing teachers' work with work in other occupations: Notes on the professional status of teaching', *Educational Researcher*, **23**, 6, pp. 4–17.

SCHÖN, D. (1983) *The Reflective Practitioner: How Professionals Think in Action*, New York, Basic Books.

SCHÖN, D. (1991) *The Reflective Turn: Case Studies in and on Educational Practice*, New York, Teachers' College Press.

SHULMAN, L.S. (1986) 'Those who understand: Knowledge growth in teaching', *Educational Researcher*, **15**, 2, pp. 4–14.

SHULMAN, L.S. (1987) 'Knowledge and teaching: Foundations of the new reform', *Harvard Educational Review*, **57**, 1, pp. 114–35.

SMYTH, J. (Ed) *Critical Discourses in Teacher Development*, London, Cassell.

SOCKETT, H. (1987) 'Has Shulman got the strategy right?', *Harvard Educational Review*, **57**, 2, pp. 208–19.

SODER, R. (1990) 'The rhetoric of teacher professionalization', in GOODLAD, J., SODER, R. and SIROTNIK, K. (Eds) *The Moral Dimension of Teaching*, San Francisco, Jossey-Bass.

SYKES, G. (1990) 'Fostering teacher professionalism in schools', in ELMORE, R.F. (Ed) *Restructuring Schools: The Next Generation of Educational Reform*, San Francisco, Jossey Bass.

TALBERT, J.E. and MCLAUGHLIN, M. (1994) 'Teacher professionalism in local school contexts', *American Journal of Education*, **102** (February), pp. 123–53.

VEBLEN, T. (1962) *The Higher Learning in America*, Reprint of 1918 edition, New York, Hill and Wang.

WALLER, W. (1932) *The Sociology of Teaching*, New York, Wiley.

Chapter 2

Teachers' Work, Restructuring and Postfordism: Constructing the New 'Professionalism'

Susan L. Robertson

Introduction

In 1885 teachers were trained in classrooms to perform the specific functions of instruction and control. Over the course of the next century they had become highly educated professionals. By 1985, while still continuing with classroom instruction and control, teachers had become a body of people who were highly knowledgeable with regard to educational theory and practice, sociology, social theory, child psychology, learning theory and so on. They had become experts in their subject content; they had won the right, as a professional body, to be centrally involved in the determination and development of curriculum content, schooling practices and educational policy in general.

By 1995 they are likely to have lost, in a single decade, most of the gains made in a single century. (Kevin Harris, 1994, p. viii)

While some teachers remain committed to the belief they can shut out change by closing the classroom door, others agree that this is too simple a description of the relationship between their work as teachers and the wider society. As evidence, they point to the dramatic changes occurring outside of the classroom, and the impact on the terms and conditions of their work inside. A quick scan of the educational jargon reveals just how much. Notions such as inputs, equity, centralized bureaucracy, mass education, seniority and unionization which defined post-world-war mass schooling have been replaced by a new language: outputs, performance, added-value, choice, markets, quality, competencies, excellence, flexibility, deregulation, and school–business partnerships.

The cause? Over the past decade, teachers in countries such as Australia, Canada, the United States of America, United Kingdom and New Zealand have experienced the winds change. Hyper-liberalism, neo-conservativism and economic rationalism are just a few of the labels writers have used to describe the economic nature of these shifts (Ball and Goodson, 1985; Carlson, 1992; Harris, 1994; Barlow and Robertson, 1994; Panitch, 1994). Whatever the term, as Freedman has observed in a recent newspaper editorial, 'the evidence of the shift is everywhere reaching beyond the ballot box and deep inside the culture . . . there gusts a headwind, *blowing right*' (my emphasis) (1995, p. 47).

Teachers agree this wind has penetrated deep inside the classroom, bringing into sharp focus the 'thrill and dread of a world in which "all that is solid melts into air"' (Berman, 1982, p. 13). Within a decade, the industrial and pedagogic achievements of public-sector teachers have been reversed. The consequences have been decisive and tangible: wage roll-backs, an overall decline in salaries, increased funds to the private sector, larger class sizes, more administration, massive budget cuts, the deregulation of wages setting, teacher licensing, to name a few. A chilling wind indeed, as 'ideological compliance and financial self-reliance' defines the new reality facing teachers (Hargreaves, 1994, p. 5). Caught in this post-modern post-Fordist maelstrom, where '(s)igns and tokens of radical changes in labour processes, in consumer habits in geographical and geopolitical configurations, in state powers and practices, and the like, abound' (Harvey, 1990, p. 121), teachers have been swept along. The juxtapositions of hope, despair, opportunity, and dismay fill the staffrooms and classrooms, as one of the central institutions of late modernity and monopoly capitalism — the educational bureaucracy — is systematically dismantled and replaced with devolved forms of school-based management, new technologies and school–business–community partnerships.

Clearly this is no ordinary storm. Rather, as national states and corporate capital experiment with new markets, technology and forms of work organization (Barlow and Robertson, 1994) to compete in the global economy, the spotlight has inevitably turned to the role of education and the work of teachers in this transition. Despite the obvious dislocations within education, some reform analysts have argued the current crisis offers a perfect opportunity for teachers to have their 'professionally-preferred cake and to eat it too'; an opportunity to move beyond the organizational paradigm which has structured modern schooling — of 'eyes front, lips-buttoned, sit-up-straight classroom cottages' (Ashenden, 1992, p. 5) — which has dominated much of this century. Teachers could, according to Ashenden, adopt new patterns of work organization which challenge the cottage model of mass education. In learning to work in smarter ways, such as delegating some tasks to other (cheaper) education workers or using a range of alternative teaching approaches, teachers would have a real chance to move in from the margins and become real professionals.

Ashenden is not alone in arguing that the current round of restructuring offers teachers new hope for that elusive title of 'professional' (Porter, 1990). In fact, the educational restructuring proposals in Australia and elsewhere, for example, have been liberally sprinkled with the promise of a new professionalism for teachers (Robertson and Trotman, 1992). Not surprisingly, many Australian teachers have found this rhetoric seductive, particularly in such hard times. This, despite the growing body of evidence that crucial aspects of the restructuring, such as self-management, have been little more than a 'deliberate process of subterfuge, distortion, concealment and wilful neglect as the state seeks to retreat in a rather undignified fashion from its historical responsibility for providing quality education' (Smyth, 1993, p. 2).

The current round of changes to teachers' work, including proposals such as those offered by Ashenden, must be investigated and debated by the educational community. Critics from the left have long argued that the industrial model under-pinning public schooling, with its privileging of ruling-class culture, has provided limited scope for critical teacher practice (Aronowitz and Giroux, 1985). The question is, can the reorganization of time and space within schools be transformed to more democratic ends? This chapter seeks to contribute to that debate through an analysis of the restructuring of teachers' work and the proposed conditions for this new 'professionalism'. In particular I ask: Have the current restructuring initiatives, in the name of a new professionalism, created the conditions for teachers to work as autonomous intellectuals? The focus in this chapter will be directed toward a critical examination of the restructuring of teachers' labour in Australia on the premise that — given the historical specificity of both the State and the capital–labour compromise — developments in one polity cannot be read off against another.

My analysis draws upon three theoretical bodies of work. Firstly, that of the French regulation school and in particular the work of Alain Lipietz (1992) and Bob Jessop (1989, 1990, 1993) who analyse transformations in the welfare State and political economy within western capitalism toward what they argue is a new post-Fordist economy.[1] Although others have insights into this complex process, the French regulation school has gone furthest in developing those concepts useful for my purpose.

Secondly, I draw upon the work of Larson (1977, 1988) and others concerned with understanding the complex phenomena of professionalization and its crucial links to the restructuring of society. In particular, I have found Larson's (1988) elaboration of professionalism, based upon Foucault's analysis of the knowledge–power relations, helpful. Larson observes that professionals have their authority constituted within a discursive field which is infused with power relations. Discourses are about what can be said and thought, but also about who can speak, when and with what authority (Ball, 1990, p. 2). Seeing teacher professionalism as constituted within a discursive field of knowledge-power helps us understand the way in which words and concepts which define teachers' work can change and how teachers can be discursively repositioning as non-experts by powerful and vested interests. Further, Larson argues that some groups within an occupational field are located in the core region and therefore are positioned as more expert than others. These theoretical insights help us pinpoint not only the centrality of discourse to understanding the positioning of teachers, but also the fact that there are unequal relations between teachers which can be manipulated for strategic purposes.

Finally, I draw upon Christer Fritzell's (1987) analysis of relative autonomy within educational theory to illuminate the complex relationship between the internal structuring of schooling and the educational functions of social reproduction within capitalist economies. In particular, Fritzell's development of structural, functional and critical forms of correspondence between schooling and the economy are a useful heuristic in understanding the kinds of relationships between teachers, the State and the economy. Fritzell (1987) describes structural forms of correspondence as those relationships where the properties or internal relations of one system can be derived from the corresponding features in another, for example, the process of streaming which structurally equates to the primary and secondary division of labour. Functional forms of correspondence describe the internal penetration of one system by another external system of control, for example the production of skilled workers for the economy. In both cases of correspondence described so far, they can take on positive and negative forms. That is, as a set of direct (or positive) relationships from one site to the other, such as hierarchical authority relations, or by excluding or preventing (or negating) certain potentially critical tendencies, such as the scope for conflict.

Critical correspondence, on the other hand refers to the potentiality for social change. This potentiality can be realized when the dynamics of contradictions are made explicit. When teachers stand to lose many of the extrinsic (for example, status and wages) and intrinsic rewards (such as relationships with students) which teachers associate with teaching, as is the case during periods of crisis and transition, a critical correspondence between schooling and the economy is more likely to emerge. This opens the space for teachers to hold a more critical view of the proposed reform. Within this framework we can see how teachers' class allegiance might change with time as the contradictions within the system of reproduction become most apparent.[2] As the crisis deepens and the terms of the new settlement struggled over, teachers, whose role is crucial as knowledge producers/reproducers, are an increasingly unreliable ally.[3] This period of transition, because it offers scope for counter-hegemony, must be carefully managed by the State. This chapter explores precisely how this process has been 'managed' within Australia in the implementation of the post-Fordist accumulation regime.

Before turning to this task, however, I want to suggest that it is important to maintain a sense of historically located perspective with regard to the changing nature of teachers' work. For one thing, it is easy to romanticize the past and the 'golden years' in education and in doing so, overlook the rigidities of bureaucratic control and the limitations of professional ideology which have also shaped teachers' work during this period (Hargreaves, 1994, p. 10). For another, an historically located perspective helps bring into sharper focus the way in which new discourses, structures and struggles about the nature of teachers' work are layered upon and between old ones. Teachers, while active agents, are also constituted as subjects within a particular socio-political and historical context (Connell, 1985). The outcome of this struggle, despite a powerful ideology of professionalism which has produced considerable compliance and which has also been used by teachers for their own ends (Grace, 1987, p. 195), can never be predetermined. Finally, as Harvey notes, there is a real danger in confusing the transitory and ephemeral with more fundamental transformations in political and economic life (1990, p. 124). Viewing critically what is left behind as well as understanding the concreteness of what is, allowing us to see more clearly the distinctions between the ephemerality of 'reform rhetoric' and the substance of 'reform action' and thus the precise nature and the extent of the changes (Ginsburg and Cooper, 1991, p. 370). In this way, a counter-hegemonic (Aronowitz and Giroux, 1985) or reconstructivist (Harris, 1994) position will be informed by an understanding of the past.

Restructuring Teachers' Work: The Case of Australia

The unambiguous message over the past decade in Australia has been that schools and teachers must change. And radically! These pressures for change to teachers' work have emerged from the complexity of the present political and economic crises confronting most advanced nations. The result has led to fundamental trans-formations in the productive sector at the level of the global economy and the firm (McGrew, 1992), the development of new trading and cultural alliances (Harvey, 1990; Jessop, 1993), and the changing architecture of the nation State (Cerny, 1991; Lipietz, 1992; Jessop, 1993). Translated by an array of self-styled school-reform gurus, the message goes something like this. Schools are large, bureaucratic organizations. Like all bureaucracies, schools have top-heavy hierarchies, limited accountability, and a myriad of rules and regulations. Teachers are not only out of date, they fail to demand that the basic skills in education are covered. In short, teachers are out of touch with the needs of kids, the community and the nation at large. Efficiencies in the provision of educational services will be made if people (as consumers), not government, determine how their money is to be spent. It is only when the principles of the market-place are allowed to operate that teachers will have greater freedom for relevant teaching and community involvement. This will lead to a genuine teacher professionalism. We need to reinvent government and restructure our organizations to provide flexibility, diversity and choice within the marketplace.[4]

This rhetoric, at first glance, is powerful. Of course teachers want fewer regu-lations, less hierarchy, more opportunities for relevant teaching and a chance to regain the public's respect! However, as I will outline, the potential demise of teachers as bureaucratic workers and their reconstitution as a smaller cadre of flexible and professional teachers supported by a large group of deskilled teachers with the new label of 'cheaper educational worker', needs to be understood against a backdrop of shifts toward a post-Fordist development model. Closer scrutiny of this model, I will argue, expose real dangers facing public-sector educators. To understand the precise nature of these shifts, I would like to turn to a brief analysis of teachers as bureaucratic workers during the post-war period in Australia.

Teachers as Bureaucratic Workers and the Fordist Development Model

The prolonged boom following World War II — the 'golden era' — which saw a dramatic expansion in the provision of mass education had largely collapsed by the

1970s. The development model which underpinned the period following World War II consists of what Lipietz (1992, p. 2) describes as 'three legs of a tripod'. This model is widely referred to as the Fordist development model. These three legs or aspects of development refer to:

- a labour process model based upon Taylorist principles of scientific management;
- a regime of accumulation where macro-economic relations are based upon mass production and mass consumption; and
- a mode of regulation involving all of those mechanisms which try to adjust the contradictory and conflictual behaviour of individuals and workers to the collective principles of the regime of accumulation.

The later difficulties facing the Fordist model of development, which by and large was spectacularly successful within the developed nations, can be captured by the notion of rigidity. With the saturation of markets and over-accumulation, capital soon came to realize that the Fordist system was particularly rigid (Harvey, 1990, p. 142). Labour relations, consumer markets and methods of production all needed to be more flexible to facilitate exploitation of limited and unstable markets. This meant substituting the principle of 'just-in case' with the principle of 'just-in-time'.

The principle of 'just-in case' was central to the development of mass schooling. The post-war State undertook an important role in not only producing future workers and consumers for the mass-production society, but in creating the conditions for the reproduction of the capitalist relations of production. The values of the new post-war liberalism — equity and rationalization — were given a parliamentary face through welfare legislation (Beilhartz, 1989, pp. 141–2). The provision of public schooling, embedded within the welfare State, was crucial to this process. In large part, the State was able to guarantee the structural and functional correspondence of education to the economy through a mass expansion of education and through universal access. Despite the rhetoric of equity and uniformity, the streaming of students into 'ability' categories of academic (middle- and upper-class) and non-academic (poorer working-class) learners within the rapidly growing secondary comprehensives throughout this period paralleled the wider stratification of labour into primary and secondary labour markets. However, the dynamics underpinning the growth of schooling were not just economic. As Connell *et al.* (1982) observed of the time:

> The coalition favouring growth had a number of elements. People of a liberal mind had long been urging that more education meant social uplift. Critics and researchers in the 1940s pointed out the class biases in the education system, and a natural response was to eliminate them by extending more schooling to those who had been excluded ... Above all, there was popular support. For most people in the 1940s, more education was

one of the hopes they had for a better and more equal postwar world. (Connell *et al.*, 1982, p. 19)

The expansion of schooling, underpinned as it was by the contradictory social relations of efficient accumulation (the commodity form) and the pursuit of common democratic and general interests (the non-commodity form), created the conditions for conflict. Nowhere was this more apparent than in the growing inequality of schooling outcomes. Despite two decades of rhetoric about uniformity and equity within public education, a convincing body of evidence by the late 1970s pointed to the facts. Schools were active producers of inequality (Rist, 1970; Anyon, 1980), exposing 'a thinly strung welfare safety-net', rather than a set of arrangements recognizing citizens as active agents, not passive objects, of welfare (Beihartz, 1989, p. 141).

These debates on schooling inequality placed teachers on centre-stage. Were teachers agents of the State and capital? What was teachers' class location? Did the ideology of professionalism politically immobilize teachers? What was teachers' status *vis-à-vis* other professional groups? Throughout the post-war period teachers in Australia had consistently sought social recognition and economic reward from the State in exchange for their possession of scarce knowledge and skills. In fact, teachers' right to bargain for better working conditions had been accepted in all provincial states within Australia by the late 1940s. However teacher unions increasingly sought settlement through a system of arbitration rather than direct employer negotiation (Spaull, 1990, p. 12). This resulted in the highly centralized unions of this period largely being incorporated into most state educational apparatus, effectively neutralizing them.

The capacity of public-sector teachers to create a protected institutional market for their services, in comparison to doctors and lawyers, has only ever been partially successful and teachers remained on the periphery in relation to other professional occupations. The reasons for this are crucial to understanding the 'border' existence for teachers as a 'core' profession in Australia. To begin, teaching in Australia, as in many other countries, is a feminized occupation. Around two-thirds of teachers are female, with the bulk of women located in the elementary and early childhood areas of teaching (Schools Council, 1990, p. 34). Further, teaching is widely conceived as structurally equating to the labour of females in the household — caring for children. Clearly then, as Larson (1988, p. 25) reminds us, individuals and groups have differential capacities to appropriate authoritative and authorizing discourse, and it is 'this differential capacity [which] constitutes a singular and characteristic dimension of social inequality' both within professions and between different occupational groups. Within education, those teachers (i) whose knowledge embodies the rationality of science, (ii) who are in male-dominated areas, and (iii) in close proximity to authority and power (as in private schools), have greater authority to speak as educational professionals. Foucault (1980) refers to this as the knowledge–power relation. Within education, discipline areas dominated by males, such as science and mathematics (buoyed by powerful professional associations), or teachers in private schools, have been more successful in claiming and being constituted as more 'learned' and therefore more expert. The professional teacher during this period, armed with the ideology of scientific management and an array of objective instruments for promoting reason and testable outcomes, embodied the logic of science.

A second reason for the border-line status of public-sector teachers flows from the fact that the public sector has traditionally attracted to it fractions of the upper working and lower middle classes in what has been an important avenue for social mobility (Connell, 1985, p. 199). Up until 1973, higher education in Australia was not free. Students either funded their way through winning scholarships, or were required to pay substantial tuition fees. Through a system of bonding to the State, whereby the cost of tuition was paid in exchange for a specified period of service following graduation, students could enrol in college-based teacher-training programmes staffed and administered by the Department of Education. Teachers were trained for a minimal period of time, exiting with a two-year diploma and were obligated to take up an appointment wherever the State required. This cheaper alternative to university-based training provided around three-quarters of the teachers for the system. It is hardly surprising that 'bonding' (an almost feudal relationship between the State and the future worker) was an attractive occupational route for working class and female students; many would have faced considerable difficulties in accessing a 'respectable' career. The decision by the socially progressive federal Labor[5] government, elected in 1973, to remove higher education fees, provide federal funding to teacher-training colleges and grant a measure of autonomy to the college sector, went some way to opening up the teacher-training programme to a diversity of intellectual ideas (including a critique of meritocracy and an analysis of the links between schooling and stratification).

This period marked a temporary shift away from the strictly prescribed regimen of bureaucratically based rationality: rules, routines and regulations in the name of system uniformity and equity. The fact remained, however, that despite some freeing up of the system of teacher training, the majority of teachers still acquired their expert knowledge in the lower-status college rather than the university system of the higher education binary in Australia. Nonetheless, the (illusory) promise of professionalism was sufficient to guarantee the co-option of many teachers to the hegemonic project, thereby preventing large numbers of teachers from seeing that their interests were the same as that of the labouring classes. Thus teachers entered into a set of class relations by offering their expertise to a system which, legitimized by the ideology of meritocracy, continued to reproduce the unequal social relations of capitalism (Connell, 1985, p. 192).

This is not to suggest that all teachers in Australia are mere agents at the behest of the State and capital. As in all settlements, the total subordination of workers to the systemic requirements is never completely successful, and for teachers it was no different. By the early 1970s, teacher unions had successfully argued for the removal of barriers, such as marriage and family responsibilities, to permanent employment for women (Spaull, 1990, p. 12). In addition, teacher unions across Australia increasingly became embroiled in a number of public and electoral opinion campaigns over a range of issues, such as federal government funding to private schools (Spaull, 1990, p. 12), and formed a strategic alliance with other unions under the umbrella of the Australian Council for Trade Unions (ACTU). On the agenda were issues such as wage parity for females. The decision by the Federal Arbitration Commission in 1974 to increase female wages to approximately 80 per cent of male wages was to have important political and economic ramifications in Australia. A flight of capital at a time of global recession was accompanied by a hastened process of de-industrialization, as industries dependent upon cheap female labour (for example in the footwear and clothing industries) sought new havens for profitability (Catley, 1978). The popularist government stepped up its public-sector spending in an effort to inject much needed funds into the system and at the same time meet the demands of its large constituency of voters. However, the imminent fiscal crisis of the State and the resultant political turmoil not only forced the controversial dismissal of the Whitlam government in 1975, but laid the foundations for a highly pragmatic form of politics within the Labor party on its return to power in 1983 (Beilhartz, 1994).

The early 1970s heralded a period of political ferment in Australian education (Beilhartz, 1989). The increasingly obvious economic inequalities and social injustices produced by the system of public and private education were not lost on some teachers (Connell *et al.*, 1982, p. 197). The views of a number of the teachers in Connell's study examining the complex relations of gender and class and educational inequality were clearly at odds with the dominant ideology of meritocracy. However, teachers still resisted seeing inequality in class terms (Connell, 1985, p. 198). This fact is crucial in understanding the barriers to teachers' potential for class action. Despite this, the significant injection of federal funds to state-funded schools, underpinned by the twin ideologies of socially progressivism and centralist federalism, did have an important impact upon the work of teachers by providing an opportunity for some change within schools.[6] For a brief period, federal funds provided a mechanism for innovative teachers to side-step the weight of bureaucratic regulation at the State level. A small band of active and committed teachers and principals seized the opportunity, creating school environments where innovation, creativity, pedagogy and collegiality culminated in a grass-roots school-development reform movement (Robertson, 1990). Recasting the knowledge–power relation, these scattered groups of practitioners committed themselves to make a difference to those students the system had succeeded in marginalizing. However, as Beilhartz (1989) notes, at best the Whitlam reforms were only an enlightened liberalism, where 'positive equality remained essentially meritocratic liberalism bathed in a rosy hue — the focus on health and education as preconditions of individual achievement and social performance . . . For Whitlam this meant, in naive yet touching pathos, that every child should have a desk, a lamp and privacy in which to study' (1989, p. 144). In other words, the essential message was about opportunities within the existing social relations.

As a result, the more pressing problems of teachers, such as problems of authority, dilemmas of curriculum content and student motivation refused to go away. The failure to substantially renovate the curriculum, despite a massive injection of funds, meant large numbers of children encountered either useless or irrelevant knowledge. Added to this were twin realities; first, that teachers had been drawn into competition for credentials as a profession but had limited means to win higher prices for their services, and second, that their 'uncertain professional self-images were insulted by conditions of work that routinely included overcrowded class-rooms and staffrooms, temporary buildings, and bureaucratic control by their employer' (Connell *et al.*, 1982, p. 23). This resulted in a heightened level of volatility, militancy and widespread strikes in Victoria and New South Wales. While some teachers clearly realized that their interests and that of their students lay in an association with other workers, for the most part the insidious controls of professionalism and 'being a good teacher' were largely unproblematic and went unchallenged (Watkins, 1992, p. 46).

Given, as Larson has observed, the 'complex social project of modern professional reform thus intertwined market and non-market orientations, disparate intellectual and ideological resources that feed back on each other' (1988, p. 27), then the brief but politically more open environment of this period provided some space for a diversity of discourses amongst teachers and teacher educators. In an effort to co-opt criticism and dissent, some state education departments attempted to manage the process by implementing limited forms of community participation, decentralization, reviewing the relevancy of curricular, and implementing more progressive teaching methods (Connell *et al.*, 1982, p. 16). Educational provision had briefly become a more critical discursive field made up of experts and a lay public, often with conflicting points of view, but nonetheless unified by a common concern: the social and economic education of children.

However, the relationship of schools to the labour market had changed by the late 1970s, leading Connell and his colleagues to observe that 'a programme for a drastic reform of schooling in a socially conservative direction is emerging' (1982, p. 16). It was increasingly difficult to disguise that the effective displacement of growing numbers of people, including youth, into the category of socially redundant (and unemployed) with no place in society was the product of a poor work ethic.

Teachers as Flexible Workers and the Post-Fordist Development Model

Following the collapse of the Fordist grand compromise, the whole of the education system — including teacher education — was under the political microscope. Critics launched successively more vicious attacks on teachers' competence, while teachers' vulnerability over their alleged failure to be more scientific, and therefore professional, was exploited. A profession which could not make explicit the scientific basis of its knowledge and practices was no profession at all! The fact was, the rules of the game had changed.

At the heart of the attack was the need to reorient schooling, and therefore the work of teachers, to the emerging model of development observers have called post-Fordist (Harvey, 1990; Lipietz, 1992; Jessop, 1990; 1993). This new model is based upon the crucial 'triad': a global regime of capital accumulation based upon the principle of flexibility as a result of intensified competition for diminishing markets; an increasingly flexible labour process centred in the principles of core, contracted and contingency labour and a new set of production concepts based upon teamwork, self-management and multiple but basic skills; and, finally, modes of regulation which are in the main governed by the ideologies of the free-market, individualism and private charity. The crucial issues facing the State and corporate capital were now two-fold: firstly, how to align the schooling system with the new system requirements, and secondly, how to limit the margin for manoeuvre of teachers — and therefore the potential for resistance and contestation — in an environment where teachers would seek to claim expertise and have their authority constituted.

Writing about post-Fordism more generally, John Holloway (1987) has identified three phases in its evolution. First an initial Keynesian and social-democratic phase which seeks to coordinate the efforts of managers, government and workers toward growth and productivity. However, recognition of the difficulties faced, and the less than satisfactory outcome of this approach, usually results in a second phase; a more macho approach by industrialists and politicians aimed at reasserting managerial power and facilitating a new strategy for growth. According to Holloway, the second phase is largely a transitional one, 'well suited to destroying the vestiges of Fordism/Keynesianism but not suitable for establishing the . . . patterns of the brave new world' (1987, p. 157). The aim of the third phase is to build upon the defeats achieved in the second phase in constructing a new consensus and new forms of integration, based upon the new division between core and marginalized workers.

This three-phase process can clearly be detected in the implementation of the post-Fordist development model in Australia and the reconstruction of teachers' labour. However, the implementation of this model has been politically mediated by an Accord involving corporate capital, peak interests within the labour movement and the State. Since 1983, the Prices and Incomes Accord has been the centrepiece of Labor's electoral strategy and a mechanism to guide Australia through the social and economic crisis (Watts, 1989, p. 104). The Accord has influenced the pace, direction and immediate outcome of the transition to post-Fordism. This strategy of 'progressive competitiveness', as an alternative to 'hyper-liberal globalization', has been described by Panitch as conforming to the principles of global competitiveness but which is also linked to the interests of peak social groups.

> In this way, key social groups that would otherwise become dangerously marginalised as a result of the state's sponsorship of global competitiveness may become attached to it by the appeal a progressive competitiveness strategy makes, especially through the ideology and practice of training, to incorporating working people who are unemployed and on welfare (or who soon might be) as well as the leaders of unions, social agencies and other organizations who speak for them. (Panitch, 1994, p. 84)

This strategy of progressive competitiveness is clearly evident in the reorganization of teachers' labour in Australia. A number of the key initiatives to restructure teachers' work have taken place under the auspices of the Accord partners. As a result, in comparison to the aggressive restructuring that has taken place in New Zealand and Great Britain, the process in Australia has been somewhat more muted. However, as Panitch also observes, this strategy has not offered an alternative to the logic of global competitiveness but rather is a 'subsidiary element in the process of neo-liberal capitalist restructuring and globalization' (1994, p. 85). In essence, the strategy of progressive competitiveness, while a more humane version, is typically a cosmetic means of buying off domestic opposition. Its effect at the school-level has been to produce teachers in a state of 'subdued agency'; a consensus seeking teacher who lays out the available options and facilitates a process of choice (Harris, 1994, p. 4).

Clearly teachers are a potential source of opposition during a period of transition. The potential for conflict arises during periods of fundamental restructuring when the prevailing ideology of an occupational group differs sharply from that of the new regime. Having been steeped in more than three decades of the ideology of the welfare state and notions of 'social uplift', teachers are likely to question those reforms which legitimize private rather than public interests, and which might lead to further inequity and social injustice. This poses potential problems for the new regime. For one, not all teachers can be dismissed for non-compliance. For another, training programmes cannot be hastily reshaped without some struggle. Thus, regulatory mechanisms are sought which significantly increase the degree of control over teachers, thereby limiting the space available for reflection, critique and contestation. Given that teachers are to implement the new reforms, what is required is greater control over the margin of discretion in their work. Further, the majority of teachers must be encouraged to embrace the new reforms. Three key regulatory tools have been crucial in this process in Australia: first, the promise of a new level of professionalism given concrete form by the introduction of new work practices (largely administrative); second, the implementation of a competency-based, outcome-oriented pedagogy which corresponds functionally to the world of work; and third, school–community (and business) partnerships. These tools have worked together, reinforcing each other.

Implementing Change

At one level, effecting change in teachers' work is no easy task. Teachers are one of the largest and most unionized occupational groups in Australia. They also make up approximately 3 per cent of the total labour force (Schools Council, 1990, p. 34). A quarter of a million teachers teach in around ten thousand primary, pre-primary and secondary schools spread across seven states and territories. Politicians, ever mindful of the pragmatics of party politics (which generally means staying in office), could be swayed by a powerful teachers' lobby. At another level, teachers' sensitivity to their marginal professional status can be used to impose an agenda which is, in reality, antithetical to their interests as autonomous workers. As it happened, when events unfolded in the 1980s, the reassertion of managerial power in the form of devolved administrative practice and the

Table 2.1: *Policy Directions and Discursive Shifts in Restructuring Teachers' Work in Australia*

Periodization	First wave Late 1970s	Second wave Early 1980s	Third wave Mid to late 1980s	Fourth wave 1990s
Focus	System	System	System/School	School/Classroom
Policy Directions	Keynesian • curricula adjustment • teacher supply • community confidence • professional development	Destabilization of existing settlement	Macro-restructuring • devolution • centralization • performance management	Micro-restructuring • labour flexibility • deregulation of schools
Discourse	• community • change • professionalism	• quality • outcomes • efficiency	• quality • outcomes • efficiency • professionalism • collegiality • entrepreneurialism	• quality • outcomes • professionalism • flexibility • work teams • competency
Outcomes	• system maintenance	crisis of confidence in teachers	• managerial control • standardization • market driven • labour intensification • greater managerial responsibility	• deregulation of labour • tiered labour structure • market driven • pedagogical deskilling • greater managerial responsibility • differentiation (student and curriculum)

imposition of school–community partnerships under the banner of professionalism, distracted teachers and concealed from them the fact that power had been further centralized. More importantly, many teachers did not connect these developments to the real agenda: a class war that had resulted in the restructuring of workplaces across the country. The result was that many teachers failed to understand the potential gravity of the changes within Australian society (Robertson and Soucek, 1991).

The restructuring of teachers' work which pushed teachers into the new world of post-Fordist flexibility appears to follow the evolution detailed by Holloway (1987) above. I have identified four phases (see Table 2.1) in the restructuring of teachers' labour in Australia (see also Robertson, 1994).

The first phase, coming at the end of the 1970s, was largely directed toward system maintenance. In the context of the curriculum, the official state line was that if teachers were engaged in work-experience programmes, better career counselling, school-to-work transition programmes, and highlighting the value of the work ethic and good manners — in other words, tinkered around the edges — that this would be sufficient to reorient the structural and functional relationship between schools and the economy (c.f. the Williams Report, 1979). With regard to teacher education, a series of reports focused their concerns upon issues such as teacher supply, managing change, community confidence and the professional development of teachers. In large part, however, the reports were underpinned by the Keynesian solution of altering the supply factors to alter the educational outputs. Many educators failed to be impressed by what was implied in these reports; that they had produced the crisis in education. So were some provincial governments; some refused to accept the generous federal programme funds, although the conflict was largely the result of federal–provincial tensions, rather than a more substantive critique of federal educational policy.

Destabilizing the Teaching Profession

The second phase of the restructuring grew from the failure to align schooling provision to shifts within the productive sector. The fiscal crisis of the State, a result of the diminution of the State's capacity to draw in a share of corporate profits as a result of de-industrialization and financial deregulation, together with the growing burden of unemployment (Watts, 1989, p. 106), saw the State turn to pruning a range of citizenship entitlements within the social-policy arena, including education. Despite the fact that Labor governments dominated federal and provincial politics throughout the 1980s, and that teachers had actively campaigned for the Australian Labor Party, it did not curtail the attack on education. Restructuring education, the State argued, was essential to produce a skilled and flexible labour force enabling Australia to become internationally competitive (Dawkins, 1988). However, there is also no doubt that the State's capacity to drive down education expenditures was limited by the current wage-award structures which underpinned teachers' wages. As in other parts of the workforce, wage flexibility was now viewed as central to market flexibility and global competitiveness.

This required a more radical change both in the organization and the terms and conditions of teachers' work. In other words, the labour process of teachers' work needed to be reworked. This could only be done by destabilizing the existing cultural and regulatory frameworks surrounding teachers' labour through an ideological attack on teacher competence. The most significant of the reports was the 1985 Federal *Report of the Quality of Education Review Committee* chaired by Professor Peter Karmel. While acknowledging the lack of supporting evidence, the Report nonetheless argued that teachers lacked the skills to develop fundamental competencies in students (reading, writing, conversing, calculating), rigour in teaching, and curriculum consistency (1985, p. 119). In other words, an efficient or professional teacher was concerned with the 'science' of teaching and learning for greater economic returns. This science could find concrete expression in measured student outcomes, public accountability through standards, and attention to the basic skills. Teacher professionalism was now constituted within a very different framework which was linked to changes within the economy.

Implementing the New Regime and Managing Dissent

Under the guidance of the corporate sector and key interests within the State (Pusey, 1991) the intent of the third phase (which was well underway by the late 1980s in almost all provincial states of Australia) was to spearhead an aggressive implementation of new managerialism within the administrative structure of education. Not only did it wipe out the potential for internal dissent, as those within the bureaucracy scrambled for jobs, but many of the new appointees at senior level were members of the technocracy; a professional managerialist class with no allegiance to teachers. This occurred concurrently within the federal and provincial arenas. In bureaucratic parlance this phase became known as the 'reorg' (Ashenden, 1990).

The intended purpose of this phase was to embed the tools (such as strategic planning, performance monitoring, site-based management and student outcomes) central to the new post-Fordist regime (efficiency, markets, entrepreneurialism) within education through a reassertion of managerial control and professional imperative. State-level devolutionary reforms in Australia tended to follow a similar pattern where the contradictory logics of corporate managerialism (flatter structures, decentralized decision-making, management information systems) and the professional imperatives of educational and organizational progressivism (school–community partnerships, site-based management, collegiality, self-determination) were grafted together. But as Harris notes, within this 'larger process of adopting forms and processes of corporate managerialism, professionals such as teachers are being redefined as straight-out contracted workers subject to direct management and becoming positioned in such a way that their expertise and professional knowledge is decreasingly called upon with regard to decision-making in areas central to the needs and requirements of those whom they teach and serve' (1994, p. 3).

Some teachers were wooed by the promise of a new professionalism. Others were forced to embrace the new practices when the new ideology found definition in the system of 'merit' promotion. However, in a remarkable show of solidarity, huge numbers of teachers went on strike in protest (Robertson and Soucek, 1991; Luzeckyj, 1992; Isaacs, 1993). They received little sympathy from the media who presented their dissent as the expected outpourings of over-paid, over-holidayed and underworked public servants. With teachers' claim to expert knowledge marginalized in the public mind, teachers' capacity to mobilize the laity — and therefore some support to their cause — was diminished. However, as Spaull has argued, 'the breadth of teacher union politics, and their willingness to prosecute them on as many fronts as are available, is certainly a new feature of contemporary unionism' (1990, p. 14). In an interesting turn of events, while other unions have declined in number, teachers' unions have increased. Spaull suggests that a combination of factors are involved in this, including the realization by teachers that they need to protect their working conditions, that they might be able to exploit the politics of devolution to increase control over their work situation, and that they can and should be social critics of society. Indeed, Isaacs (1993) draws upon evidence gathered in Victoria to argue that in comparison to the post-war period, Victorian teachers, at least, display a shift in class affiliation from the middle- to the working-class.

The solidarity of teachers was certainly apparent during the period of 1989 to 1993 in traditionally conservative states such as Western Australia. Despite the general lack of public support, outraged teachers and principals rallied in massive numbers (Robertson and Soucek, 1991). In some of the largest demonstrations in Australia since the troubled days of the Vietnam war, teachers took to the streets. In an ongoing campaign of active resistance, huge numbers of teachers waged a bitter battle of strikes, work-to-rules, lockouts, and the length of the working day. The struggle over the working day, as Harvey notes (1990, p. 230), has long been the familiar landscape of industrial capitalism in battles over minutes and seconds, and the intensity of work schedules. Rifts soon appeared between teachers, nourished by the image of the 'good teacher' who ignored the time-clock and remained dedicated to the organization, no matter what. But the failure of teacher unions to deliver either public acknowledgment of teachers' efforts as competent professionals or political recognition of their increased productivity by way of salary increases, resulted in many teachers losing the momentum which they had mobilized. The crucial issue for teachers seems to be that while their numbers have grown and their class affiliation has shifted, they must also develop a political programme to influence the course of events and construct their own futures (Harris, 1994).

Embedding the new post-Fordist rules has had the effect of tightening of the structural correspondence between education and the economy. In essence, the changes have meant teachers can participate in making decisions over a limited range of technical issues, not the big ticket items such as: What is it that we want children to know? How do we provide opportunities for students to genuinely participate in the learning process? What does it mean to educate a critical citizenry? Instead teachers have been left to dream up schemes as to how they can work smarter to increase student performance, compete for scarce students with neighbouring schools, raise money from the business sector, or access new technology for the school through school–business partnerships. At the same time it has marginalized teachers' dissenting voices and reduced their scope for critical practice and autonomy. Harris describes this as a process of repoliticizing of teachers 'away from the broader concerns of determining curricula, formulating educational goals and promoting social reconstruction and toward the realm of efficient school management within an educational marketplace' (1994, p. 4). This is not to suggest that some teachers are not able to see the extent to which markets and managerialism have eroded their already precariously balanced marginal autonomy. Examples of teachers protesting these changes are numerous. Teachers have pointed out the contradictions between good nutrition and the installation of Coke and Pepsi machines on the school grounds and have successfully campaigned to have McDonalds banned from forming school–business partnerships. However, the really insidious controls over the work of teachers have slipped in, as if they were invisible.

It is important at this point to reflect upon precisely what it is that teachers have lost control over. The work of Derber (1982) is useful here in understanding the dual forms of control over workers like teachers. He terms these two forms of control: ideological and technical. The loss of autonomy in these two spheres can be described as 'ideological' and 'technical proletarianization' (Derber, 1982, p. 30). The former involves teachers losing control over the goals, objectives and policy directions of their work. The latter refers to a loss of control over the skills, content, rhythm and pace of their work, for example with the introduction of various forms of technology in the classroom.

The loss of ideological control has occurred in a number of ways in the current round of restructuring. For example, the government has typically refused to engage in any level of prior consultation with teachers, their unions or teacher educators on the precise shape of key administrative, organizational or curriculum changes within education. The consultation which has occurred has been tightly managed and after the fact. The fact is, the goals, objectives and policy directions for schools are not for teachers to determine. Rather, the organization of schooling and teachers' work must take its cue from the needs of industry. An array of committees and forums, such as the Finn Committee under the chairmanship of Brian Finn (IBM General Manager) reviewing post-compulsory schooling, the Meyer Committee to implement the competency-based curriculum under the Chairmanship of Eric Meyer (National Mutual Life Insurance), the Industry Education Forum with representatives from all the large transnational corporations, and the federal Economic Planning and Advisory Council (a coalition of state, corporate capital and peak unions) have all laid out the ideal worker for the new regime: multiskilled, efficient, self-reliant, team-oriented, adaptable and flexible. The task for teachers is to develop new approaches to teaching which efficiently produce the ideal worker.

There are many instances which illustrate the technical proletarianization of teachers as well. For example, teachers have increasingly lost the scope to choose methods for determining how well students meet predefined goals. Rather, a national curriculum and standardized testing to monitor through student performance are the mechanisms by which teachers are now controlled. The advance of computer technology, as well as the onslaught of corporate-funded television programming for students in schools, are further instances of technical proletarianization.

The intensification of teachers' labour, an outcome of this third wave of educational restructuring, has certainly limited the opportunities for teachers to engage critically with their students. In a study on the impact of devolution on teachers in Western Australia, teachers reported the need to constantly attend meetings as a result of collegial and managerial demands, the escalation of accountability and control initiatives, the pressure to be more entrepreneurial, and an increasing scarcity of resources which led to intense rapid politicization. All of these activities took considerable time. In order to meet their commitments teachers worked longer hours per day and more days of the week (Robertson and Soucek, 1991).

The compression of time and space leading to an intensification of teachers' labour has resulted from a complex of factors. These include bigger classes, the addition of new managerial tasks at the school level, new technology such as fax machines moving information in and out of the school, new information systems in the school which monitor student and map school performance, increased activity around business partnerships, more intense entrepreneurial activity, a constant cycle of assessments, to name but a few (Smyth, 1993). The intensification of teachers' work inevitably leads to the prioritizing of those activities which are rewarded over those that are not. This is only human. Given that the reward structures for teachers are now based upon being able to generate market competitiveness, it is obvious where the sacrifices will be made. However, the more distant teachers become from their students, the more depersonalized their teaching. This leads inexorably to an even further alienated relationship between themselves and their students. Their relationship takes on all of the characteristics of the commodity form (Grace, 1989). It is the logic of the market — the commodity form — which has penetrated deep inside the schools, and constituted the authority of the new professional. The new professional has embraced a new science; the commodity form in the schooling market-place.

The commodity form can be seen in a myriad of ways: the direct involvement of business in the school by funding computer equipment and sponsoring industry-based scholarships, the encouragement of entrepreneurial teachers in the school, the development of niche courses such as aeronautics and art/fashion, and in marketing of the school's performances to the wider community. The outcome is that niche schools are able to provide, under the guidance of the corporate sector, a small band of suitably skilled workers to work in specialized industries. This trend toward market specialization in schools, based upon the principle of 'just-in-time', 'marks a bid by a new ideological configuration . . . educators are asked to base the curriculum on market trends which in turn are grounded in market forecasting' (Aronowitz and Giroux, 1985, p. 192).

The emerging entrepreneurial culture within the schools has not advantaged all teachers in the same way. We found winners and losers in our study of the effects on teachers of devolution (Robertson and Soucek, 1991). The winners were teachers who embraced the market, new managerialism and technology, setting into place the structural and functional correspondence between schools and the economy. They were the new entrepreneurs — the new professionals amongst teachers. Their values corresponded to the values of the post-Fordist regime, and they were rewarded accordingly. The losers were those teachers who failed to exploit the new opportunities, either for ideological reasons or because they were in areas where their expertise was no longer needed or valued. These teachers had fewer resources and marginal influence.

However, responding to market niches raised problems for teachers which had not been anticipated. The highly specialized programmes in the school attracted an *élite* group of male-student outsiders. Their presence in the school increased the divisions within the school resulting in conflict between the *élites* and the local 'lads'. In order to counter an emerging gender imbalance, the school offered a programme of specialized science and technology to an *élite* group of females. Again the programme attracted mainly outsiders. These female imports, however, were unhappy about establishing themselves in this new environment, and the programme was disbanded. In both cases, the idea of importing students did not sit well with all teachers. In our interviews, some teachers were firmly committed to the idea of a school servicing its local community. This view stands in opposition to the competitive school which provides specialized services within the educational market-place.

Embedding the New Commonsense

A final phase in the restructuring of teachers' work in Australia — beginning in the 1990s and still underway — is concerned with embedding the new commonsense of the post-Fordist model of development. Here the labour process, regime of accumulation and modes of regulation must work together to close the hegemonic circle. With ideological controls in place through the new management framework, thereby limiting the possibility for critique and autonomous action by teachers, the corporate sector and reform technocrats have challenged willing schools and teachers to 'trial' and 'experiment' with new work practices which might carry the new curriculum (National Project on the Quality of Teaching and Learning, 1991).

This phase has been paralleled by crucial changes to the industrial-relations legislation. The conditions for the deregulation of wage bargaining, pressed for by the corporate sector, took form in March 1987 when the federal Industrial Relations Commission (IRC) handed down their historic decision that wage increases were conditional upon productivity gains (Niland, 1992, p. 33). This marked a turning point in Australian industrial relations. Wage increases over the past century in Australia have rested in the judicial principles of uniformity across industries. This decision has opened the way for the deregulation of wage bargaining.

By late 1993 the new industrial-relations legislation was in force. Teachers in Victoria faced massive lay-offs, extensive school closures, and the deregulation of all wage bargaining. Western Australia is rapidly following suit. Wages are now determined in the market-place, with no guarantee of a bottom-line or safety net.

The thin strings of the welfare state have been severed altogether. For teachers, the outcome has been fear and compliance. The new professional must now sit up straight, with lips buttoned and eyes forward! The flight of teachers from provincial to federal awards offers teachers short-term protection. However, if teachers are covered on one federal award, teachers *en masse* are likely to be highly vulnerable to a change in political party. Despite the limitations of federal–state relations, the politics which flow from this relationship have sometimes been a source of protection from some forms of political control.

A crucial ideological theme in this phase of the restructuring is the notion of flexibility and adaptability. However, flexibility now has a very particular meaning. In outlining the federal government's view of flexibility, the Schools Council locates flexibility within a managerial and market-oriented framework rather than a pedagogical one. That is, flexibility is:

> ... the skilful *management* of human and physical resources in response to identified educational needs which results in increased *effectiveness* (e.g., improved student learning outcomes) and *productivity* (e.g., improved school performance. (my emphasis) (Schools Council, 1992)

The teacher is now constituted as the 'manager' of resources which might lead to pre-specified learning outcomes and targeted performances. And while learners are to be enterprising, self-directed, work in multi-level groups, and progress on an individualized basis (Schools Council, 1989, 1992), their endeavours within school are almost exclusively directed toward their 'flexible' participation world of work rather than participation within the wider society. Here the functional requirements of the economy are made explicit. Further, the School Council outlines a structural alignment or correspondence between the organization of teachers' labour and the organization of labour within the wider workforce; the increased segmentation in teachers' work to enable staffing flexibility and cost efficiencies (Schools Council, 1992, p. 16).

However, there is no discussion by the School Council of the more dysfunctional relations within schools and which affect teachers' work; in essence, the contradictions that are revealed by the growing number of economic and social losers in the system. For example, how should teachers cope with the increased levels of stress in the classroom — the result not only of hunger, violence, abuse, and drugs, but an intense sense of hopelessness and alienation amongst an increasing number of students. The fact is, many of these students are never likely to enter the core or contract labour market. Rather they will be unceremoniously directed toward an insecure contingency labour market with basic skills and few chances but a healthy dose of the new ideology: adaptability and market flexibility. Teachers, with their reconstituted professional status authorized within the market-place, will be expected to play a key role as agents in this process.

And this outcome is precisely what the federally funded National Schools Project (NSP) is intended to achieve; to embed a new set of work practices within schools which works toward realizing the industry-endorsed worker competencies, while at the same time aligning the organization of schooling with the organization of the workplace. This requires that teachers review those work practices which are now dysfunctional and replace them with new ones directed to achieving the new system imperatives. However, providing a context for teachers to experiment with these new practices is quite a challenge. The brief for individual schools around Australia has been to investigate how changes in work practices can lead to improved student outcomes whilst working within current levels of resourcing.[7]

The NSP has several distinct features. Project schools operate in a 'deregulated zone' where the regulatory framework for teachers and their work is suspended. Further, the Project framework is also tightly prescribed — further evidence of ideological proletarianization. Teachers must accept a model of curriculum which is outcome-oriented and concerned with workplace competencies.[8] In addition, the focus for reforms must be on work practices rather than on the curriculum. The unit of change, to use the NSP jargon and borrowed directly from the post-Fordist literature, must be the 'systems work unit'. However, reframing teachers' central concerns as those of management rather than pedagogy has caused considerable unease, as is evident from this NSP teacher:

> To effect change for education for the 21st Century we need to change the relationship between teachers and students. But when we probed . . . (NSP official) on this point in terms of pedagogy he said the project was not about pedagogy, it's about work organization. His argument was that you can change pedagogy all you like and change teachers' professional development and have wonderful new programs going but they only last as long as teachers' interest in them. Whereas what he wants is change embedded in the organization. I think they have to go hand in hand. I can't see that just a change in structure is going to have a significant influence on student learning outcomes unless you have an associated complimentary change in the process. This is why I'm becoming more convinced that the only way to go is to adopt the philosophy of student centred learning, because if we do everything in terms of that, then we will both achieve. (Chadbourne, 1992, p. 51)

The teacher in Chadbourne's study reported above can see the need for changes to the organization of schooling. However, what is clear is that state officials believe pedagogical change should flow only from managerial change, rather than the other way around. In other words, it is still the case of the managerial tail waving the pedagogical dog. The crucial change is that the rhythm of the new managerial tune is now determined by the post-Fordist market-place!

The NSP's strategic separation of pedagogical concerns from managerial processes represents confused thinking about what ought to be the central and real interests of teachers. Teachers cite their immediate concerns such as problems of student literacy and numeracy, student behaviour, oversized classrooms, lack of resources, and the overtly top–down approach to innovation and change as the more significant barriers to learning (Chadbourne, 1992, pp. 30–1). Were teachers in the NSP to tackle issues such as what to do about growing student alienation within schooling, or what might constitute a set of outcomes for students which are linked to socially oriented goals, then teachers could be said to be moving toward creating the space for some intellectual autonomy. The fact that teachers have largely failed to do this, despite their increased level of unionization, is evidence of a further diminution of their already reduced capacity for critical autonomy.

By far the NSP's most controversial proposal for regulatory change has concerned the flexible deployment of non-teaching staff to assist teachers in a more diverse array of tasks. These propositions are also at the core of Ashenden's (1992) proposals. To begin, Ashenden argues that teachers' work is badly designed and managed, and there are too many trivial tasks. However, these 'trivial' tasks, like writing letters to parents about a student's behaviour, arise not so much as a result of the way in which teachers' work is organized, but as a result of the organization of schooling in general. Schools, as institutions, are structures of power. Further, many of the constant infractions arise as a result of the contestation of class/gender/ ethnic relations within the school (see Connell *et al.*, 1982). This affects teachers' relationships with students. And as Ashenden himself reminds us (1992, p. 57), relationships with students can be spectacularly conflicting, upsetting and humiliating. These relations border on a constant movement in the classroom from consent to coercion, from resistance to compliance and pragmatism (Connell *et al.*, 1982). Unless the proposed changes to the organization of schooling confront the underlying relations of power, then little will alter.

Ashenden also argues that unless staffing is made more flexible, teachers will be unable to deliver increased student productivity (measured in student outcome terms). Ashenden proposes to reduce the number of professional staff in the school by more than one-third, and use the surplus funds to employ a range of other flexible educational workers in para-professional roles (parents, student teachers, consultants, teacher aides) on a casual or short-term contract basis. According to Ashenden, teachers do too much busy-work which is not real teaching. Teachers would also be encouraged to explore new options for the delivery of education, including the use of large groups, new technologies, learning packages, and peer tutoring.

What can be seen emerging here is a core and peripheral workforce typical of post-Fordism: a core of trained teachers and the periphery made up of expendable units of semi-skilled and cheaper labour, in this case parents, the unemployed and interns (c.f. Harvey, 1990). The remaining teachers would be required to do more of the 'real' teaching, while those skills which can be separated off will be embedded in a machine or given to cheaper workers to perform. It is this process, described so graphically by Braverman (1974), centred on the deskilling and devaluing of labour power which describes the essential features of proletarianization; the 'economic process of devaluation of labour power from skilled to average levels' (Harris, 1994, p. 1). While it is to be hoped that the peripheral workforce that operates within the school remains dedicated and available to the school, the low rates of pay make this doubtful. If it is the case that they stay, the school will be able to devote its main energies to curriculum as opposed to staffing issues. If not, these energies will be dissipated, and the school will operate on a constant training cycle.

In a study which explored teachers' views on these proposals (Chadbourne and Robertson, 1992) in a junior primary school, we found that most staff would like the support of para-professionals. However, teachers opposed increased salaries if it meant an erosion of other conditions, such as an increase in class sizes or an escalation in the number of multiple-ability groups. These teachers argue that moving to larger classes would reduce their contact with students and limit their teaching strategies and relationships with students. They argued that an inevitable outcome of these changes would be a burgeoning managerial (and supervisory) role for teachers, taking them out of the classroom and interaction with students. These teachers were reluctant to see a further division in their labour, arguing that there was very little which could be further delegated without significantly deskilling them and eroding their relationships with the students. The proposed expansion of technology within the school also worried them. Aside from the costs of computer technology being outside of the reach of many financially constrained schools, teachers also observed that the software available was educationally limited.

Some elements of the Ashenden proposal have merit. For too long teachers have engaged in teacher-centred pedagogy. A shift away toward a more learner-centred pedagogy would be a highly desirable move. But this would have to take the form of a shift toward a critical pedagogy which is built upon a relationship of trust and a genuine interest in the child as citizen, rather than as a commodity in the market-place. Unless the underlying relations of power upon which schooling is built are confronted, then the sorts of proposals offered by Ashenden will only momentarily obscure the social relations which schools are asked to reproduce. The problem with Ashenden's proposal, and his is the only one example amongst a growing number in the same vein, is that the model is essentially undemocratic. These proposals begin with the system imperatives of adaptability and flexibility for the economy rather than the needs of the life world and the child.

A New Professionalism for Teachers?

The evidence is overwhelming. The current restructuring initiatives — in the name of a new professionalism — have not created the conditions for teachers to work as autonomous intellectuals. Rather, I have shown that teachers have become a special target for control, because of their crucial role in the production of knowledge and labour power for the new post-Fordist settlement. As Harris (1994) reminds us — in a single decade, teachers have lost a great deal! The outcome of the reorganization of teachers' work is increased segmentation for the purposes of organizational flexibility, pedagogical deskilling, a new conception of professionalism linked to managerial activity, the reconstruction of teacher as learner-manager, an expansion of tasks to include management activity, and tighter external controls. These developments create a qualitatively different terrain on which teachers must work. The development model which underpinned Fordism has given way to a new post-Fordist ethos: the authority of the highly competitive market-place. Teachers' workplace is also now a market-place, as education takes on the commodity form. Teachers are the new saleswomen and salesmen for the economy; the only catch is that like in all market-places, not all buyers have equal power if the full force of labour deregulation and labour flexibility take their toll.

Teacher flexibility and professionalism have been cast in a new light in the new settlement. Flexibility in schools is not driven by pedagogical concerns, depite the fact that the rhetoric borrows heavily from the critique of schooling launched almost three decades ago. The fall-out for schools already includes larger classes, the increasing use of technology within the school, business–school relationships, the privatization of key services, and a segmented and cheaper teaching force. There is little scope in the promise of professionalism to wrest a degree of autonomy because the crucial margin for determination — that is ideological control — has been unceremoniously split from teachers' work and placed in the firm hands of administrators, politicians and transnational capital. The margin of indetermination is now located at the level of decisions to meet the system-specified outcomes, rather than at the point of judgment about what might constitute an adequate framing of knowledge. Gains to teachers are thus largely illusory. Teachers will be weighed down by the pressure of management, time constraints, larger classes and the management of other workers. What flows from this is a depersonalized authority — an outcome teachers have confused with professionalism. Teachers have not been provided or promised an opportunity to negotiate the changing shape of their work. Rather, their work has increasingly been moulded by economic imperative and expediency, and is the outcome of the State's need to establish the new conditions for accumulation.

Reconceptualizing the Space for Teacher Autonomy

The period of transition creates the conditions for a critical correspondence between teachers, the State and the economy. The dramatic curtailing of teacher autonomy in order to control teachers reveals a further erosion of teachers' already licensed autonomy. This period creates a unique space in which to insert an agenda which seeks to have the voices of teachers also constituted as those with authority to speak in the educational interests of children. But a crucial question remains to be addressed. Are the objective conditions created by the increased tendency toward proletarianization sufficient for teachers to mobilize and act in counter-hegemonic ways. I wish to argue that while Derber's (1982) two forms of proletarianization, technical and ideological, are useful in beginning to conceptualize the erosion of teacher autonomy, it is insufficient to help us understand neither the precise nature of that autonomy, nor the basis from which the possibility for educational change might emerge. That is, a notion of autonomy versus proletarianization does not fully reveal the kind of relationship between teachers, the economy and their students. Can we argue, for example, that a teacher who participates in a forum to discuss the outcomes of a particular set of policies but who has been blinkered by an ideology of professionalism, is acting autonomously? At one level it might appear to be the case. But at another level, the failure of the teacher to interrogate the basic relationships between schooling and the economy, such as the principle of meritocracy, would suggest otherwise. Dale has called this 'regulated autonomy' (Dale, 1982, p. 146). In this case, the basic character of the relationship between the teacher and the State has been mediated by an ideology of professionalism which results in a positive correspondence between schooling and the economy. On the other hand, if the basic character of the relationship between the teachers and the economy is one of critical correspondence, that is, where the teacher is able to see the penetration of the commodity form into the organization of their labour and classroom practice, then this, together with the objective conditions of proletarianization, are more likely to lead to forms of critical resistance and intellectual autonomy.

My argument is that the processes which lead toward the proletarianization of teachers' work, particularly during periods of crisis and transformation, may provide the conditions for, but will not necessarily lead to, a more critical practice within schools. Rather, the shift toward intellectual autonomy and a more critical practice will occur only when teachers are able to recognize and conceptualize the various ways in which the proletarianization of their work is the result of the penetration of the commodity form into schooling and the labour process. This project should be the starting point for future political action by all educators and intellectuals.

Notes

1 Peter Watkins provides a very good account of the different post-Fordist positions, including the French regulation school (1994).
2 I am accepting here that while teachers do occupy a contradictory class location, it is more useful to ask the question that Connell *et al.* (1982) poses: What class relations do teachers enter into? In this way teachers' class relations are seen as more fluid and dynamic rather than being necessarily overdetermined by the material relations of production.
3 John Hinkson (1991), however, argues that schools are increasingly less important as sites of socialization as this role is increasingly taken on by the mass media and television culture.
4 See for example J. Lewington and G. Orpwood, (1993) *Overdue Assignment: Taking Responsibility for Canada's Schools*, Ontario, John Wiley and Sons; A. Nikiforuk (1990) *Schools Out: The Catastrophe in Public Education and What We Can Do About It*, Toronto, Macfarlane Walker and Ross; J. Chubb, T. Moe (1990) *Politics, Markets and America's Schools*, Washington, DC, The Brookings Institute.
5 The Australian Labor Party was formed almost one hundred years ago to represent the interests of labour. In the main its constituency is drawn from the laboring classes and segments of the middle classes.
6 Ironically, it was the federal ideology of political centralism, infused with an economically derived nationalism, which has later profoundly impacted upon the nature of teachers' work in Australia. By 1988, the Federal Government had proposed a national curriculum, national testing and standards, and National Teaching Council. This despite the fact that the Federal Government has no constitutional authority for its

involvement in schooling provision, and that teachers' salaries and appointments are provincial rather than federal affairs.

7   In 1992, over 60 schools joined the NSP. There is funding however for time release for key staff in each of the schools.

8   As identified in the Finn, Mayer and Carmichael reports. The limitation of the overtly economic focus thus is picked up in the construction of these new school cultures and patterns of work organizations.

References

ANYON, J. (1981) 'Social class and the hidden curriculum of work', in GIROUX, H., PENNA, A. and PINAR, A. (Eds) *Curriculum and Instruction: Alternatives for the Future*, Berkeley, McCuthchan.

ARONOWITZ, S. and GIROUX, H. (1985) *Education Under Siege*, Massachusetts, Bergin and Garvey.

ASHENDEN, D. (1990) 'Award restructuring and education', *QTU Professional Magazine*, **8**, 1, pp. 8–13.

ASHENDEN, D. (1992) 'New forms of work organisation for teachers and students: Some developments and possibilities', IARTV Seminar Series, Melbourne, Incorporated Association of Registered Teachers in Victoria.

ANYON, J. (1980) 'Social class and the hidden curriculum of work', *Journal of Education*, **162**, pp. 67–92.

BERMAN, M. (1982) *All That is Solid Melts into Air*, New York, Verso.

BALL, S. (1990) 'Introduction Monsieur Foucault', in BALL, S. (Ed) *Foucault and Education: Disciplines and Knowledge*, London, Routledge.

BALL, S. and GOODSON, I. (1985) *Teachers' Lives and Careers*, Basingstoke, Falmer Press.

BARLOW, M. and ROBERTSON, H. (1994) *Class Warfare: The Assault on Canada's Schools*, Toronto, Key Porter Books.

BEILHARTZ, P. (1989) 'The Labourist tradition and the reforming imagination', in KENNEDY, R. (Ed) *Australian Welfare*, China, Macmillan.

BEILHARTZ, P. (1994) *Transforming Labor: Labour Tradition and the Labor Decade in Australia*, Australia, Cambridge University Press.

BRAVERMAN, H. (1974) *Labour and Monopoly Capital: The Degradation of Work in the Twentieth Century*, New York, Monthly Review Press.

CARLSON, D. (1992) *Teachers and Crisis: Urban School Reform and Teachers' Work Culture*, New York, Routledge.

CATLEY, B. (1978) 'Socialism and reform in contemporary Australia', in WHEELWRIGHT, E. and BUCKLEY, K. (Eds) *Essays in the Political Economy of Australian Capitalism: Volume Two*, Sydney, Australian and New Zealand Book Company.

CHADBOURNE, R. (1992) *The National Schools Project at Belmont Senior High School: A Formative Review of the First Nine Months*, Perth, International Institute for Policy and Administrative Studies.

CHADBOURNE, R. and ROBERTSON, S. (1992) *Dean Ashenden's Proposal for Restructuring Teachers' Work: A Junior Primary Perspective*, Perth, International Institute for Policy and Administrative Studies.

CERNY, P. (1991) *The Changing Architecture of Politics: Structure, Agency and the Future of the State*, Wiltshire, UK, Sage Publications.

COMMITTEE OF ENQUIRY INTO EDUCATION AND TRAINING (Williams Report) (1979) *Education, Training and Employment, Vols 1 and 2, Report* (B. Williams, Chair), Canberra, AGPS.

CONNELL, B., ASHENDEN, D., KESSLER, S. and DOWSETT, G. (1982) *Making the Difference*, Sydney, Allen and Unwin.

CONNELL, B. (1985) *Teachers' Work*, Sydney, George, Allen and Unwin.

DAWKINS, J. (1988) *Strengthening Australia's Schools*, Canberra, AGPS.

DALE, R. (1982) 'Education and the capitalist state: Contributions and contradictions', in APLE, M. (Ed) *Cultural and Economic Reproduction in Education*, London, Routledge and Kegan Paul.

DERBER, C. (1982) *Professionals as Workers: Mental Labour in Advanced Capitalism*, Boston, Massachusetts, G. K. Hall.

FOUCAULT, M. (1980) *Knowledge/power: Selected Interviews and Other Writings*, New York, Pantheon Books.

FRITZELL, C. (1987) 'On the concept of relative autonomy in educational theory', *British Journal of Sociology of Education*, **8**, 1, pp. 23–35.

FREEDMAN, J. (1995) 'New Right tackles social wrongs under guise of cultural warriors', *The Edmonton Journal*, 5 February, pp. A7.

GINSBURG, M. and COOPER, S. (1991) 'Educational reform, the State and the world economy: Understanding and engaging in ideological and other struggles', in GINSBURG, M. (Ed) *Understanding Educational Reform in Global Context*, New York, Garland.

GRACE, G. (1987) 'Teachers and the State in Britain: A changing Britain', in LAWN, M. and GRACE, G. (Eds) *Teachers: The Culture and Politics of Work*, East Sussex, Falmer Press.

GRACE, G. (1989) 'Education: Commodity or public good', *British Journal of Educational Studies*, **37**, 3, pp. 207–21.

HARGREAVES, A. (1994) *Changing Teachers, Changing Times*, Wiltshire, Cassells.

HARRIS, K. (1994) *Teachers: Constructing the Future*, Basingstoke, Falmer Press.

HARVEY, D. (1990) *The Condition of Postmodernity: An Enquiry into the Origins of Cultural Change*, Oxford, Basil Blackwell.

HINKSON, J. (1991) *Postmodernity, State and Education*, Geelong, Deakin University Press.

HOLLOWAY, J. (1987) 'The red rose of Nissan', *Capital and Class*, **32**, pp. 147–65.

ISAACS, D. (1993) 'Shifting class identity and industrial practice: The case of Victoria secondary teachers', *Discourse*, **14**, 1, October, pp. 65–74.

JESSOP, B. (1989) 'Conservative regimes and the transition to post-Fordism: The cases of Great Britain and West Germany', in GOTTDIENER, M. and KOMNINOUS, N. (Eds) *Capitalist Development and Crisis Theory: Accumulation, Regulation and Spatial Restructuring*, Macmillan, London.

JESSOP, B. (1990) 'Regulation theories in retrospect and prospect', *Economy and Society*, **19**, 2, pp. 153–216.

JESSOP, B. (1993) 'Towards a Schrumpeterian workfare state?: Preliminary remarks on post-Fordist radical economy', *Studies in Political Economy*, **40**, Spring, pp. 7–39.

LARSON, S. (1977) *The Rise of Professionalism: A Sociological Analysis*, Berkeley, University of California Press.

LARSON, S. (1988) 'In the matter of experts and professionals, or how impossible it is to leave nothing unsaid', in TORSTENDAHL, R. and BURRAGE, M. (Eds) *The Formation of Professions: Knowledge, State and Strategy*, Newbury Park, Sage.

LIPIETZ, A. (1992) *Toward a New Economic Order: Post-Fordism, Ecology and Democracy*, New York, Oxford University Press.

LUZECKYJ, M. (1992) 'Teachers and industrial relations in South Australia', in RILEY, D. (Ed) *Industrial Relations in Australian Education*, Wentworth Falls, Social Science Press.

McGREW, A. (1992) 'A global society?', in HALL, S., HELD, D. and McGREW, T. (Eds) *Modernity and its Futures*, Oxford, The Open University Press.

NATIONAL PROJECT ON THE QUALITY OF TEACHING AND LEARNING (1991) *The National Schools Project*, Canberra, NPQTL Secretariat.

NILAND, J. (1993) 'The light on the horizon: Essentials of an enterprise focus', in RILEY, D. (Ed) *Industrial Relations in Australian Education*, Wentworth Falls, Social Science Press.

PANITCH, L. (1994) 'Globalisation and the State', in MILIBAND, R. and PANITCH, L. (Eds) *Between Globalism and Nationalism: Socialist Register 1994*, London, The Merlin Press.

PORTER, P. (1990) 'World restructuring has put education in crisis', *QTU Magazine*, **8**, 1, pp. 3–7.

PUSEY, M. (1991) *Economic Rationalism in Canberra: A Nation-building State Changes its Mind*, Sydney, Cambridge University Press.

RIST, R. (1970) 'Student social class and teacher expectations: The self-fulfilling prophecy in Ghetto Education', *Harvard Education Review*, **40**, 3, pp. 411–51.

REPORT OF THE QUALITY IN EDUCATION REVIEW COMMITTEE (1985) *Quality of Education Review* [Chair: Professor P. Karmel], Canberra, AGPS.

ROBERTSON, S. (1990) 'The corporatist settlement in Australia and educational reform', Unpublished doctoral thesis, University of Calgary.

ROBERTSON, S. (1994) 'An exploratory analysis of post-Fordism and teachers' labour', in KENWAY, J. (Ed) *Economising Education: Post-Fordist Directions*, Deakin University Press, Geelong.

ROBERTSON, S. and SOUCEK, V. (1991) 'Changing social realities in Australian schools: A study of teachers' perceptions and experiences of current reforms', A paper presented at the Comparative and International Education Society Conference in Pittsburgh, Pennsylvania.

ROBERTSON, S. and TROTMAN, J. (1992) 'A spoke in the wheels of professionalism', *Education Links*, **42**, pp. 23–9.

SCHOOLS COUNCIL (1989) *Teacher Quality: An Issue Paper*, Canberra, AGPS.

SCHOOLS COUNCIL (1990) *Australia's Teachers: An Agenda for the Next Decade*, Canberra, AGPS.

SCHOOLS COUNCIL (1992) *Developing Flexible Strategies in the Early Years of Schooling*, Canberra, AGPS.

SMYTH, J. (Ed) (1993) *A Socially Critical View of the Self-managing School*, Basingstoke, Falmer Press.

SPAULL, A. (1990) 'Is there a new teacher unionism?', A paper presented to the Annual Meeting of AERA, Boston.

WATKINS, P. (1992) *Class, the Labour Process and Work: A Focus on Teaching*, Geelong, Deakin University Press.

WATKINS, P. (1994) 'The Fordist/post-Fordist debate: The educational implications', in KENWAY, J. (Ed) *Economising Education: Post-Fordist Directions*, Deakin University Press, Geelong.

WATTS, R. (1989) 'In "fractured times": The Accord and social policy under Hawke, 1983–7', in KENNEDY, R. (Ed) *Australian Welfare*, China, Macmillan.

Chapter 3

Teacher Professionalism and Curriculum Control

Gill Helsby and Gary McCulloch

The professionalism of teachers and their control over the curriculum are often assumed to be closely linked to each other. In the English context, moreover, there have been frequent criticisms that the recent emergence of a prescriptive and centralized National Curriculum has undermined this supposedly intimate relationship. The present article seeks to examine such assumptions and criticisms by investigating the changing and contested nature of the relationship between 'teacher professionalism' and 'curriculum control'.[1] It will also highlight some of the concerns expressed by teachers in this regard as a result of recent curriculum initiatives undertaken by the British government, especially the National Curriculum, and will suggest a research agenda of related issues that deserve further and deeper consideration in the years ahead.

Teacher Professionalism and Curriculum Control

The school curriculum provides an important point of entry for inquiry into the nature of teachers' professionalism. This is especially the case if we accept the thrust of the distinction that has recently been drawn between 'professionalization' and 'professionalism' in relation to teachers. Professionalization denotes issues of status that have tended to preoccupy historians and sociologists. These include in particular the quest of teachers to be publicly acknowledged as 'professionals', and of teachers' unions and associations to establish teaching as a recognized 'profession' on the same level as, for example, medicine and law. By contrast, professionalism refers to teachers' rights and obligations to determine their own tasks in the classroom, that is, to the way in which teachers develop, negotiate, use and control their own knowledge. Drawing on suggestions developed in recent published works in the United States, Linda Eisenmann asserts a need to focus on questions about 'how and what teachers actually taught in the classroom and how they exercised their professionalism' (Eisenmann, 1991, p. 224). This kind of focus on the idea of teacher professionalism emphasizes different forms of knowledge and how they have been interpreted in the classroom and in other contexts. It therefore implies an important role for issues that involve the relationship between teachers and 'what counts as knowledge' in the school curriculum viewed in its broadest sense.

This relationship has special resonance in the context of the education system in England and Wales. Over the past fifty years, the supposed rights of teachers to exercise control over the school curriculum have come under detailed scrutiny, and to all outward appearance they have recently been sharply curtailed. In the 1940s, at a time of extensive educational reforms, it was generally accepted that the State should not be involved in an active way in prescribing the details of the school curriculum, but that this should be a matter for the teachers and schools themselves. This did not amount to complete curricular freedom for the teachers, since there were several constraints and wider influences including those of examinations and of the different types of secondary school (grammar, technical and modern) that were officially endorsed. Religious education was also made compulsory for the first time. Overall, however, the rights of teachers in relation to those of the State could be celebrated as a distinctive feature of English education, and certainly as one that contrasted with the authoritarian state curriculum initiatives of such nations as Germany and Italy (McCulloch, 1994, Ch. 6).

This situation continued to exist until at least the beginning of the 1960s. Denis Lawton has described the period from the 1944 Education Act until the 1960s as 'the Golden Age of teacher control (or non-control) of the curriculum' in Britain (Lawton, 1980, p. 22). It may be argued, as does Lawton, that teachers by and large failed to assert effective control over the curriculum, or to take responsibility for curriculum change, when they had the opportunity to do so during this period. According to Lawton, indeed, 'It might be said that the teachers had their chance to take control of the curriculum, but failed to take it' (ibid). On the other hand, there were several major initiatives in curriculum reform during the 1950s that were led by teachers, usually through subject-teaching associations. In the area of science education, for example, the Science Masters' Association and the Association of Women Science Teachers (later combined to form the Association for Science Education) were strongly influential in a campaign for curriculum change that led in the early 1960s to the rise of the Nuffield Foundation Science Teaching Project. Even in the case of this influential national curriculum project of the 1960s, however, it is arguable that the role of the subject association as the 'guardian' of the curriculum (Layton, 1984) was subverted by the involvement of independent and detached 'experts' (see McCulloch, Jenkins and Layton, 1985, Chs. 3 and 5).

Throughout the 1960s, high expectations of teacher autonomy with regard to the curriculum were generally maintained. For instance, it was suggested in 1963 that 'one of the major features of the English educational system has been the freedom assigned to the teacher in regard to the planning and development of the curricula and methods in our schools' (*Educational Research*, 1963). The historian Brian Simon argues, indeed, that the 1960s 'are commonly assessed as marking a striking growth in teacher autonomy, especially in relation to the curriculum' (Simon, 1991, p. 311). In retrospect, this was also the time when the apparatus of the State gradually began to become more actively involved in matters directly related to the curriculum. Certainly, the introduction of the Curriculum Study Group in 1962 revealed clear intentions of at least some administrators and politicians in this area to adopt a more centralized and assertive role, although this initiative was effectively resisted by teachers and local interests and was supplanted in 1964 by a more broadly based body, the Schools Council for the Curriculum and Examinations, that emphasized the representation and interests of teachers. Overall it is still largely true, as Chitty asserts, that a 'concerted effort' on the part of civil servants and politicians to displace the role of teachers in this regard did not develop until the mid-1970s and the crucial intervention of the Prime Minister, James Callaghan, in a speech at Ruskin College in October 1976 that led to a self-styled 'Great Debate' (Chitty, 1988, p. 327). The educational reforms of the Conservative governments in the 1980s and 1990s have extended and consolidated this process of direct and active intervention on the part of the State. In particular, the Technical and Vocational Education Initiative (TVEI), launched in 1983, was intended to strengthen education–industry lines, to develop an enhanced four-year curriculum for 14 to 18-year-olds, and to prepare young people for adult and working life. This particular initiative aroused fears that teachers' 'professional prerogative to think and to plan' would be increasingly undermined (Proud, 1984; see McCulloch, 1987 on the early development of the TVEI). Such anxieties seemed to be confirmed with the rise of the National Curriculum under the Education Reform Act of 1988.

In its original form, the English and Welsh National Curriculum consisted of ten subjects, which took up a large proportion of the timetable, and which would be assessed on a national basis through testing of all school children at the ages of 7, 11, 14, and 16. Kenneth Baker as Secretary of State for Education was a strong advocate of this 'broad-based' curriculum, and he denied that it would undermine the accepted role of teachers. In the House of Commons debate on the Education Reform Bill in December 1987, Baker noted the concerns of 'some teachers' that the National Curriculum would 'prescribe how they go about their professional duties'. He sought to 'put such fears at rest', and emphasized: 'We want to build upon the professionalism of the teacher in the classroom — the professionalism of the many fine and dedicated teachers throughout our education system.' Baker added that 'We do not intend to lay down how lessons should be taught, how timetables should be organised, or which textbooks should be used.' On the contrary, he expressed confidence that the National Curriculum would 'provide scope for imaginative approaches developed by our teachers' (House of Commons Debates, 1987, col. 774). It is clear, however, that his aim was to restrict the influence of teachers, which he distrusted. As he has recalled in his memoirs, he favoured a 'full prescribed curriculum' partly to avoid schools being left 'adrift in a sea of fashionable opinions about what students should not, rather than should, be taught and at what age' (Baker, 1992, p. 192), and partly because in his view 'Vagueness and lack of detail will allow an inadequate and lazy teacher to skip important parts' (Baker, 1992, p. 198).

Over the following five years, the attempt to impose a centrally prescribed National Curriculum fostered several public controversies. These problems reached a climax in 1993 when there was a widespread teachers' action to boycott tests for 7- and 14-year-olds. The underlying reasons for the teachers' protest were widely recognized as being 'a battle over who controls the nation's classrooms, the way children are tested and how far the government should prescribe what pupils are taught' (*Sunday Times*, 1993). More specifically, as *The Independent* noted, 'The two points on which the overwhelming majority of teachers agree are that the introduction of the curriculum has placed a heavy extra burden on their time, and that their professional concerns have been casually disdained.' (*The Independent*, 1993). On this view, the State had moved in on the classroom, hitherto regarded as the province of the teacher, with the effect of downgrading the teacher's role to that of merely implementing decisions reached elsewhere.

The long-term general process through which the relative freedom enjoyed by teachers in England and Wales in the post-war years was seen to be curtailed and replaced in the 1990s by rigid State prescription, suggests a straightforward theoretical model or hypothesis for teacher professionalism. In this general model, teachers' professionalism has been eroded as their control over the curriculum has been subverted and taken over by the State. This leads on to two general propositions. First, causation is asserted: teachers' professionalism has been eroded *because* their control over the curriculum has become subverted and taken over by the State. Second, by deduction, teacher professionalism is assumed to reside in their control over the curriculum; such control is the *source* of their professionalism. At the same time, associations that have developed to provide an instrument and public forum for teachers' control over the curriculum, such as subject-teaching associations, become central, as they are taken to represent teachers' aspirations for professionalism.

Gerald Grace's notion of 'legitimated professionalism' develops a sociohistorical model that supports these general propositions. According to Grace, in the earlier part of this century, school teachers fought for and won effective control over one major sphere of their work, that of the curriculum, and this has been the basis for their 'legitimated professionalism'. He suggests that 'The legitimated professionalism which emerged in the 1930s was a form of educational settlement which implicitly involved an understanding that organised teachers would keep to their proper sphere of activity within the classroom and the educational system and the state, for its part, would grant them a measure of trust, a measure of material reward and occupational security, and a measure of professional dignity' (Grace, 1987, p. 208).

Grace notes that in the 1950s and 1960s, this situation gave rise to considerable professional autonomy in relation to the curriculum despite setbacks in teachers' terms and conditions of service, to the extent that 'In contrast to highly centralised and controlled systems of state schooling in other socio-political contexts, the decentralised autonomy of British teachers with respect to curriculum selection and pedagogic methods was taken to be a distinctive feature of British democracy and schooling' (Grace, 1987, p. 212).

By the mid-1980s, however, in Grace's terms, successive state initiatives appeared to have eroded this kind of professional autonomy no less than they had weakened the position of teachers in other areas such as their terms and conditions of service. At least one initial objection may fairly be raised to this general thesis on the character and decline of teacher professionalism. It may be argued that recent State interventions in the curriculum, whatever their aims and rhetoric may have been, have had little impact on teachers' professionalism in practical terms, or that they may even have tended to enhance rather than to undermine it. This kind of analysis would tend to emphasize an important distance between 'policy' as constructed by the State and its agencies, and 'practice' as understood and experienced by teachers.

In relation to the Technical and Vocational Education Initiative (TVEI), for example, Janet Harland has observed what she calls the 'central paradox' of 'the simultaneous emergence of two apparently or potentially conflicting features: on one hand, strong central control of a kind which has permitted the detailed intervention of a central government agency right down to the level of the classroom; and on the other a teacher response which is, in many of the pilot schemes, creative and innovative, and often indeed experimental and downright risky' (Harland, 1987, p. 39).

TVEI, she argues, defies the 'dogma' that 'creativity, innovation and willingness to experiment depend upon professional autonomy and a good degree of personal security and freedom from authoritarian intervention' (Harland, 1987, p. 39). Harland describes the teachers 'leading the TVEI crusade' as 'released prisoners'. These, however, are a 'very particular set of teachers', many of them drawn from the practical/technical/applied areas of the curriculum, who have 'in many schools led rather isolated and low-status professional lives' (Harland, 1987, p. 47). Therefore, she suggests, 'on the whole those teaching in the technical and vocational areas will be more likely than others to support the government's avowedly utilitarian and instrumental policies for education because for them the price of opposition would be very expensive in terms of their professional identity' (Harland, 1987, p. 48).

On this view, teachers interpret state policy in different ways, often leading it in directions unanticipated by its initiators. They also have differing and even competing professional interests, and may have different experiences and memories of the so-called 'Golden Age of teacher control'.

In relation to the National Curriculum, Stephen Ball and Richard Bowe have developed the notion of a 'policy cycle' consisting of 'significantly different arenas and sites within which a variety of interests are at stake' (Ball and Bowe, 1992, p. 98). There is in this analysis continual slippage and contestation in the role of the teachers in 'interpreting the texts'. They suggest, indeed, that 'the substance of existing curriculum structures and the current institutional practices *may well not only remain in place but be reinforced by the way in which the National Curriculum is being introduced*' (Ball and Bowe, 1992, p. 102). In some cases, according to Ball and Bowe, 'teachers' priorities, experience and professional expertise were set over and against the structure, content and progression of subject knowledge presented in the National Curriculum documents' (Ball and Bowe, 1992, p. 105). Moreover, they argue, the 'whole notion of teacher professionalism' may provide at least in some instances a basis for resistance, and establishes 'a powerful critical vocabulary of aspects of the National Curriculum' (Ball and Bowe, 1992, p. 108). The extent to which different teachers experience the possibilities implied in this, and the processes that are involved, remain open for further research.

In the United States, too, an unproblematic model in which major extensions of state control over the school curriculum effectively eclipse teacher professionalism has also been challenged. Archbald and Porter, for example, argue that teachers retain a strong belief that they are in control of the most important aspects of the curriculum, despite the effects of state policies. Indeed, they claim, 'clearly teachers did not feel that their professional discretion was sharply curtailed' by district-wide curriculum control over programmes and policies (Archbald and Porter, 1994, p. 36). While outside observers of policy would assume that prescribed changes at a district level were exerting 'a strong determining influence in shaping curriculum and instruction', from the perspectives of the teachers themselves 'central policies tend to be remote, often not well-understood, and easy to ignore with impunity'. Thus, according to Archbald and Porter, official curriculum policies 'pale in significance compared with the day-to-day curriculum planning, instructional activities, and social demands making up teachers' working lives' (Archbald and Porter, 1994, p. 36).

Such correctives restore the role of teacher agency that is in danger of being lost from a rigid theoretical model of teacher professionalism. They tend to support the idea that 'teacher professionalism' is indeed bound up with teachers' 'curriculum control', but they also suggest scope for action and responses among teachers to maintain or develop their role even in the rapidly changing policy context of the 1980s and 1990s.

Teacher Autonomy and the National Curriculum

These notions are supported and given further depth in a recent empirical study of teachers' perceptions of change and influences upon change. This suggests that the effects of the 1988 Education Reform Act (which brought in the National Curriculum) and subsequent legislation had a significant impact upon the professional confidence of many teachers, and consequently upon their ability to maintain control of their working lives. The study was undertaken by Gill Helsby and Murray Saunders as part of the TVEI Evaluation Programme at Lancaster University's Centre for the Study of Education and Training. It involved the use of a wide-scale survey, targeted at all teachers of 14–18 year olds in three local education authorities, as well as an intensive programme of semi-structured teacher interviews. One-to-one interviews were conducted in all secondary schools and colleges in two of the three authorities, and typically included the head or principal, the TVEI co-ordinator and two teachers, one from the arts/humanities area and one from the science/technology side: in large colleges, a greater number of staff from a range of curriculum areas were interviewed. In total over 2,000 completed questionnaires were received, and nearly 200 teacher interviews were conducted.

What the study immediately confirmed was both the extent and speed of recent developments: nearly 90 per cent of the survey group said that there had been a lot of changes in their subject area over the last two to three years, and nearly three-quarters also reported changes in teaching and learning styles over the same period.

In both cases the National Curriculum was seen as the major influence for change. This suggests that one of the effects of this centrally prescribed initiative has been to prompt the vast majority of teachers to make adjustments to their practice in the most fundamental areas of their day-to-day work, areas in which they would formerly have been deemed to have had authority and expertise.

When asked about the main professional site of recent changes, teachers in the survey group put even more emphasis upon curriculum structures than upon either subject content or pedagogy. The evidence suggests that a move towards shorter units of teaching might be relevant here, since nearly three-quarters claimed that they organized their teaching into modules with some of their students. Findings from an earlier study (Helsby, 1987) suggest that the fixed content and recording procedures and short timescales implied in modular approaches are likely not only to create additional work pressures but also to limit teacher flexibility to respond to needs which arise during the course of teaching: in other words their freedom to make professional judgments within the course of their practice is constrained by prior, self-imposed curricular prescriptions (see also Apple and Jungck, 1992).

The spread of new curriculum structures with pre-specified and short-term learning outcomes, coupled with changes in everyday practices as a result of a new and compulsory National Curriculum, would certainly seem to point towards a possible decline in teacher autonomy. However, this might not be the case if teachers were supportive of the changes and actively involved in promoting them. Here, the evidence is very mixed: when asked whether they believed that recent changes in the curriculum were for the better, only 37 per cent of the survey group agreed, with the other 63 per cent being uncertain or disagreeing. Moreover, considerable doubts about the desirability of the changes were repeatedly expressed by teachers both in the interviews and in the open comments section of the questionnaire. Some objected to what they saw as 'ill thought out national decisions':

> The rate of change over the past few years and the half baked ideas have had a disastrous effect on all aspects of education, particularly on pupils.

> ... nothing seems to have been clearly thought out nor effectively applied. I deplore the emphasis on training rather than on education.

At the same time many took exception to the centralized planning of the National Curriculum, emphasizing the lack of consultation with teachers over its introduction and content:

> ... in many cases change has come by imposition from above whereas it should occur as a result of shop-floor practice and needs.

> National Curriculum change ... has systematically under-valued the professional voice.

There were also numerous suggestions that current developments ran counter to the professional pedagogical beliefs of respondents and were actually undermining what they saw as existing good practice:

National Curriculum is resulting in a return to rote learning and a move away from exploration and 'real learning'.

If anything, teaching styles are being forced into reverse by the National Curriculum.

The National Curriculum was also thought to impose constraints upon teachers' professional freedom of action:

National Curriculum . . . acts as a content-based straitjacket. Because of the legislation, league tables and immense fears you're forced backwards.

National Curriculum assessment means you're teaching more to a test or exam, there's a loss of flexibility. The investigative approach in science is laid down in a particular way in the National Curriculum . . . it's become so rigid and formalized.

I feel hemmed in by criteria laid down by the National Curriculum. It's like teaching in a box.

Thus, far from being a site of professional creativity, the evidence suggested that many teachers felt disempowered by the developments which they were legally, if reluctantly, forced to implement. Many emphasized that it was not the principle of a National Curriculum or even of national testing that they objected to, but the way in which this particular National Curriculum had been designed and implemented.

Another reason for the feelings of disempowerment can be found in the fact that change had come to be seen as a constant feature of professional life over the last few years; as one teacher put it:

The changes keep changing and changing and changing. No time given to organize the extra work the changes involve. Everything is hurried, incomplete, chaotic.

Such a feeling of 'shifting sands' and lack of time for consolidation clearly created feelings of pressure and uncertainty amongst large numbers of our respondents:

Any changes should be implemented slowly as it disturbs a system from its equilibrium. Too much disturbance causes a situation of chaos, which is not conducive to progress. Over the last five years, courses and systems have changed so much that both teachers and students have become unsure of the ground rules, resulting in disillusionment by both.

Headteachers whom we interviewed were frequently only too well aware of the pressures placed upon their staff and were often struggling to alleviate this as best they could:

There's a danger that everything becomes a knee-jerk reaction. One of my biggest jobs is to maintain the sanity of my staff and the stability of the curriculum, to see a way through.

My job is to control as best I can the rate of change, to ensure that changes are manageable, to avoid 'innovation overload'. I can't control the shifting goalposts — I need to assess which target is the most important to hit, I need to prioritize and focus on the basis of the best information available.

The theme of 'shifting goalposts' was one which recurred with some frequency amongst respondents. This was particularly true for science teachers, who had been one of the first groups to be involved in the National Curriculum and who had been subjected to repeated changes in national requirements. Whereas many science teachers had initially put considerable effort into planning the first year of National Curriculum science, the subsequent changes had rendered much of this work irrelevant:

Much time wasted with National Curriculum science in changes made in attainment targets, preparation work of high quality largely discarded and money wasted on purchase of books relating to seventeen attainment targets now obsolete. Morale rock bottom.

One of the results of this was that teachers were becoming much more wary of expending effort on curriculum planning, which might soon become redundant:

I feel that I have reached the point of not preparing for change until the changes are in practice — too much preparation for changes that then don't take place in the past.

It's very much in turmoil, we're trying to keep up with it all. You can't plan from one year to the next.

The planning role's been diminished because of the National Curriculum in the last two to three years . . . I believe that planning has moved down from broad sweeps to mere detail.

In some cases, this left teachers in a position of considerable uncertainty, waiting for some central directive:

I'd be happy with the National Curriculum if someone, somewhere, would tell me what to do.

This pattern of responses is very much in line with Taylorist principles of 'scientific management', which involve a separation of 'planning' and 'doing' in the interests of production-line efficiency (Helsby and Saunders, 1993). Indeed it is possible to identify several features of Taylorist philosophy in recent educational developments, including a recurrent pattern of centrally devised and standardized programmes, divided into readily managed units to be 'delivered' by teacher/ workers and inspected by outside efficiency experts and finally judged by 'consumers' rather than by the teachers themselves. Littler (1978) has linked Taylorism with 'an accelerated dynamic of deskilling', and certainly any decrease in the involvement of teachers in curriculum planning can be seen as a threat not only to their professional autonomy but also to the maintenance of these very specific skills.

The evidence from the Lancaster study, however, suggests a further erosion of professional confidence because of the growing intensification of teachers' working lives caused by increased workloads (Apple and Jungck, 1992; Hargreaves, 1994). Additional tasks and responsibilities arise partly from the plethora of new initiatives and partly because of growing bureaucratic demands; either way the result is severe pressure upon teachers' time:

Too much going on at once and totally impossible to cope with change because of lack of time and all the other pressures.

More and more of my time is taken up with record-keeping and assessment and less and less time with actual teaching.

The point about having less time for classroom teaching was made by many respondents, and is significant because it represents a key site for the exercise of professional expertise:

I feel under great pressure to try to deal with all the initiatives and form filling involved in so many of the changes in education. Worst of all I feel that much of my energy is being diverted from my classroom teaching which is, in the end, the most satisfying and fulfilling part of my work.

Lack of time often forced teachers to cut corners and made it difficult to do a 'professional job', which was a cause of considerable dissatisfaction:

Most institutions are not giving teachers time to properly initiate and develop the many and varied prescribed practices, therefore they are always under-developed and unsatisfactory.

What was particularly striking were the apparently low levels of professional confidence across the survey group: of the 2,010 respondents, three out of five said that they were having difficulty keeping up with current demands whilst a half claimed that there were important gaps in their professional expertise. Low morale, stress, despair and inability to cope were mentioned frequently:

> I feel despair at all the changes — they could not all be implemented properly even if staff and pupils were there twenty-four hours a day. I have taught English, up to [Advanced] Level, for nearly twenty years. I am able and efficient — but I cannot cope with all the trash hurled at us.

> No time for consolidation . . . feeling of shifting sands, never quite in control of any one aspect any more. How many more balls can I be asked to juggle at once? Staff morale at lowest ever since I began teaching and no sign of any improvement.

> After teaching for twenty plus years, I have never been so exhausted, nor so pessimistic about my ability and competence to cope with what is now expected of me.

In the light of all of the new demands and pressures, teacher support might be supposed to be of key significance. The evidence here, however, suggested that many teachers felt that such support was inadequate: less than one in three felt that they had received sufficient professional development in their curriculum area and well over a half claimed that they rarely had the opportunity for personal professional development. In recent years there has been a sharp movement away from externally provided in-service teacher training towards more institutionally based development; however, less than one in three believed that the system of school- or college-based training worked well, or that the system had improved over the last two to three years. This, coupled with the fact that 70 per cent of respondents reported regular planning meetings with colleagues, seems to point to the possible use of 'contrived collegiality' (Hargreaves, 1992) to ensure administrative control, rather than to provide the effective kind of teacher support that can come through a genuinely 'collaborative culture'. As one teacher put it of the compulsory school-based training days:

> There's more emphasis on 'you've got to do . . .', but I query the value . . . why couldn't we spend the time on more useful topics? Even when we're working in departments, we're told what to work on.

The situation has been exacerbated by the dominance of national priorities in funded INSET, which has meant that most courses have been concerned with the implementation of National Curriculum or National Vocational Qualifications or, alternatively, with management training. As a result, many generic areas of concern to teachers have been neglected. The evidence also suggests that access to courses has been uneven, tending to increase in accordance with a teacher's status in the hierarchy. Even the traditional support given by Local Education Authority advisers has been diminished because of financial cutbacks and also as a result of their new responsibilities for monitoring compliance with the demands of the National Curriculum:

> People are more suspicious of advisers because of the inspectorial role. The relationship has changed.

An interesting deviation from this rather pessimistic picture of teacher morale arose amongst one particular group of respondents. The construction of the questionnaire enabled the identification of a small group of 231 teachers who had been strongly influenced by TVEI, and of another 379 who had definitely not been so influenced. In comparing the responses of these two groups, some remarkable differences arose, with the 'TVEI' group strikingly more satisfied with their lot and more confident in their ability to manage change. Thus, for example, although they were more likely to claim involvement in what might be termed 'innovative' activities, such as recording of achievement, student-centred inquiry work, work experience placements for students or the use of adults other than teachers in the classroom, yet they were significantly less likely than the 'non-TVEI' group to claim that they were experiencing difficulty in keeping up with current professional demands (53 compared to 65 per cent). They were also much more confident that the system of professional support had improved in recent years (57 per cent compared to 15.7 per cent of the non-TVEI group) and that they themselves had received adequate professional development (41.6 per cent compared to 24.2 per cent). At the same time they were more than twice as likely to believe that recent changes were for the better (52.4 per cent as against 25.5 per cent).

The data themselves do not reveal the reasons for such disparities. The TVEI group is almost equally balanced in terms of gender and includes a good range of subject specialisms, although humanities teachers are in a clear majority, comprising over a third of the group. The fact that senior managers are over-represented in the TVEI group may clearly be significant. Interestingly, however, there was also evidence of a more collaborative culture amongst the TVEI group, which may relate to the notion of 'professional communities' as a significant factor in teacher professionalism (Little, 1992). Thus, for example, 47.8 per cent of the TVEI group claimed that they often taught alongside other colleagues, 81.9 per cent that they worked with colleagues from other subject areas as a matter of course and 80.8 per cent that they were involved in meetings with teachers from other schools: this compares with figures of 25.2 per cent, 43.4 per cent and 42.7 per cent respectively amongst the non-TVEI group.

The interview data also suggest that many of those who had had a close involvement in TVEI, especially TVEI co-ordinators, held unusually strong convictions and were able to articulate a clear view of what counted as good practice in curricular terms, whether with regard to school–community links, pedagogy or curriculum content. Accordingly they were more likely to approach the requirements of the National Curriculum as something which needed to be 'fitted in' to existing structures and practices, rather than as something which would direct activities in new directions:

> The experience of TVEI gives me more confidence in what I'm pushing.

In some cases, this was expressed in terms of struggle or contestation:

> There is a big pressure (from the National Curriculum), you have to watch it doesn't force you to become didactic to cover the topics. We have to fight to keep fieldwork. The practical work is also under threat, we need to preserve this.

TVEI was also referred to as something which had enabled and encouraged teachers to think for themselves and to make their own curricular decisions:

> It encouraged colleagues in school to work together, to link in with a whole-school approach. TVEI made us question how we did things and then offered support.

> It's generated discussion about the curriculum and the way we are delivering it.

> (TVEI has) given us a broader base, a widened perspective for making decisions.

This certainly accords well with earlier findings which suggest that TVEI in practice, far from representing strong, centralized control of the curriculum, actually encouraged grassroots creativity in curricular design amongst some teachers (Harland, 1987; Helsby, 1989). Interestingly, one of the interviewees was led to speculate as to whether the National Curriculum could be subverted in the same way:

> TVEI was an attempt to get us into line, but we made it our own. I wonder if we'll do the same with the National Curriculum?

Issues and Agendas

The results of the Lancaster study are striking in terms of what they suggest about the relationship between teacher professionalism and curriculum control. For many of the teachers involved, the introduction of a centralized and prescriptive National Curriculum appears to have weakened their professional confidence, lowered morale and left them uncertain both of their ability to cope and of their right to take major curriculum decisions. These findings are consistent with the view of increased state control of the curriculum undermining teacher professionalism. Indeed, many of these teachers appear almost as victims of government policies, adopting a largely reactive, rather than proactive, role in their responses.

However, not all of the teachers in the study reflect such a sense of dis-empowerment, suggesting a variety of responses to National Curriculum policy amongst different groups of teachers, in line with the earlier findings of Bowe and Ball (1992). In particular, the responses of the TVEI group point towards a more problematic and contested relationship between teacher professionalism and curriculum control, which highlights the dangers of over-simplification in this area. It underlines the importance of taking into account the question of agency and the spaces which some teachers are able to create to exert their professionalism in curricular matters. Moreover, it does much to highlight the differences in personal experiences and career histories among teachers themselves. The relationship between these variables, on the one hand, and the ideals and realities of 'teacher professionalism' and 'curriculum control' seems of central importance for further study in this area.

Developing further research along these lines should not only provide greater detail of teachers' professional lives. It needs also to assist in testing and elaborating the general conceptual framework surrounding 'teacher professionalism' and 'curriculum control'. At the same time, it needs to remain closely related to broader theoretical, social, political, and historical issues. Fulfilling these aims will mean attempting to come to terms with an extensive agenda of problems and themes for research that are so far relatively unexplored.

The first of these problems concerns methodology. In relating teachers' views and experiences in a systematic fashion to wider and more long-term frameworks, it will be necessary to make use of a number of research methods, including documentary research, questionnaires, and interviews of various kinds. If these different techniques are to be employed towards a common project, they clearly require similar vocabularies and a shared notion of what is problematic. While they may not ask the same questions, they need to ask questions that are complementary in order to advance the project as a whole. These requirements raise difficult issues of research management in a field that has not been notable for the coherence of the 'micro' and the 'macro'.

Moreover, the use of teacher interviews in seeking to understand the relationship between 'teacher professionalism' and 'curriculum control' also raises important methodological issues. It is by no means straightforward to encourage teachers to articulate their 'practical consciousness' of aspects of their everyday working lives that tend to be taken for granted. At the same time, in the interviews themselves contested notions such as 'professionalism' need to be problematized rather than taken for granted. It is important also to allow scope for alternative frameworks to emerge from the experiences of teachers, and thus to begin to develop grounded categories that may or may not cohere with the assumptions of policy makers and of the existing published literature.

Further research in this area needs also to take account of a rapidly changing context in terms of curriculum policy. The heavily prescriptive National Curriculum that gave rise to the teacher-led protests of 1993 has been reviewed and revised through the Dearing Report on the National Curriculum and its assessment. The then Secretary of State for education, John Patten, conceded that 'teaching methods' were to be left to the 'professional judgment of teachers' (*TES*, 1993). The Dearing Report, published at the end of 1993, also acknowledged a limited role for teachers in determining the actual content of the curriculum, within the constraints imposed by the National Curriculum. It recommended that the National Curriculum should be 'slimmed down' in order to allow 'scope for professional judgement' (Dearing, 1993, p. 20). An increased margin of time outside the reduced statutory National Curriculum and religious education would allow room for 'optional material which can be taught according to the professional judgement of teachers' (Dearing, 1993, pp. 21–2), although the Report also emphasized that 'increased trust in teachers' should also be 'matched by accountability to parents and society, including that from simple tests in the core subjects' (Dearing, 1993, p. 25). The extent to which these shifts in national policy will affect the position of school teachers remains to be seen, but they should provide new opportunities to observe the relationship between 'teacher professionalism' and 'curriculum control'. Already, however, it has been argued that the revisions establish the basis for 'a new partnership founded on a balance between professional discretion and public accountability, a partnership that would have at its heart the continual improvement of teacher quality' (Barber, 1994). This view suggests the possibility of a potential renewal of the 'legitimated professionalism' that Grace perceives in relation to the 1950s and 1960s (Grace, 1987).

Another set of unresolved issues that need to be taken into account in further research relates to the territory or sphere of the curriculum. In assessing the relationship between 'curriculum control' and 'teacher professionalism', the contested and problematic characteristics of the curriculum itself need to be clarified. In particular, the views of teachers themselves on the most important features of the curriculum over which they might wish to exert effective control are highly relevant to a more detailed understanding of this relationship. The relative importance of classroom control and of influence over curriculum policy in the development of teachers' professionalism is one important issue in this regard. The role of teachers' identities in relation to the subjects that they teach, in relation to their pedagogy and to their pastoral and other teaching duties, is another.

By the same token, exploring the contested borders or margins of teachers' authority in relation to the curriculum also offers opportunities for a more detailed understanding of their 'sphere of influence'. For example, the role of teachers in relation to assessment and examinations has often been fiercely disputed with other interest groups such as university examining boards. The Norwood Report on the curriculum and examinations in secondary schools, published in 1943, championed a central role for the 'judgement of the teacher' by recommending the development of internal examinations, 'conducted by the teachers at the school on syllabuses and papers framed by themselves' (Norwood Report, 1943, p. 140). It argued that this would be in the interests both of the 'individual child' and of the 'increased freedom and responsibility of the teaching profession' (Norwood Report, 1943, p. 140). Predictably enough, the university examining boards proved hostile to this proposal. It is, notable, however, that many teachers were also lukewarm, which seemed to reflect 'some unwillingness on the part of teachers to shoulder the responsibility which would fall on them' (Smith, 1942). In such cases, teachers appear to have tended to define their sphere of authority in a somewhat restricted way that reflects only limited ambitions (see also McCulloch, 1993), although there may be a more complex pattern over the longer term in respect to this kind of disputed border country.

Another key set of issues for further exploration involves the relationship between teachers and the associations that have been established to defend and represent their professional aspirations. To some extent, this may be achieved through comparing the views of different kinds of teachers' organizations. For example, Gaskell and Rowell have documented how a subject-specialist organization such as the British Columbia Science Teachers' Association may emphasize 'collective control by teachers over the content and methods of the curriculum', whereas a more generalist teachers' organization such as the British Columbia Teachers' Federation may tend to stress 'control of the curriculum by individual teachers making judgements in the context of a particular community and students' (Gaskell and Rowell, 1993, p. 70). They contend, indeed, that:

> while not all subject specialist and generalist teachers' organizations develop strategies similar to the two studied, generalist organizations are likely to be more open to emphasizing the individual autonomy of teachers and subject-specialist organizations are likely to be more open to emphasizing collective control over a standardized curriculum. (Gaskell and Rowell, 1993, p. 71)

More research of this kind should be most helpful in gauging the relationship between teacher professionalism and the school curriculum. At the same time, it remains important to continue to investigate the views of the teachers themselves. In particular, recent research has highlighted the influence of subject-teaching associations in the development of particular areas of the school curriculum (e.g., Goodson, 1988, McCulloch, 1992). David Layton has focused on science teaching associations on the basis that the curriculum can be viewed as 'the site of intense micro-political activity', and that 'outcomes of this in relation to the control and management of classroom knowledge are important for any understanding of what takes place in schools and colleges' (Layton, 1988, p. 16). However, it is arguable that such research has tended to be too uncritical of the claims of subject teaching associations to represent teachers' professional interests (see e.g., Mbhalati, 1993). It is necessary, therefore, to search out ways to explore teachers' own views of such associations, of alternative resources on which they can draw in constructing the curriculum, and of their freedom and constraints in this regard.

Much of the research already developed in this area has tended to focus on the position of secondary school teachers, although the distinctive meanings of 'professionalism' for primary school teachers in England and France has also been pursued in recent studies (Broadfoot and Osborn, 1993). Further work is needed to take account of the varying problems and issues relating to different areas of the education system, including nursery schools, primary schools, further education, and universities. The relationship between 'teacher professionalism' and 'curriculum control' is likely to vary in each case.

In many ways, however, the most fascinating as well as the most difficult dimension with which further research must struggle to contend is that of teachers' cultures. As Andy Hargreaves has recently noted:

> We now know quite a lot about particular teacher cultures — like the culture of English teaching or the culture of developmental teachers, for example — but we know little about the overall classification and configuration of teacher cultures throughout the occupation more generally. (Hargreaves, 1992, p. 218)

In the process of developing this more detailed and sophisticated awareness, there are further opportunities for light to be shed on the nature of the relationship between 'teacher professionalism' and 'professional control'. Specific aspects of teacher culture that may well provide a basis for such exploration include tensions between subject specialism and broader curriculum development, subject hierarchies and the position of teachers within these hierarchies, the interplay between teachers' personal and professional identities, and the role of gender as a category.

Overall, therefore, the development of socio-historical frameworks and some useful empirical research have provided a helpful basis for the study of the relationship between teacher professionalism and curriculum control. This research suggests the existence of a very close relationship, recognized by education policy makers and by many of the teachers themselves. It tends to support the general view that the growth of active involvement of the State in the curriculum has posed an important challenge and indeed a potential threat to teachers' professionalism, although teachers as individuals and in groups have been able to mediate or even redirect this process. At the same time, there are still several extensive areas that remain to be explored and mapped out in the years ahead, which may well serve to challenge existing assumptions about teachers' professional lives.

Note

1   We would like to acknowledge the support of the Economic and Social Research Council for the research project 'The professional culture of teachers and the secondary school curriculum' (R000234738); also the helpful and constructive comments of our colleagues in this project, Peter Knight, Murray Saunders, and Terry Warburton.

References

APPLE, M. and JUNGCK, S. (1992) 'You don't have to be a teacher to teach this unit: Teaching, technology and control in the classroom', in HARGREAVES, A. and FULLAN, M.G. (Eds) *Understanding Teacher Development*, London, Cassell.
ARCHBALD, D. and PORTER, A. (1994) 'Curriculum control and teachers' perceptions of

autonomy and satisfaction', *Educational Evaluation and Policy Analysis*, **16**, pp. 21–39.

BAKER, K. (1992) *The Turbulent Years: My Life In Politics*, London, Faber and Faber.

BALL, S. and BOWE, R. (1992) 'Subject departments and the "implementation" of National Curriculum policy: An overview of the issues', *Journal of Curriculum Studies*, **24**, pp. 97–115.

BARBER, M. (1994) 'Union's testing boycott threatens drive to raise standards', *Sunday Times*, 22 May.

BOWE, R. and BALL, S. (1992) *Reforming Education and Changing Schools: Case Studies in Policy Sociology*, London, Routledge.

BROADFOOT, P., OSBORN, M., GILLY, M. and BUCHER, A. (1993) *Perceptions Of Teaching: Primary School Teachers In England And France*, London, Cassell.

CHITTY, C. (1988) 'Central control of the school curriculum, 1944–87', *History of Education*, **17**, pp. 321–34.

DEARING, R. (1993) *The National Curriculum and its Assessment: Final Report*, London, School Curriculum and Assessment Authority.

EDUCATIONAL RESEARCH (1963) editorial introduction, 'Curriculum study and the freedom of the teacher', **5**, pp. 83–4.

EISENMANN, L. (1991) 'Teacher professionalism: A new analytical tool for the history of teachers', *Harvard Educational Review*, **61**, pp. 215–24.

GASKELL, P.J. and ROWELL, P.M. (1993) 'Teachers and curriculum policy: Contrasting perspectives of a subject specialist and a generalist teachers' organisation', *Historical Studies In Education*, **5**, pp. 67–86.

GOODSON, I. (1988) *The Making of Curriculum: Collected Essays*, London, Falmer Press.

GRACE, G. (1987) 'Teachers and the State in Britain: A changing relation', in LAWN, M. and GRACE, G. (Eds) *Teachers: The Culture and Politics of Work*, London, Falmer Press, pp. 193–228.

HARGREAVES, A. (1992) 'Cultures of teaching', in HARGREAVES, A. and FULLAN, M. (Eds) *Understanding Teacher Development*, London, Cassell, pp. 216–40.

HARGREAVES, A. (1994) *Changing Teachers, Changing Times: Teachers' Work and Culture in the Postmodern Age*, London, Cassell.

HARLAND, J. (1987) 'The TVEI experience: Issues of control, response and the professional role of teachers', in GLEESON, D. (Ed) *TVEI and Secondary Education: A Critical Appraisal*, Milton Keynes, Open University Press, pp. 38–54.

HELSBY, G. (1987) *A Modular Approach to the Secondary Curriculum*, Evaluation Report of the North West Regional TRIST Project, Wigan, North West TRIST.

HELSBY, G. (1989) 'Central control and grassroots creativity: The paradox at the heart of TVEI', in HARRISON, A. and GRETTON, S. (Eds) *Education and Training UK 1989: An Economic, Social and Policy Audit*, Newbury, Policy Journals.

HELSBY, G. and SAUNDERS, M. (1993) 'Taylorism, Tylerism and performance indicators: Defending the indefensible?', *Educational Studies*, **19**, pp. 55–77.

HOUSE OF COMMONS DEBATES (1987) **123**, 1987–8, 1 December.

LAWTON, D. (1980) *The Politics of the School Curriculum*, London, Routledge and Kegan Paul.

LAYTON, D. (1984) *Interpreters of Science*, London, Association for Science Education.

LAYTON, D. (1988) 'Subject teaching associations and curriculum control in 19th-century England: The case of science', *History of Education Review*, **17**, pp. 15–29.

LITTLE, J.W. (1992) 'Opening the black box of professional community', in LIEBERMAN, A. (Ed) *The Changing Context of Teaching*, Chicago, NSSE, pp. 157–78.

LITTLER, C.R. (1978) 'Understanding Taylorism', *British Journal of Sociology*, **29**, pp. 185–202.

MCCULLOCH, G. (1987) 'History and policy: The politics of the TVEI', in GLEESON, D. (Ed) *TVEI and Secondary Education: A Critical Appraisal*, Milton Keynes, Open University Press, pp. 13–37.

McCULLOCH, G. (Ed) (1992) *The School Curriculum in New Zealand: History, Theory, Policy and Practice*, Palmerston North, Dunmore Press.

McCULLOCH, G. (1993) 'Judgement of the teacher: The Norwood Report and internal examinations', *International Studies in Sociology of Education*, **3**, pp. 129–43.

McCULLOCH, G. (1994) *Educational Reconstruction: The 1944 Education Act and the 21st Century*, London, Woburn Press.

McCULLOCH, G., JENKINS, E.W. and LAYTON, D. (1985) *Technological Revolution?: The Politics of School Science and Technology in England and Wales Since 1945*, London, Falmer Press.

MBHALATI, C.F. (1993) 'Teachers and the Association for Science Education', MA dissertation, Lancaster University.

NORWOOD REPORT (1943) *Curriculum and Examinations in Secondary Schools*, London, HMSO.

PROUD, D. (1984) 'Nothing but vinegar sponges', *Times Educational Supplement*, 14 December.

SIMON, B. (1991) *Education and the Social Order 1940–90*, London, Lawrence and Wishart.

SMITH, F. (1942) 'Oral evidence to Norwood Committee, 26–27 June', Incorporated Association of Assistant Masters Papers, Institute of Education, London, E1/1/file 3.

SUNDAY TIMES (1993) report, 'Patten's big test', 11 April.

TES (*Times Educational Supplement*) (1993) report, 'Patten "does trust teachers"', 22 October.

THE INDEPENDENT (1993) leading article, 'Boycotts and other distractions', 24 April.

Chapter 4

Are Professional Teachers a Good Thing?

Tomas Englund

Introduction

During the last decade the concept of 'profession' has increasingly come to be associated with teaching. In Sweden, for example, the decentralized school system that is now emerging will, it is said, place a heavy burden on the professionalism of teachers. Is there anything to be gained from calling teachers professionals or advocating a shift towards professionalism and/or professionalization of teaching staff? Can teachers become professionals or are they perhaps already professionals? Are they on their way to becoming professionals? If so, is this a desirable development?

The answer to all these questions depends on how we define the concept of teaching as a profession. Quite clearly, this concept has no unequivocal meaning, and it has been used by different groups to achieve different aims. The concept of (teaching as a) profession is, rather, a buzzword and a tool that has been used in attempts to create legitimacy for different developments. In a setting where the concept of teaching as a profession is so ambiguous, it is uncertain whether and how it should be used.

Against this background, the central aim of my chapter is to make it clear how ill-defined the concept of teaching as a profession is. I will discuss and exemplify this by analysing the Swedish context in historical perspective. I will proceed by the following stages:

First, I wish to stress the distinction between (teacher) professionalization and professionalism, a distinction that is often neglected and confused in the perpetual intertwinement of the two terms. This confusion in fact gives rise to the overriding problem of this chapter. In short, I will characterize professionalization as a sociological project, relating to the authority and status of the (teaching) profession, and professionalism as a pedagogical project, concerned with the internal quality of teaching as a profession.

Secondly, I will refer to some classic texts on professionalism/professionalization which offer a spectrum of different interpretations and shed light on the possible confusion of the terms.

Thirdly, I will try to examine the central area of tension within the theory of teachers as professionals, namely the tension between teacher autonomy and the task assigned to teachers as professionals by the State.

Finally I will contextualize my discussion by analysing the history of Swedish education and the present situation. Historically, there has been a tension between two types of teachers, entailing different conditions for, and meanings of, teaching as a profession, but in recent decades a new, more complex pattern has emerged. In short, my fear is that the sociological project of teacher professionalization and the rhetoric about teachers as professionals/teacher professionalization — implying a narrow, technical-rational view of teachers' effectiveness — will over-shadow the pedagogical project of teacher professionalism — teachers as reflective practitioners.

Professionalization — Professionalism

First of all, I want to stress the distinction between (teacher) professionalization and professionalism.[1] Of course, these two terms cannot be kept totally apart, since they are related. The distinction between them is often neglected, however. In the rhet-oric of educational policy especially, the two terms are (consciously?) confused (Telhaug, 1990; Popkewitz, 1991).

The distinction that I would propose is to view professionalization as a soci-ological project, relating to the authority and status of the (teaching) profession, and professionalism as a pedagogical project, concerned with the internal quality of teaching as a profession. I thus regard professionalization as a manifestation of the historical and social ambition of an occupational group to achieve status and a position in society. Professionalization is, in that sense, a measure of the societal strength and authority of an occupational group. Professionalism, on the other hand, focuses on the question of what qualifications and acquired capacities, what competence, is required for the successful exercise of an occupation, in this case, teaching — which, in the last instance, is assessed by external forces. There is, furthermore, an ongoing discussion about the essence of teaching. The demands of both teacher professionalization and teacher professionalism confront each other in the shaping of teacher education. Consequently, the two concepts are not mutually independent, but intertwined, although they can, and should, be distinguished.[2]

I thus regard professionalization primarily as a sociological concept that says nothing about the inner qualities of teaching. Professionalization is a reflection of the symbolic strength of the profession and its possible exclusiveness, measured in terms of status etc. and protected by trade-union activities. In the sociological theory of professions, the professionals' autonomy over their branch of knowledge is emphasized. Their autonomy also entails a certain responsibility and the need for professional ethics. The theory also presupposes that professionals have clients.

With the concept of professionalism we come closer to what, as regards teaching as a profession, we can call the pedagogical project: the desirable com-ponents of teaching as practice. The question raised is what real competence the professional teacher ought to have. In parenthesis, one could ask here whether the competence concept is not better suited to this discussion than the sociologically influenced concept of profession, since we necessarily end up back with the professionalization of teachers and the sociological dimensions of this concept. However, we have to remember — despite the differences stressed — that the internal quality of teaching, teacher professionalism, is constantly intertwined with the sociological aspect, professionalization, as a result of the different ways in which different groups define these concepts. Of necessity, the authority of professions rests on a societally based legitimacy. It is, moreover, in the context of the ongoing struggle over its definition that the concept of profession can take on a dynamic force; but, when power is unevenly distributed, it can also block change and development.

Thus we cannot obtain a clear-cut picture of the phenomenon of teaching as a profession. A tendency towards professionalization is always present when different groups attempt to assert their interests and/or to represent certain of their characteristics as being more closely associated with their profession than others. We can uncover these complex relationships only by analysing them in their historical and social context. As Torstendahl (1989) underlines, there is 'good reason to break open the theory of professionalization in its prevalent form and develop it into a theory about the positions and actions of different knowledge-based groups in different societal settings' (p. 36).

Before turning to the historical and social context that it is natural for me to study, that of Swedish society, we can note that there is one area of tension which seems to recur when we are dealing with state professionals and/or the role of professionals in society. That is, the tension between the professionals' demand for autonomy, for an independent right to draw up and discuss the rules and ethics of professional practice, and control of this practice by the (democratic) State. Does professionalization mean that democratic influence via the State is undermined? Or is this putting the question the wrong way? Is professionalization necessary to the development of teachers and schools?

To gain a better understanding of these issues and to discover the presuppositions that underlie them, we need to go back to the theoretical starting-points and subsequent development of the theory of professionalism and professionalization.

Points of Reference for a Theory of Professions

Analysing the modern society that was evolving around the turn of the century, the French sociologist Emile Durkheim suggested that the professions should constitute a link between the central authority/state power and the development of civic morals by individuals/citizens. In Durkheim's view, the professions would represent a balance which could maintain and develop democracy by, on the one hand, avoiding the danger of the State becoming too far removed from the individual — 'if the State is not to oppress the individual' (Durkheim, 1992, p. 96) — and on the other hand, preventing the State becoming 'societified' (Petterson, 1988) — 'if the State is to be sufficiently free from the individual' (op. cit.).

In his works *Professional Ethics and Civic Morals* (Durkheim, 1992) and

Durkheim on Politics and the State (Durkheim-Giddens, 1986), the author lays bare some of the fields of tension which have since become increasingly conflict-ridden, e.g., the one mentioned between the professions' demand for autonomy and the task assigned to them by the State. This specific area of tension, as conflicts past and present show us, is politically charged. And even if attempts are made, from time to time, to define in principle the dividing line between politicians' and professionals' fields of decision making, this is more or less an impossible task.[3] It is also in a further extension of Durkheim's theory of the professions that the crucial borderline between public and private concerning the character of the professions can be discerned.

The interpretation of the (Durkheimian) concept of profession that dominated sociology up to the 1960s was formulated by the American sociologist Talcott Parsons (1963). The interesting thing about his theory of professions — in the light of what has been said here — is that it interconnects the two aspects which I have distinguished. They are interconnected, however, because of a specific underlying societal perspective, a perspective of consensus which can be seen as a structural functionalist interpretation of Durkheim's theory. It is perhaps on the basis of such a perspective, more or less exploited for rhetorical purposes, that the two aspects are confused and recent, more critical views of the problematic of professionalism/professionalization are neglected. It is also from such a vantage point that a demarcation of the political and professional fields may appear unproblematical, which it is not. The practice of teaching always has political implications, and teachers are constantly making choices with political implications (Englund, 1986).

Professionalization of an occupational field has thus generally had the result that the influence of the State/the politicians over the professionals has decreased and the professionals themselves have been given or assumed the power to decide. Even if professional practice has historically been subordinate to the task assigned by the State, gradual professionalization has resulted in looser coupling and greater scope for interpretation. Should this development be seen as a necessary precondition for more thoroughgoing professionalism, or is it the other way around?[4]

Professional Autonomy: The Task Assigned by the State with a Focus on the Teacher

Tendencies to professionalize teaching in the United States, where teachers have attempted to use the profession concept to strengthen their position and authority (compared with Sweden, the status of teachers in the US is quite low and the proportion of women in teaching is higher), have prompted the following warning from American researchers:

> Rather than relying on an undemocratic concept that connotes privilege, special status, and the superiority of mental over manual labor, teachers should look to other bases for organization. A progressive strategy would emphasize the common purposes and commitments to education that we

must build in a democracy and place these squarely in the public domain, not within the professional associations of an occupational elite. (Burbules and Densmore, 1986)

These researchers represent, as I see it, a fairly prevalent and critical view of teacher professionalization. They consider as a threat the tendency of teachers to develop — independently of the State — their own conditions for teaching practice, ethics etc., rather than seeing these conditions as dependent on public objectives and the democratically controlled State.

One fundamental issue can be raised here. In what way are professionalization and professionalism related to the question of teaching and education as parts of the public and private spheres?

The critical views of Burbules and Densmore on the tendency towards professionalization can be ascribed to the fact that their concept of professionalization is based in a critical historical-sociological tradition which has emphasized the élitist tendencies and market factors associated with a process of professionalization.

The historical-sociological tradition of professionalization research appeared in the second half of the 1970s represented by Sarfatti-Larson (1977), Collins (1979) and Parkin (1979), among others. In Sweden, it was established by a project on 'Professionalization and conflict theory' in the late 1980s (Selander, 1989; Torstendahl and Burrage, 1990).

An exciting application of this critical, historical-sociological tradition in the United States, mixed with a Foucault-inspired angle on the teacher profession, is the work of Labaree (1992). He argues that the consequences of a professionalization of teaching are technological rationalization and a standardized version of teaching. And Labaree's analysis forms the background to my own fears that the rhetoric of teaching as a profession will lend support to the type of teaching to which he refers. Those fears are also reinforced by the positive and often simplistic views of teacher professionalism/teacher profesionalization that many Swedish educationalists have advanced during the last decade. One of their sources of inspiration has been the American sociologist Lortie (1975). His critical analysis of the (American) teaching profession concludes that it is characterized by conservatism, individualism and presentism. One of Lortie's points is that teachers never become bearers of collective knowledge. Rather, they develop on a personal basis and fail to create any kind of professionalism.

Transferred to the Swedish context, researchers have compared Lortie's characterization with normatively founded and curriculum-based definitions of teacher professionalism and professionalization. Colnerud and Granström (1989) emphasize two aspects, professional ethics and professional language. The offensive on teacher professionalism has been developed by Berg (1981, and many later works, e.g., 1983, 1989). Berg and Wallin (1983) have used the profession concept to express a desirable development (according to their interpretation of the curriculum) from 'restricted' to 'extended' professionalism.[5]

Carlgren and Lindblad (1991), however, problematize teacher professionalism as a field of tension between loyalty and independence. They suggest that what has long been emphasized in the Swedish debate on professionalism/professionalization is the desire to make teachers faithfully accept the task they have been set in accordance with the demands of the National Curriculum, rather than perform it in line with the (narrow) tradition of their occupation.

What is now happening in the Swedish context, however, is that the preconditions and demands for teacher professionalism and professionalization are changing very fast. While teachers in Sweden have long been looked upon as a specific type of profession (Brante, 1990), what we can call public welfare professionals, this characterization is now in flux as a result of the gradual establishment of private schools. Simultaneously, rhetorical use of the concept of teachers as professionals is growing, but it is unclear what it means and what its implications are. For example, what will it mean if (private) market factors increasingly replace (public) democratic organs (Englund, 1991a; Englund, 1994a) as the mechanisms that control schooling, and especially its content, and how will it affect views of what it means to be a professional teacher?

Teacher Professionalization and Teacher Professionalism in Sweden

Historical Perspective

The movement towards professionalization among Swedish elementary school teachers can be said to have begun around the turn of the century, and was closely connected with a hierarchization and a gender struggle within the occupation (Florin, 1987). Their endeavour was at the same time conditioned by their relationship to the historically stronger secondary-school teachers — not until 1897 was there any link between these two types of school.

In recent decades, too, moves towards professionalization among teachers in Sweden have been closely connected with differing union aims — with one teacher union traditionally representing secondary school/subject specialist teachers with a university education and another traditionally associated with elementary school teachers — implying different views of teacher autonomy and the task assigned by the State. The crucial difference between these two teacher unions has been their differing views of the job given to teachers by the State and, more specifically, of the general aims of the curriculum and the demand for 'extended professionalism'. Should teachers accept the role of local developers and cooperative planners, or should they just stick to teaching their subjects?

Secondary school/subject specialist teachers have historically developed one of the professional characteristics — autonomy — which has been used as a form of resistance to the National Curriculum's aims of collectivity, analysis of the social role of schools, etc. Elementary-school teachers on the other hand, who during the first half of this century did achieve some, albeit not fully accepted (professional?) status, have, on becoming teachers in the compulsory nine-year comprehensive school (like the subject specialist teachers recruited alongside them in recent decades), gradually been deprofessionalized, as many would see it. They have been controlled by a National Curriculum and told by experts what to do and how. Simultaneously, as we have seen, there have been calls for teachers to act as professionals, guided by the National Curriculum.

Present Tendencies

In recent years teaching as a profession has once again been put on the agenda. The emerging decentralized school system is said to be dependent on teacher professionalism. But the question that can now be asked is whether it is the traditional, individually autonomous teachers (who have often opposed the general aims behind the curriculum) who will be given more scope, or whether those teachers who have long been loyal to the aims of the curriculum, the ones envisaged by educational researchers as professional, collectively autonomous teachers, will take the scene? Of course this characterization is perhaps oversimplified, but what is crucial in the present situation is that, with the new curriculum on its way, educational-policy intentions/curriculum intentions are shifting and that a new situation for 'the professional teacher' is in the making.

What seems to be happening at the syllabus level is a gradual retracing of the educational philosophical triangle back to its starting-point of traditional essentialism (Englund 1986 for an introduction to an educational-philosophical analysis of Swedish educational history). The curriculum introduced in 1962 for the common compulsory school, and especially for its senior level, was clearly inspired by the essentialist tradition of the *realskola*, with its strictly subject-based structures and its focus on preparation for further study and the labour force/working life.

The 1969 curriculum brought a shift in the self-understanding of schooling towards progressivism, i.e., a stronger emphasis on taking the experience of pupils as the starting-point for developing their knowledge. An attempt was made to go beyond the strict subject structure by introducing integrated studies. Yet at the same time educational–technology approaches to teaching were proposed. This curriculum thus made an ambivalent impression.

What distinguishes the National Curriculum of 1980, which is still in force, is that it rose above the self-understanding that had predominated under its predecessors. It also established — in line with the government bill that preceded it — a form of schooling involving active and critical preparation for citizenship, in that it related the content of education to the overriding goal that the compulsory comprehensive school should offer a complete citizenship education. Various environmental questions, for example, were related to the science and social-studies subject areas as a whole. The aim of the curriculum was to relate activities in schools and the content of education more closely to the realities of society, its development and its conflicts.

In the recent proposals for a new curriculum, the conflict perspective and the critical approach is missing. The report of the curriculum committee seems to bring us back to the traditional, narrower self-understanding of schools and also to the essentialist interpretation associated with it (for a more detailed account of the recent changes in Swedish education policy, see Englund, 1993a, Englund, 1994b).

Professionalization and/or Professionalism of Teachers: Meanings and Consequences

If teacher professionalization means that the individual, autonomous teacher strengthens his or her position in relation to a teacher professionalism of a traditional technological type, and there are clear tendencies in that direction (Säfström and Östman, 1992), there is an obvious risk that already well established ways of looking at the work of teachers will be reinforced. These include conceptions of cumulativity — the possibility of becoming qualified by accumulating knowledge; notions about consensual development and growth (Sundgren, 1991); and also metaphors such as solid knowledge, basic knowledge and a core curriculum (Säljö, 1990). Greater demands for teachers' work to be evaluated will naturally fuel such a trend, which is unlikely to result in any problematization of the content of education.

However, even the other form of teacher professionalism, the one more closely related to the general intentions of the National Curriculum and a 'collective autonomy', seems relatively biased. As Colnerud and Granström (1989) document from their studies, teaching teams deal with the types of questions laid down in the National Curriculum, but questions concerning choice of subject-matter are seldom dealt with. 'Traditional teacher knowledge, instructional methods and subject knowledge' would appear to be timeless, immutable and unambiguous.

I have doubts about both these 'professionalized' futures. The different demands for professionalism/professionalization are more a rhetorical way of dealing with an antagonism with which we already are very familiar. The future design of teacher education is a highly relevant example of this antagonism between different approaches to teacher professionalism (between essentialism and progressivism).

What I find crucial is that both these views of teaching as a profession miss what Swedish educationalists, especially, refer to as the 'didactic aspect' — the posssible problematization of the content of education, of teaching and learning. Both views take content for granted. The term professional fails to focus on the didactic aspect; it merely expresses the old positions and problems in a 'new' rhetorical language.[6]

At a superficial level, teachers are being given greater autonomy, but at the same time there are more vociferous demands for teaching practice to be evaluated. What kind of teacher role will be supported by these demands? I see an obvious risk that the 'traditional' calls for pupil evaluation will predominate. Decentralization and increasingly pronounced demands for economic efficiency, together with 'steering by goals', are tending to link the language of schooling to efficiency, economics and administration. Such a development will naturally mean less scope for reflection upon curriculum intentions and didactic questions.[7]

Didactic Competence as an Alternative to Teacher Professionalization and Teacher Professionalism

I therefore find an endeavour to develop the didactic competence of teachers (Englund, 1991b) preferable to the rhetorical and contradictory aims of professionalization/professionalism. However, even a term such as 'didactic competence' is, like 'the professional teacher', open to differing interpretations. What is fundamental to the didactic perspective and to didactic competence is that the emphasis is on the content of education. The didactic perspective thus meets a central requirement in terms of the traditions and the development of the teaching occupation. It links onto, and seeks to develop further, the inner meaning of teachers' work: as a teacher you teach a specific content within a specific subject field and/or to a specific age range.

The next step, the teacher's attitude to that content, is crucial, however. This attitude can be anything from an unreflecting and possibly also authoritarian, content-affirming attitude to one of critical questioning and constant scrutiny. I consider there to be a manifest risk that, with the current aims and rhetoric of educational policy, the professional teacher will evolve into a technological figure, a perfectionist who always knows what content should be chosen and how it should be taught, and who also has the professional authority to assert his or her standpoint, often without listening to others (Labaree, 1992; Popkewitz, 1991). The didactically competent teacher, on the other hand, will constantly problematize and scrutinize what is to be taught, be open to different solutions, and preferably be aware of, and knowledgeable about, the consequences of different choices of content and methods (for a fuller discussion, see Englund, 1991b).

The difference between these two attitudes to content, then, is that the authoritarian, affirming attitude looks at the content of education as decontextualized. The content is not really contextualized in a way that gives it a conscious social meaning, but is seen as meaningful in itself, e.g., scientific concepts in the natural sciences.

The problematizing perspective, on the other hand, relates the content of education to a variety of contexts, giving it different social meanings. A more detailed presentation of this perspective can only be made in relation to specific (school) subject areas. The didactics of foreign languages, of Swedish as a first language, of mathematics, social studies, science and so on all have their specific starting-points and problems. Within every subject area, different didactic typologies, different ways of approaching the content, can be developed and distinguished, creating different preconditions for choosing the content and the meanings that it creates. The didactically competent teacher will be interested in, and aware of, these different possibilities, because school knowledge/classroom communication is necessarily something other than a recitation of decontextualized subject theory/scientific knowledge.

Within this perspective there is of course an awareness of the professional aspects that educationalists have emphasized for a long time — the need to consider and reflect upon one's practice in relation to the aims underlying the curriculum.

A curriculum which, in Sweden at least, is in fact the democratically agreed document on which the activities of schools are to be based.

Thus, what I particularly want to emphasize is the need to reflect upon, and problematize, not only the content of education, but also the intentions behind the curriculum. In line with the perspective I have outlined, school knowledge as such can be seen as a question of democracy which invites an ongoing discussion about what to study and from what angle. It also raises the question of the balance between established and alternative subject areas, e.g., environmental and media studies, and of how the latter can be given legitimate space and how they are to be studied.

Some Consequences of the Perspective Outlined

Of course the role of the teacher educator is central to developing the didactic competence of teachers. Teacher educators are their natural vanguard. They therefore have to move — if they have not done so already — from a focus on methods of instruction, on teaching the 'right' way to teach, to a didactic perspective. With a didactic outlook, you distance yourself from the methods perspective and realize that the method you are choosing is one of many, comparable possibilities, possibilities which can be made the subject of didactic studies. In the same way, a textbook (or parts of it) can be seen as a choice among different, comparable possibilities and, again, be subjected to didactic investigation.

Thus, to be able to develop a distanced, didactic perspective, a comparison is needed. This can be performed most systematically by means of different didactic methodologies, such as those based in curriculum theory and history, qualitative (e.g., phenomenographic) methods and text-analytical approaches.[8]

Conclusion

Once again, then, are professional teachers a good thing? Yes, if that means that they will be didactically competent. The main thrust of my article has been to show that the concept of teaching as a profession tends to obscure a necessary discussion of the future competence of teachers, since it can lend legitimacy to different courses of development. A debate on the meaning of teaching as a profession, teacher professionalism, is very important (and indeed appears to be unavoidable), but at the same time some of the dark shadows of (teacher) professionalization theory are also there in the background. These shadows, the sociological and the rhetorical project, tend to draw the debate in other directions than that of discussing the complex questions of the meaning of (teacher) competence and questions concerning the content of education.

As I see it, a discussion about good teachers (professional teachers?) has to begin with, but also to go beyond, the traditional role of the teacher, namely that of passing on knowledge and creating an optimal climate for learning. From this starting-point, teaching practice can be set in the wider context of collective reflection upon different possible courses of action. The content of education is the key to these different possibilities, and what we need to do is relate our choice of content to what we want our teaching to achieve, what kind of meaning we are trying to create.

Notes

1 The distinction between professionalism and professionalization has been made earlier, but I have been influenced here by Eisenmann (1991), Herbst (1989) and McCullogh (1992).

    While reading the proofs of this chapter, I came across and began to study Hugh Sockett's *The Moral Base for Teacher Professionalism* (1993). From reading this book I learnt that the distinction I have made in my chapter between teacher professionalization and professionalism, a distinction I had a feeling had been made earlier, was in fact identified by Hoyle as early as in 1980. Hoyle characterizes professionalism as the quality of a person's professional practice and sees professionalization as concerned with the status of the occupation. As Sockett (1993) underlines, Hoyle (1980) 'sensibly distinguishes (the) conception of "professionalism" from "professionalization", which is the process whereby an occupation (rather than an individual) gains the status of a profession; but a teacher's professionalism is apparent in his or her practice' (Sockett, 1993, p. 9).

2 The concept of professionalization is also often used to refer to an individual's route to becoming a teacher/professional, but I see that process more in terms of teacher socialization.

3 I will not attempt to discuss Durkheim's theory of professions further here, but I find it important to stress that it cannot be dismissed as necessarily conservative and organismic. What is exciting and progressive about Durkheim's theory is that his professionals are located in a collective context which also can be interpreted in a 'democratic socialist' way, with the public good in sight (Gouldner, 1962).

4 Let me take an example from another occupational field. Dentists — who in many ways do a fairly manual type of job — have historically 'succeeded' in their professional ambitions and are often, like doctors, regarded as having professional status. But what happens to the knowledge development and practice of the dentist in a one-person private practice compared with those working in the public dental service? If the private dentist continues to just mend and pull teeth, while the public service develops a preventive, community dentistry-based approach to dental care — which is the most professional? What is professionalization and professionalism in this case (Freidson, 1970)?

5 As yet, however, no concerted effort to address teacher professionalism/professionalization has been made by Swedish educationalists.

6 This is not to say that the didactic aspect has no chance at all of asserting itself in the teacher education and teaching practice of the future. The professionalization/professionalism strategy does not appear to create the best conditions for its development, though. For a fuller analysis of the different didactic traditions in the Swedish context, see Englund, 1993b.

7 For an account of recent developments in Sweden as regards these matters, too, see Englund, 1993a; Englund, 1994b.

8 In Sweden, the fast growing field of didactic research bears a major responsibility alongside teacher educators and teachers themselves. Fundamental to the development of didactic competence is the opportunity to reflect in writing upon one's teaching practice, one's choice of content etc., and here, in my view, didactic centres and courses have an important part to play.

References

BERG, G. (1981) *Skolan som organisation* (The school as an organization), Uppsala, Almqvist and Wiksell, Uppsala Studies in Education, **15**.

BERG, G. (1983) 'Developing the teaching profession: Autonomy, professional code, knowledge base', *The Australian Journal of Education*, **27**, 2, pp. 173–86.

BERG, G. (1989) 'Educational reform and teacher professionalism', *Journal of Curriculum Studies*, **21**, 1, pp. 53–60.

BERG, G. and WALLIN, E. (1983) *Skolan i ett utvecklingsperspektiv* (Schools in the perspective of development), Lund, Studentlitteratur.

BRANTE, T. (1990) 'Professional types as a strategy of analysis', in BURRAGE, M. and TORSTENDAHL, R. (Eds) *Professions in Theory and History: Rethinking the Study of Professions*, London, Sage.

BURBULES, N. and DENSMORE, K. (1986) 'The limits of making teaching a profession', *Educational Policy*, **5**, 1.

BURRAGE, M. and TORSTENDAHL, R. (Eds) (1990) *Professions in Theory and History: Rethinking the Study of Professions*, London, Sage.

CARLGREN, I. and LINDBLAD, S. (1991) 'Lärarprofessionalism: Lojalitet eller självständighet?' (Teacher professionalism: loyalty or independence?), *Didactica Minima*, **16**, pp. 6–16.

COLLINS, R. (1979) *The Credential Society*, Academic Press.

COLNERUD, G. and GRANSTRÖM, K. (1989) *Läraryrkets professionalisering: Yrkesetik och yrkesspråk — två viktiga aspekter* (The professionalization of teaching: ethics and language — two important aspects), Skolöverstyrelsen, F 89:5, Vad säger forskningen.

DURKHEIM, E. (1957/1992) *Professional Ethics and Civic Morals*, London, Routledge.

DURKHEIM, E./GIDDENS, A. (1986) (Eds) *Durkheim on Politics and the State*, London, Heinemann, Polity Press.

EISENMANN, L. (1991) 'Teacher professionalism: A new analytical tool for the history of teachers', *Harvard Educational Review*, **61**, 2, pp. 215–24.

ENGLUND, T. (1986) *Curriculum as a Political Problem: Changing Educational Conceptions with Special Reference to Citizenship Education*, Lund, Studentlitteratur/Chartwell Bratt.

ENGLUND, T. (1991a) 'Education as a citizenship right: A concept in transition', Contribution presented to the symposium 'Growing into the Future: The Social Significance of Education', organized by the Institute for Future Studies, Sweden and the National Agency for Education, October.

ENGLUND, T. (1991b) 'Didaktisk kompetens' (Didactic competence), *Didactica Minima*, **18**, 19, pp. 8–18.

ENGLUND, T. (1993a) 'New, international trends for Swedish schools: Marketization, privatization, religious-ization, language-ization . . .', Paper presented at the First Comparative Seminar: 'New Policy Contexts for Education: Sweden and the United Kingdom', 22–24 April, Uppsala, Sweden.

ENGLUND, T. (1993b) 'Narrow and broad didactics in Scandinavia: Towards a dynamic analysis of the content of schooling', Paper presented at a symposium on 'Didaktik and/ or Curriculum' at the IPN Institute, Kiel, Germany, October.

ENGLUND, T. (1994a) 'Education as a citizenship right: A concept in transition; Sweden related to other western democracies and political philosophy', *Journal of Curriculum Studies*, **26**, 4, pp. 383–99.

ENGLUND, T. (1994b) 'Communities, markets and traditional values: Swedish schooling in the 1990s', *Curriculum Studies*, **2**, 1, pp. 5–29.

FLORIN, C. (1987) 'Kampen om katedern?: Feminiserings- och professionaliseringsprocessen inom den svenska folkskolans lärarkår 1860–1906' (Who should sit in the teacher's chair?: The processes of feminization and professionalization among Swedish elementary school teachers 1860–1906), *Umeå Studies in Humanities*, **82**.

FREIDSON, E. (1970) *Profession of Medicine*, New York, Harper and Row.
GOULDNER, A. (1962) *Introduction to Durkheim, E. (1962): Socialism*, New York, Collier Books.
HERBST, J. (1989) *And Sadly Teach: Teacher Education and Professionalization in American Culture*, Madison, University of Wisconsin Press.
HOYLE, E. (1980) 'Professionalization and deprofessionalization in education', in HOYLE, E. and MEGGARY, J.E. (Eds) *The Professional Development of Teachers*, London, Kogan Page, pp. 42–57.
LABAREE, D. (1992) 'Power, knowledge, and the rationalization of teaching: A genealogy of the movement to professionalize teaching', *Harvard Educational Review*, **62**, 2, pp. 123–54.
LORTIE, D. (1975) *Schoolteacher: A Sociological Study*, Chicago, University of Chicago Press.
MCCULLOGH, G. (1992) 'School subjects and teacher professionalism', Paper presented at the first PACT Conference in San Francisco, USA, April.
PARKIN, F. (1979) *Marxism and Class Theory: A Bourgeois Critique*, London, Tavistock.
PARSONS, T. (1963) 'The professions and social structure', in PARSONS, T. (Ed) *Essays in Sociological Theory*, New York, Free Press.
PETTERSON, O. (1988) *Metaforernas makt* (The Power of Metaphors), Stockholm, Carlssons.
POPKEWITZ, T. (1991) *A Political Sociology of Educational Reform: Power, Knowledge in Teacher Education and Research*, New York, Teachers College Press.
SÄFSTRÖM, C.A. and ÖSTMAN, L. (1992) 'Den nya utbildningsretoriken' (The new educational policy rhetoric), *Utbildning och Demokrati*, **1**, 2, pp. 47–55.
SÄLJÖ, R. (1990) 'Språk och institution: Den institutionaliserade inlärningens metaforer' (Language and institution: The metaphors of institutionalized learning), *Forskning om Utbildning*, **17**, 4, pp. 5–17.
SARFATTI-LARSON, M. (1977) *The Rise of Professionalism*, University of California Press.
SELANDER, S. (1989) (Ed) *Kampen om yrkesutövning, status och kunskap: Professionaliseringens sociala grund* (The struggle over occupational practice, status and knowledge: The social basis of professionalization), Lund, Studentlitteratur.
SOCKETT, H. (1993) *The Moral Base for Teacher Professionalism*, New York, Teachers College Press.
SUNDGREN, G. (1991) 'Är lärare professionella?' (Are teachers professional?), *Didactica Minima*, **16**, pp. 17–33.
TELHAUG, A.O. (1990) *Den nye utdanningspolitiske retoriken* (The new educational policy rhetoric), Oslo, Universitetsforlaget.
TORSTENDAHL, R. (1989) 'Professionalisering, stat och kunskapsbas: Förutsättningar för en teoribildning' (Professionalization, state and knowledge base: Preconditions for the construction of a theory), in Selander, S. (Ed), pp. 23–36.
TORSTENDAHL, R. and BURRAGE, M. (1990) (Eds) *The Formation of Professions: Knowledge, State and Strategy*, London, Sage.

Chapter 5

Historical Notes on the Barriers to the Professionalization of American Teachers: The Influence of Markets and Patriarchy[1]

Andrew Gitlin and David F. Labaree

Introduction

In the last half dozen years, an educational reform movement has emerged in the United States with the goal of professionalizing teachers. The Holmes Group and the National Board for Professional Teaching Standards are two of the organizations currently leading this movement, which draws on such diverse groups as colleges of education, teacher unions, and educationally oriented foundations. Within the movement, there is widespread agreement around three basic propositions:

- teaching in the US is not structured as a professional occupation (i.e., teachers exercise a limited role in educational decision making, work in relative isolation from each other, lack the opportunity to develop and transmit an appropriate knowledge base, and suffer from inadequate status);
- quality education cannot exist without a professionalized teaching force and therefore;
- any effort to improve education must include a component that promotes the professionalization of teaching.

However, like many educational-reform efforts in the past, this one has not examined adequately the historical roots of the problem it addresses. In this chapter, we seek to sketch out two major factors that played a particularly significant role in erecting barriers to the professionalization of American teaching. The first factor is *markets*. It was the market rather than the State that exerted the strongest impact on the occupational development of teaching in the United States, creating conditions that put a premium on quantity over quality and on the acquisition of educational credentials rather than professional knowledge. As a result, these market factors undercut the ability of education schools to foster teacher professionalism, diminishing and diffusing the content and reducing the status of teacher-preparation programmes. The second factor is *patriarchal structures and values*. These structures and values shaped the professionalization projects undertaken by normal schools and schools of education in ways that not only cast doubt on teachers' abilities, skills, and ultimately their authority, but also fragmented the educational community by furthering gendered divisions of labour. In this sense, the infusion of patriarchal interests into teacher professionalization projects imbued these projects with internal tensions and limited any unified attempt to professionalize teaching. Instead, these professionalization projects came to be dominated by self-interested efforts aimed at organizational survival and enhancement.

We fully recognize the limitations of this chapter. It covers a wide expanse of educational history in a rather hasty and uneven fashion, it slights a number of key factors that limited professionalization efforts, and it relies almost entirely on secondary historical sources. The aim here, however, is not to provide a comprehensive history of American teaching but to develop a preliminary and selective look at the barriers to professionalization in the history of American teaching. The chapter is necessarily an effort to sketch broad themes from this history rather than to define precise explanations of discrete events. We hope it will be judged on the basis of whether it provokes fruitful discussion about the nature of professionalism, the occupational character of teaching, and the peculiarities of both in the context of American history.

The discussion that follows is organized into two major sections. In the first, we examine the impact of markets on the history of American teaching; in the second, we explore the way patriarchal structures limited professionalization projects and how these projects strengthened gendered divisions of labour. While we treat these factors separately for the purposes of this analysis, we want to emphasize that in practice markets and patriarchy interacted intensively, each reinforcing the effect that the other had in limiting projects of teacher professionalization. However, before we discuss these barriers to professionalization, it is important to say a few words about professionalization itself.

Professionalization

Professionalism is a social construct that has changed dramatically over time. Before the rise of institutionalized centres of higher learning, for example, affiliation with a guild was the primary mechanism by which a person came to be seen as a specialist, an expert of some kind. Once universities were established, however, 'association with the university . . . distinguished the "learned professions" from the craft guilds' (Larson, 1977, p. 3). While notions of professionalization continue to evolve, what is common to most if not all constructed views of professionalization is the idea of authority. Broadly defined, authority is something that is given to professionals in exchange for confidence and trust in their abilities, skills, and more importantly their knowledge about a particular endeavour (Howsam *et al.*, 1976, p. 6). When an occupational group is considered to be an authority of one sort or another, it sometimes attains professional standing, which means that it is 'granted autonomy in control of actual work of the profession and the conditions which surround it' (Howsam *et al.*, 1976, p. 7). What tends to be the contested terrain of professionalization, therefore, is not the idea of authority, but the criteria by which groups make claims about their knowledge, abilities, and skills.

One factor that affects the success or failure of a professionalization project is the extent to which members of an occupation group can restrict access to their ranks. That is, an aspiring profession must corner the market for a particular service. This monopoly both raises the status of the service givers, because of their membership in an exclusive organization, and enhances their value in the occupational market-place, because of artificial scarcity. Unfortunately for the professional aspirations of American teachers, they faced market conditions that were highly unfavourable to the accomplishment of these ends. Access to teaching has always been wide open; and once they attained access, teachers found themselves members of a mass occupation rather than an exclusive guild.

Another factor affecting an occupational group's claims to professional status is the way in which members of the group are perceived by those in dominant positions in society. Where members are viewed through the narrow lens of cultural stereotypes, these stereotypes become barriers to professionalization. Furthermore, when these perceptions are systemic and materially based, they acquire structural force. Because of the growing numerical dominance of teaching by women during the late nineteenth century, teacher professionalization projects became merged with stereotyped views of women (devaluing their abilities, skills, and knowledge), which contradicted the view that, as professionals, teachers have a right to authoritative control over their work.

Market Influences on Teaching and Teacher Education

In the history of American teachers, professionalization efforts ran into two different kinds of barriers deriving from the job market for teachers. One came from employers, whose demands served to structure both teaching and teacher education around the demands of social efficiency. The other came from educational consumers, the students at normal schools and teacher colleges, whose demands served to undercut professional education for teachers and elevate general education for social mobility.

Employers, Markets, and Social Efficiency

The American common school movement emerged in the second quarter of the nineteenth century with the goal of incorporating all young people within each community into a locally governed and financed public elementary school. It succeeded in transforming a heterogeneous array of private schools, charity schools, dame schools, and individual tutors into a series of locally inclusive and increasingly similar district schools administered by local public authorities. One result was to create a chronic shortage of teachers, which persisted throughout the nineteenth and early twentieth centuries (Warren, 1985). In part this shortage was the result of the rapid expansion of public-school classrooms, which created a steadily increasing demand for teachers. But in part it was also due to the unattractiveness of teaching as an occupation, with low pay, uncertain tenure, and a short school year. For men, teaching served largely as a temporary position to tide them over while pursuing their own education or until a real career position came along. For women, teaching was more attractive, since it represented one of the few legitimate and respectable forms of employment open to them. Yet women too usually had a brief tenure in the classroom, limited to the short period of time between the completion of their own schooling and entry into marriage. For the most part, teaching in this period served as a career only for older unmarried women and widows.

Conditions in the job market for teachers, therefore, put employers in a difficult position. Thousands of local school districts were under pressure to hire someone, anyone, to fill newly constructed classrooms and to replace teachers who were leaving existing classrooms. Growing demand exacerbated by high turnover meant that they had to be concerned more about quantity than quality. As a result, the examination of the qualifications of prospective teachers was perfunctory at best. For example, the following exchange constituted the entire examination of one teacher candidate before a school district in New England during the 1860s.

Chairman: How old are you?
Candidate: I was eighteen years old the 27th day of last May.
Chairman: Where did you last attend school?
Candidate: At the Academy of S.
Chairman: Do you think you can make our big youngsters mind?
Candidate: Yes, I think I can.
Chairman: Well, I am satisfied. I guess you will do for our school. I will send over the certificate by the children tomorrow. (quoted in Sedlak, 1989, p. 261)

As Sedlak notes in his analysis of the job market for teachers in the mid nineteenth century,

A general teacher shortage, combined with wildly fluctuating and inconsistent prerequisite qualifications, virtually assured any prospective teacher some sort of job, and secured someone for most communities needing a teacher. (Sedlak, 1989, p. 262)

Market conditions during this period could hardly have been less conducive to the development of teaching into a profession. However a group of educational reformers at mid-century nonetheless sought to do just that, by creating a series of normal schools that were designed to provide prospective teachers with a solid programme of professional education. Cyrus Pierce opened the first public normal school in Lexington, Massachusetts in 1839, and by 1860 there were a total of twelve such institutions concentrated in the north-east and upper mid-west of the USA (Elsbree, 1939, p. 152). Looking back on his pioneering effort a few years later, Pierce spelled out the way in which the normal school was intended to promote the professionalization of teaching.

> I answer briefly, that it was my aim, and it would be my aim again, to make better teachers, and especially, better teachers for our common schools; so that those primary seminaries, on which so many depend for their education, might answer, in a higher degree, the end of their institution. Yes, to make better teachers; teachers who would understand, and do their business better; teachers who should know more of the nature of children, of youthful developments, more of the subject to be taught, and more of the true methods of teaching; who would teach more philosophically, more in harmony with the natural development of the young mind, with a truer regard to the order and connection in which the different branches of knowledge should be presented to it, and, of course, more successfully. (Borrowman, 1965, p. 65)

The effort by normal school leaders 'to make better teachers' and thereby turn teaching into a true profession was doomed to failure by the exigencies of the job market. The fact was that the number of graduates produced by these professional schools was tiny relative to the existing demand, and therefore school districts were compelled to hire teachers for the most part who had little or no professional preparation. Some had undergone a brief course in pedagogy at the high school or a teacher institute, but many had no qualifications at all except the ability 'to make our big youngsters mind'. This market situation presented normal school leaders with an uncomfortable choice. They could preserve the normal school as an exclusive institution for the professional preparation of an élite cohort of teachers, but this would mean standing on the sidelines while the bulk of the teachers entered the classroom through alternative routes that required a much less extensive professional education. Or they could expand the normal schools to meet the demand for teachers, running the risk of diluting the professional rigour of the preparation provided. They chose the latter course.

From 1865 to 1890, the number of normal schools in the US increased from fifteen to 103 (Borrowman, 1965, p. 70). During this same period, states began to set certification requirements for teachers, and by 1897, twenty-eight states had come to accept normal school diplomas as evidence of qualification for a teaching certificate (Sedlak, 1989, p. 266). As a result of this rapid expansion, the normal school, which had first arisen as a model institution for the professional education of teachers, quickly transformed itself into a mechanism for mass-producing teachers. Its leaders positioned it to become eventually the primary route by which prospective teachers reached the classroom, which meant that it was under pressure to meet an increasing share of the demand coming from the growing teacher job market.

The consequences for the normal school were dramatic. In its evolving role as a teacher factory, the normal school came to be shaped by a goal of social efficiency that was antithetical to any notion of professionalism. The pressure from the job market was for it to produce a large number of warm bodies to fill empty classrooms and to do so as quickly and cheaply as possible. This meant keeping admission qualifications low; it also meant watering down the content of the curriculum to a level that minimized attrition and maximized the academic success rate. A high-powered professional programme would weed out too many candidates who were needed in the classroom and would then force school-district employers to look for teachers elsewhere. Also, given the high demand for teachers and the short amount of time that each tended to spend on the job, normal schools were under the gun to produce them at minimum expense, which put emphasis on a course of study that was relatively short and cost efficient.

These conditions in the job market for teachers, which persisted until the middle of the twentieth century, made it prohibitively difficult for teachers to pursue a successful course of professionalization. It was hard for teachers to make a claim of professionalism based on status, since professional status is in large part a function of restricted access and exclusive membership whereas normal schools made entry into teaching open and easy. And it was also hard for them to make this claim based on knowledge, when the professional education provided by normal schools suggested strongly that only minimal knowledge and skill was required to teach acceptably.

Consumers, Markets and Social Mobility

The normal school arose in response to the demand for a cost effective mechanism for producing large numbers of teachers, but one key side effect of this creation was an extraordinary expansion of educational opportunity. That is, the same job-market pressures that turned the normal school into a teacher factory also shaped it into a people's college (Herbst, 1980). Not that this was the original intention; far from it. The rapid expansion of the normal school was spurred primarily by the logic of social efficiency (as a way to fill openings in the job structure), but one key side effect of this expansion was to promote social mobility.

Women in particular benefited from this educational innovation. In the cultural and occupational world of the late nineteenth century, it was difficult to justify the investment of either public or family resources the the advanced education of women. But teaching provided such a justification, since it was a large and growing occupation that was increasingly defined as female and that required advanced education for its practitioners. Another group that benefited from the opportunities offered by the normal school was men from lower middle class, working class, and farm families, who otherwise would not have been able to afford the direct or indirect cost of advanced education.

The net result of this mixture of social-mobility and social-efficiency functions was to create a form of structural conflict within the normal school. From the perspective of the State (which paid for it) and the school districts (which hired its graduates), the normal school was a vocational training institution. But from the perspective of its students, it was potentially much more than that. Many of these students were unwilling to pursue a narrow vocational training programme designed to propel them into a single occupational slot — teaching — that offered only modest status and pay. Instead they sought a more general form of education and an advanced degree that would open doors for them to a wide range of high-status positions. (This orientation was particularly characteristic of the men who found their way into normal schools, but a number of female students also began to think of them this way.) In short, they wanted the normal school to become a real people's college and provide access to the American Dream (Herbst, 1989; Altenbaugh and Underwood, 1990).

The emerging social-mobility orientation among a sizeable portion of the students at the normal school introduced another form of market pressure that acted as a barrier to the professionalization of teaching, but this time it was coming from the consumer rather than the employer. The student consumers of the educational commodity offered by normal schools exerted considerable power. For one thing, they had other options. Students who wanted to become teachers could do so in other ways: as late as 1898, normal school graduates still only accounted for a quarter of new teachers (Tyack, 1967; cited in Urban, 1990, p. 63). And for those seeking broader credentials, normal schools were just one among many educational options open to consumers completing grammar school, including high schools, public and private liberal arts colleges, land-grant colleges, and public and private universities. This freedom of choice for the educational consumer was combined with considerable financial clout, for American institutions of higher education have always been heavily dependent on enrollments for their financial survival (via tuition payments and per-capita state appropriations) (Trow, 1988), and normal schools were no exception.

Eager to keep their customers happy, normal schools had to adapt to student demands, and for many of these students (especially the men), the demand arose for a curriculum that was more liberal than professional. The schools already had in place a course of liberal studies aimed at shoring up student knowledge in subject areas in which they would be expected to teach. But consumer pressure led to an expansion of these course offerings well beyond what was required for professional preparation and to the introduction of entire courses of study that were separate from teacher education. And the increase in liberal arts offerings only served to attract more students to normal school who treated it less as a professional school than a junior college, which served as an alternative to, or entry point into, the state university (Herbst, 1989; Altenbaugh and Underwood, 1990).

This consumer pressure on the normal school had significant consequences for the character of professional education and the potential for teacher professionalization. One such effect was to reinforce the social-efficiency pressure exerted by the job market to make teacher education both brief and easy. In order to draw students, the normal school leaders had to offer more liberal arts courses; and in order to induce many of these students to pursue teacher preparation as part of their studies, these leaders had to make it unobtrusive and undemanding, so it could be incorporated within a programme of liberal study or taken as an easier alternative to such a programme. As a result, the market pressure exerted by consumers, like that coming from employers, served to contain, marginalize, and minimize the content of the normal school's programme of professional studies for teachers. This shift both undercut the quality of professional preparation and signalled the declining status of teacher preparation among normal school students.

A second effect of consumer pressure was to undermine the social efficiency of teacher education within the normal school. After all, it was hardly cost efficient to set up an institution for the purpose of preparing teachers and then have it devote an increasing share of its resources to the provision of liberal education for students who never pursued teaching. To a growing extent, the normal school was subsidizing the individual ambitions of its students at the expense of its original broad professional mission and also its subsequent narrow vocational mission (induced by social-efficiency concerns).

A third market effect arising from student demand was a radical transformation of the location, level, and character of the normal school as an institution, which shifted teacher education into the awkward educational position that it currently occupies. Normal schools began in the mid-nineteenth century as educational institutions that were parallel to high schools. However student consumers expressed a demand for a form of accessible education that would be most effective in promoting their future social prospects, and that put an increasing premium on the acquisition of a bachelor's degree. In response to this demand, normal schools began functioning as junior colleges at the turn of the century and by the 1920s they were transforming themselves into state teachers colleges. But with the continuing demand for broad programmes of liberal studies, in the 1960s these institutions gradually changed their names to state colleges (reflecting the general range of programmes they were already offering), and by the 1980s most had become regional state universities (Altenbaugh and Underwood, 1990).

In the space of less than 100 years, therefore, the normal school underwent a remarkable evolution — ascending the educational hierarchy from high school to university, and at the same time expanding its educational function from teacher preparation to general education. As the institution moved through this evolutionary development, teacher education went along for the ride; for, although other colleges and universities have taken part in the preparation of teachers, it is the former normal schools that have continued to carry the bulk of this responsibility. The changes in the institutional setting for teacher education during the twentieth century have presented sobering problems from the perspective of teacher professionalization.

On the surface, the rise of teacher education to a university-level programme represents a significant boost in the status of teachers. However, this new location presents as many professional costs as benefits. First, teacher education occupies a marginal place within the university, which offers a wide range of programmes, in contrast with the central position it enjoyed within the normal school. This marginality is exacerbated by the way in which control of teacher preparation is spread across the university, divided between the education department and the academic departments in the various school-subject areas. Second, in the status hierarchy of the university, teacher education occupies the lowest rung. In part this is because of the modest position occupied by teachers relative to the other occupations to which college students aspire. But in part it is because of the way universities tend to value abstract academic knowledge over practical clinical knowledge of the kind that forms a central part in a teacher education programme (Lanier and Little, 1986). Third, the university has been unwilling or unable to confer on teacher education the kind of exclusivity and prestige it accords other programmes. This is so because of its need to use this programme as a cash cow — which provides high-volume education at low cost and which serves as a convenient place to park below-average students.

All in all, the location of teacher education within the university has not provided a solid platform from which to launch an effort to professionalize teaching. In fact, the impact of markets in general has been disabling to such efforts. Treating teacher education as both a mechanism for social efficiency and social mobility, market forces have deterred the development of credible and comprehensive programmes of professional education for teachers and have also undermined the social status of these programmes and their graduates. One key barrier to the professionalization of American teachers, therefore, has been the job market and the way in which it has structured the world within which teachers and teacher-preparation programmes have had to operate. Another such barrier has been patriarchy and the way in which it has likewise shaped the structure of teaching and teacher education. We now turn to examine this other major barrier to professionalization that has characterized the history of American teachers.

Patriarchy and Professionalization

Patriarchal structures and values — those structures and values which 'constitute a web of privileges and advantages [for men] which are mutually reinforcing and which pervade the many sites of social relations and social interactions' (Witz, 1992, p. 24) — acted along with market forces to constrain and distort American professionalization projects. These structures and values limited professionalization efforts in two significant ways at the turn of the twentieth century. First, while normal schools and schools of education were developing their professionalization projects at this time, the educational landscape included patriarchal structures such as the gendered differentiated high-school curriculum, and womens' limited access to higher education which bounded their efforts. Second, as these institutions developed their professionalization projects a hidden consequence was that gendered divisions of labour became institutionalized strengthening vertical divides where 'women as a group are disadvantaged relative to men in pay and the conditions under which they labour' and horizontal divides where 'women are concentrated in particular kinds of work' (Apple, 1986, p. 55).

The Differentiated High-school Curriculum

At the time that American normal schools and schools of education within universities were developing their teacher-education programmes at the turn of the twentieth century, the high school was rapidly expanding. With this expansion came questions about the purpose and function of this institution. These questions often reflected patriarchal values. Many leading educators and educational reformers, for example, argued that young women, who at this time made up almost two-thirds of the high-school population, should be discouraged from attending this institution. A high-school education, they claimed, was harmful to a woman's health and happiness (see Rury, 1991, p. 12). These patriarchal values were at the centre of arguments to limit young women's access to secondary education. Conversely, the survival of the high school required that women enter these institutions, given that men initially felt that going directly into the workforce or serving an apprenticeship had a more direct payoff than schooling (p. 34). The primary effect of patriarchal assumptions about women, therefore, was not the exclusion of women from the high school, but rather differentiation within high schools. This differentiation was supported by curricular reforms that tried to 'resocialize' women to their 'true' occupation as homemakers (p. 142). In time a differentiated curriculum was put in place that would enable young women to be more efficient in the home and help young men succeed in the public sphere. Home economics became the centrepiece of the newly developed curriculum for young women.

The differentiated curriculum was partly successful in socializing women to the private sphere. A changing labour market, however, with increased need for service workers provided a counter force to the aims of the differentiated curriculum and encouraged women to move into the public sphere. As women did move into the public sector in jobs such as clerking, and social work, and in greater numbers in teaching, the high school put into place vocational courses which would help women prepare for these types of jobs. Unfortunately, this practical approach to education 'aggravated-the existing division of labour . . . by training women for specifically female forms of labour' (Rury, 1991, p. 9) rather than increasing the overall opportunity structure for women. To make matters even worst, when women did gain a foothold in areas like clerking it wasn't long before their dominance within the occupation brought forth reform efforts to routinize and control their work (p. 95). What occurred in the area of clerking repeated itself in teaching. As women made gains in the public sphere, efforts to supervise and control their labour soon were put into place. This supervision was primarily conducted by men.

The differentiated curriculum had several implications for the professionalization projects of the normal schools and schools of education within universities. By providing vocational courses in teaching, the high school in many ways represented an alternative route for teacher certification. No longer could the normal school count on the increasing need for teachers to fill their enrolments, prospective teachers could go directly into the labour market from the high school. In many ways this competition between normal schools and high schools, forced the normal schools to maintain open-admissions policies while finding ways to attract additional students. While effective in some ways, this strategy also diverted attention from the primary objective of the normal school — instruction in the art of teaching, because a curriculum had to be put into place that would address the deficiencies of many students in basic education (Herbst, 1989, p. 85). This open policy also had implications for schools of education. Because the normal schools were training large numbers of students with minimal educational backgrounds, schools of education were more able to move in an élitist direction, by holding to high standards and focusing on the training of educational leaders. Put differently, because normal schools largely satisfied market pressures, schools of education were somewhat removed from the pressure of putting warm bodies in the classroom.

Women's Access to Higher Education

As we have mentioned the differentiated curriculum, in part, was shaped by growth in a number of new service occupations in the first two decades of the twentieth century. This developing occupational market, which included a rapidly expanding number of teaching positions, created the need for experts who could use their specialized knowledge to supervise and manage these new or expanding occupations. The universities viewed this need for experts as an opportunity to increase their student population and develop better community relations, thereby softening criticism that universities had little or no interest in local affairs. There was some pressure from within the university to avoid 'vocational' coursework that would challenge the long standing tradition of liberal arts education, but the pressures of the market, and the need to develop somewhat better relations with the community made professional schools a viable strategy. This strategic move to develop professional schools should have provided additional opportunities for women by giving them access to educational leadership positions. Unfortunately, the establishment of professional schools tended to do just the opposite, especially for those women entering the teaching profession, because they were either denied access, limited by quotas, or segregated in a sister institution. In 1910, Stanford established quotas for women. Harvard, during this same time, limited women's access by cutting back on coursework in elementary education which has been and continues to be dominated by women (Clifford and Guthrie, 1988). And, all married women were virtually barred from receiving fellowships thereby further limiting access to higher education (p. 156). The reasons given for these limits were explicitly patriarchal (see Cubberley, 1909, pp. 67–8 and Judd, 1929, p. 880). These doubts about women's abilities were so deeply ingrained that in 1909 the Harper commission, which was set up to reform schooling and teacher education, introduced a proposal to differentiate salary based on sex, with men receiving the higher salaries (Wrigley, 1982, pp. 94–6).

Over time women did enter institutions of higher education in increasing numbers. This change, however, did not so much signal a lessening of patriarchal values but rather the fact that universities had been overbuilt and women accounted for two-thirds of the high-school graduates. Not surprisingly, therefore, increased access seemed to do little to change women's relation to men in the field of education. Instead women were either informally separated from men by tracking mechanisms, such as the establishment of separate sections for administrators and teachers or more formally separated in less prestigious 'sister' institutions (Powell, 1980).

As normal schools and schools of education developed their professionalization projects in the first two decades of the twentieth century, patriarchal structures such as formal and informal tracking along with the differentiated high-school curriculum strengthened a division of labour where women were clustered on the least prestigious rungs of the educational hierarchy — the elementary school — and men were given direct access to leadership positions. Teaching not only became feminized but the patriarchal doubts about women were embedded within professionalization efforts.

Professionalization Projects and the Institutionalization of
Gendered Divisions of Labour

1 The normal school

By 1900 the normal school was a well-established institution with over half a century of experience in the field of teacher education. While the rapid development of the high school would cause the normal schools to make a number of changes in the coming years, this institution held steadfastly to its aim of professionalism (Steer, 1931, p. 192). However, as opposed to the university approach to professionalism, the normal school became a people's college 'tied closely to the local community and eager to serve students without any special desire for the high-brow culture of the traditional colleges' (Borrowman, 1965, pp. 19–20).

What the normal schools offered in terms of professional training was an emphasis on method. In fact, the term normal school comes form the French word *norme* meaning model or rule (Cushman, 1977, p. 22). Normal schools based their professionalization project on the mastery of these practical techniques of teaching and viewed experience as an important source of educational knowledge. This professionalization project with its emphasis on method and experience was in short order roundly criticized by men and in particular male administrators who felt the normal school would limit their opportunities for administrative advancement given that the 'haphazard empiricism [found within this institution] would not be accepted as truly professional by the more traditional learned professions' (Powell, 1971, p. 406). To correct this problem, it was argued that normal schools needed to put into place a more rigorous liberal arts curriculum and hire professors with a university background. In time, the normal schools tried to respond to these criticisms by introducing more liberal-arts types of courses, hiring different types of instructors, and in general trying to find ways to make the school more acceptable to men. This strategy largely failed because the inclusion of men created a divided student population. One survey of men in normal schools conducted in 1914 indicated that 78 per cent did not intend to teach and because of their lack of interest in professional training became a 'disintegrating element' (Borrowman, 1965, p. 194). In trying to make the institution acceptable to men, the normal school diluted the professional content of their curriculum and allowed patriarchal assumptions to inform their hiring policies such that women often were limited to a tutoring role while men held administrative positions and taught theory courses.

Furthermore, because the normal school also felt pressure from the community — a community that often viewed the normal school as a way for young women to prepare for married life — the normal school felt obliged to expand their curriculum to include courses that resembled those taken in finishing schools (Rutkowski, 1979). However, the inclusion of finishing courses not only led to cynicism about the professional ambitions of the normal school, but acted to reinforce stereotypes about women, especially the notion that they need to become 'finished' to meet and marry the appropriate man.

The normal schools' desire to make the institution acceptable to men, while maintaining close community relations allowed patriarchal values to become embedded within their professionalization projects and fragmented the institutional efforts in this regard. In particular, the normal schools close connection to the community, made it necessary for this institution to design a professionalization project that would not be exclusionary. The emphasis on methods and experience fit well with such a project. This emphasis, however, also was unlikely to enable those graduating from normal schools to achieve the authority associated with successful professionalization projects, if for no other reason than experience is an inclusive more so than a specialized form of knowledge. One central tension within the normal schools' professionalization project, therefore, was the conflict between the desire for open access and the exclusiveness (in terms of specialized knowledge) required by professionalization projects.

2 Schools of education

The rapid expansion of the high school at the turn of the twentieth century increased the need for teachers. For the normal school this was a mixed blessing because the increase in available students was accompanied by competition from the high school which provided a way for students to bypass the normal schools' certification programmes. The normal school responded to this dilemma by making their institution acceptable to a wide variety of students. Schools of education had a different response to the expansion of the high school. In contrast to normal school-professionalization projects that provided open access, and emphasized experience and methods, schools of education centred their professionalization projects on exclusiveness and the importance of subject-matter expertise, and scientific knowledge.

Scientific knowledge was the linchpin of this approach because it promised to provide the specialized knowledge associated with successful professionalization projects (Judd, 1929, pp. 878–9). By the beginning of the second decade of the twentieth century most schools of education based their professional teacher-education courses on the doing of scientific research. One indication of this trend is not only that statistics replaced history at Harvard in 1911, but Harvard began losing students to Teacher College as this institution rapidly moved in the direction of scientific research (Powell, 1980).

While the scientific approach gained momentum in schools of education, normal school scholars dug in their heels maintaining that this method excluded not only practitioners but the world of practice itself (Powell, 1971, pp. 408–9). Normal schools' reluctance to move in the direction of scientific research cast doubt on their professionalization project with its emphasis on experience. Judd was quite outspoken on this point.

> [Judd] considered the 10 years of teaching and administrative experience of the average recipient [candidate for a position in the university teacher education program] as evidence of a retardation of career, a handicap rather than an asset. (Clifford, 1986, p. 433)

Inglis of Harvard added to this critique of experience by saying that, 'an able person would be sick of kids by the time he was 35' [pp. 433–4]. Others at Harvard also noted that a focus on practice would attract, 'academically weak students' (Powell, 1980, p. 61).

The professionalization project of schools of education also differed from those of the normal school because they were directed at the educational élite — those leaders who would shape the nature of educational policy and administer those who were working at the level of practice. Beginning in the late 1880s and continuing into the twentieth century many schools of education including Harvard sought ways to influence the nature of education from the top–down. In practice what this meant is that Harvard would emphasis the training of administrators at the graduate level rather than training of undergraduate teachers. According to those shaping the teacher-education programme at Harvard administrators, 'seemed more important than teachers because their role was to direct education conceived of as a "social force"' (Powell, 1980, pp. 52–3). When practitioners and administrators did take similar courses, 'separate sections for prospective teachers and aspiring superintendents or high school principals' were formed' (p. 65).

In many ways the professionalization project of the schools of education more closely matched the exclusiveness associated with successful professionalization projects than the open-access inclusive policy of the normal schools. In particular, scientific research promised to produce an objective form of knowledge that would not be available to those without university training thereby helping establish trust in the schools who endorsed this approach to knowledge production and those who used this method.

As was true of the normal schools, however, patriarchal values and structures were embedded within the professionalization projects undertaken by schools of education. On the one hand, the move to scientific research had a dramatic effect on women because the one source of knowledge that women readily had available to them, teaching experience, was discounted. On the other hand, men had access to scientific knowledge through university training, and therefore were able to solidify their position as educational policy makers and supervisors of those functioning at the level of practice. In this sense, professionalization projects were shaped by patriarchal values and structures and had patriarchal implications. In part, one such implication is that the push to professionalize teaching resulted in the professionalization of teacher educators and those managing the educational process (Clifford and Guthrie, 1988). Teaching, as a practical activity, lost status and prestige because 'those with "professional" training were managing others who had for the most part gained practical knowledge at the normal schools. One indication of this loss in prestige is that training institutions such as normal schools and teachers colleges, began to change their names and remove the word teacher or normal from the title in order to retain and recruit students' (Woodring, 1958, p. 10).

The merging of patriarchal values with professionalization projects of schools of education created internal tensions within the institution. The push for teacher professionalization did help men, administrators, and teacher educators at the university gain authority. At the same time, the exclusionary nature of the professionalization project actually diminished the prestige of the most common form of teaching — elementary education. In this sense, the professionalization projects that did develop at schools of education, as well as normal schools, served the interests of institutional survival — especially those challenges posed by a changing and expanding educational market — more so than the professionalization of teachers.

The Fragmented Community

By the beginning of the second decade of the twentieth century schools of education and normal schools had established professionalization projects which embodied internal tensions and were in direct competition with each other. Normal schools tried to attract enough students to survive, while education schools focused on 'high calibre' students who could bring prestige to the institution. Viewed from the perspective of the educational community, these contrasting projects which were shaped dramatically by market forces and patriarchal values and structures fragmented the community in ways that reflected horizontal and vertical gendered divisions of labour. These divisions had much in common with those occurring in the industrial sector. For as the scientific management movement in the industrial sphere progressed not only did this rationalized approach put conceptual tasks in the hands of managers who would specify in a precise manner what workers should do but much the same process occurred between teacher-education institutions (Braverman, 1974). Universities took on the task of engaging students with aims, purposes, and educational concepts, while the normal school focused on how to do teaching, the practical side. This division was not absolute. Surely, universities paid some attention to methods and normal schools provided conceptual work. The division was significant enough, however, to help define roles and relations within schools and between school personnel and professors of education. These roles and relations were very much linked to gender stereotypes. For example, not only did the university focus its attention on administrators, superintendents and educational policy leaders, but these educators were overwhelmingly men. In contrast, the normal schools focused their attention on elementary education, and these educators were overwhelmingly women. Furthermore, the women elementary teachers were getting an education that centred around facilitating aims determined by others and the male administrators were getting an education that would allow them to be educational leaders and policy makers. Men not only supervised women, but importantly the role of teacher was seen as needing supervision, not only because of patriarchal assumptions about women, but also because teachers clearly did not have the training to forcefully assert their right to take leadership roles within the educational community.

The implications of this divide soon became apparent. It was teacher educators who were becoming professionalized by the professionalization projects of schools of education because in contrast to teachers who had difficulty making research a part of their work once they entered the intense practical environment of the public schools, teacher educators had a more flexible schedule which allowed them to continue doing research.

The fragmentation with the educational community also divided secondary and elementary teachers. Again, this was because secondary teachers were often trained in schools of education and elementary teachers in normal schools. Further, secondary teaching had many more male teachers and importantly conceived of their role in ways that reflected the subject specialization of their training. In contrast, elementary teaching was dominated by women and reflected a methods, or practical approach. Not surprisingly as the institution became more male, in this case secondary schools, it gained in prestige.

Professionalization projects undertaken by teacher-education institutions gave structural support to patriarchy. Divides along gender lines, in terms of prestige and authority, were institutionalized and strengthened. This not only worked against any unified professionalization project, but constructed professionalization in ways that benefited university teacher educators, and administrators to a lesser degree, at the expense of women, teachers, and in particular, women elementary teachers.

Conclusion

We have suggested in our opening remarks that current professionalization projects have largely overlooked the historical roots of professionalization. When this history is considered two major factors appear to limit and distort American professionalization projects: market forces and the merging of patriarchal values and structures within efforts to professionalize teaching. More recently, these factors have become mediated in a number of subtle and not so subtle ways, but they still significantly shape current teacher-professionalization projects.

Until the 1970s education has always faced teacher shortages. These shortages were due to an ever increasing student population (Kennedy, 1992, p. 66). More recently, however, only one per cent of the teaching positions in the public sector went unfilled (NCES, 1991). And the supply of teachers in gross totals has actually been well in excess of demand (Boe and Gilford, 1992, p. 29). However, while supply is at or above demand nationally in the United States, teacher shortages still present problems in terms of composition and distribution. In terms of composition there is a shortage of teachers in certain subject areas such as science and mathematics (Gilford and Tenenbaum, 1990) and in specialized training such as bilingual education (Schmidt, 1992). As a result, over 11 per cent of all teachers are uncertified in their primary teaching assignment (Carroll, 1985). Furthermore, there is still a severe shortage of minority teachers (AACTE, 1987). In terms of distribution there is a shortage of teachers in urban schools (Oaks, 1990).

The market, therefore, has changed significantly. No longer is there a need to fill classrooms with warm bodies. On the other hand, teacher shortages in distribution and composition still encourage both the State and teacher-education institutions to adopt strategies that limit and constrain professionalization projects. For example, the State has recently used two strategies to address the supply side of the problem and one on the demand side. The main mechanism on the supply side is to, 'relax qualification requirements during hiring. If a highly qualified applicant is not available to fill an open teaching position, a less qualified applicant is typically hired' (Boe and Gilford, 1992, p. 31). On the demand side, the shortage of teachers can be reduced by, 'increasing the work loads of employed teachers . . . by increasing class size and by increasing the average number of classes assigned to a teacher' (p. 32).

Teacher-education institutions have also developed policies to contend with teacher shortages of composition and distribution. One of the most dominant approaches is the Alternative Certification Program (ACP). The ACP allows those with a strong background in an area such as math and science to either skip the teacher education altogether or take an intensive summer training session before entering the classroom (Boe and Gilford, 1992). Typically, after two years of supervised practice the Alternative Certification student is awarded a teaching certificate.

These state- and teacher-education policies focus on filling a demand for a certain type of teacher rather than working in the direction of professionalization thereby influencing the terrain upon which current professionalization efforts, such as those undertaken by the Holmes group take place. As a consequence, whatever results might be gained from professionalization efforts such as those found in Holmes group proposals (professional-development schools, graduate teacher-education programmes, and teacher-initiated research) (Holmes Group, 1986), these efforts will be mediated by state strategies and ongoing teacher-education policies that create doubt about the distinctive skills, abilities, and general expertise needed to teach.

Patriarchal structures and values have also evolved and changed from the turn of the twentieth century. No longer are women denied access to higher education through quotas. No longer are women required to take home economics and other gender-differentiated coursework. And, no longer is there an ongoing tension between normal school and schools of education. While these are encouraging results, patriarchal structures have not disappeared but rather have become more complex and somewhat less overt. In many ways the trend started in the early twentieth century continues where not only are women clustered in the least prestigious institutions, but when women do gain access to high-status institutions they are separated from men, denied opportunities including salary increases, and constrained in terms of obtaining leadership positions within the institution. Evidence for this continuing trend can be found in current statistical data on teachers, administrators and university faculty.

Current census data collected in 1993 indicates that there are over four times as many women elementary teachers as men. However, as teaching gains in status, for example, in secondary school almost 40 per cent of the teachers are male. In terms of administration positions, including both elementary and secondary schools there are over twice as many male administrators than female. And as we move to higher education, which has the most status within the field of education only 27 per cent of the faculty are women. Furthermore, if we consider salaries, secondary teachers make on average $4,000 more than elementary teachers and men on average make almost $6,000 more than women if we consider both elementary and secondary public schooling (NCES, 1993).

Women's access to higher education also reflects the historic trend where access is followed by informal segregation within an institution. There are still wide disparities in womens' access, rank, salary and advancement between men and women professors. Statistics collected in 1988, for example, indicate that only 27 per cent of university faculty are women. Even in the field of education where women dominate, only 38 per cent of those faculty are women. In terms of rank in doctoral institutions only fourteen women are full professors. And where 68 per cent of men are tenured only 38 per cent of women obtain the same commitment from the university. Across all higher-education institutions, men earned an average basic salary of $42,322 and an average total salary of $53,318, women faculty, in contrast, earned an average basic salary of $31,755 and an average total salary of $36,398. In professional programmes, including business, education, engineering and the health sciences the gap in salaries is even greater with the total average income for men being $81,702 and that of women faculty $49,016 (NCES, 1991). More recent comparative data indicates much the same disparities. A survey conducted by the Utah State Office of Equal Opportunity (Shafer, 1994), for example, shows that women assistant professors on average made $4,000 less than men, women associate professors $2,500 less than men, and women full professors, $11,500 less than men. Clearly, patriarchal values continue to strengthen gendered divisions of labour.

Given that market forces and patriarchal values and structures continue to shape the educational landscape, and influence professionalization projects in ways which further gendered divisions of labour, what implications does this continuing trend have for current professionalization projects? We see two major implications. The first is that the market continues to focus attention on putting particular types of teachers in classrooms. Current, professional activities such as those endorsed by the Holmes Group which focus on extended training and specialized knowledge will be undermined in part by the pragmatic needs of markets to fill teaching needs in an ever-changing educational landscape.

Furthermore, professionalization projects undertaken on the behalf of women-dominated professions that have a public-service orientation (i.e., are closely tied to market influences) will have additional tensions. If these projects uphold dominant views of what counts as legitimate knowledge, such as the doing of scientific research, and raise standards to assure only the most 'competent' enter into the specialized professional training, given patriarchal assumptions and structures which limit womens' access and/or opportunity, it is likely that the women-dominated sectors of the occupation will not benefit. On the other hand, if professionalization strategies foster broader notions of legitimate knowledge, by looking to both experience and research, for example, as important sources of knowledge production, and provide for a more open access to teacher training, not only are these projects unlikely to satisfy the trust of dominant groups but importantly patriarchal doubts about the abilities, skills and appropriate roles for women will place a further burden of proof on these professionalization projects.

A second implication directly related to the first, is that if professionalization projects are attempted for public employees that are primarily women, such as teachers, these projects must explicitly challenge market forces and gendered divisions of labour. Challenging markets is a matter of resisting current strategies such as Alternative Certification, relaxed hiring policies, and continuing efforts to maintain and/or increase the intensified nature of teachers' work. These strategies may address supply problems of composition and distribution and decrease demand for extra teachers but they will ultimately undermine professionalization efforts. Challenging gendered divides is a matter of focusing attention on the continuing presence of patriarchy in the educational community including disparities between the salaries of men and women teachers, the clustering of women in the least prestigious institutions, the dominance of men in administrative positions, and even one of the primary patriarchal assumptions that teachers need others — usually male administrators — to oversee the aims and goals to which education is directed. Challenges such as these must go hand in hand with professionalization efforts if professionalization is going to serve the interests of teachers and enhance quality education.

Note

1 Included in this text are revised versions of arguments previously published elsewhere. (Labaree, 1995).

References

ALTENBAUGH, R.J. and UNDERWOOD, K. (1990) 'The evolution of normal schools', in GOODLAD, J.I., SODER, R. and SIROTNIK, K.A. (Eds) *Places Where Teachers are Taught*, 136–86 San Francisco, Jossey-Bass, pp. 136–86.
AMERICAN ASSOCIATION OF COLLEGES OF TEACHER EDUCATION (1987) *Minority Teacher Recruitment and Retention: A Public Policy Issue*, Washington, DC.
APPLE, M. (1986) *Teachers and Text: A Political Economy of Class and Gender Relations in Education*, New York, Routledge and Kegan Paul.
BOE, E. and GILFORD, D. (1992) 'Summary of conference proceedings', in BOE, E. and GILFORD, D. (Eds) *Teacher Supply Demand and Quality*, Washington, DC, National Academy Press, pp. 21–60.
BORROWMAN, M.L. (1965) (Ed) *Teacher Education in America: A Documentary History*, New York, Teachers College Press.

BRAVERMAN, H. (1974) *Labour and Monopoly Capital: The Degradation of Work in the Twentieth Century*, New York, Month Review Press.

CARROLL, D.C. (1985) *High School and Beyond Tabulation: Background Characteristics of High School Teachers*, Washington, DC, NCES.

CLIFFORD, G. (1986) 'The formative years of schools of education in America: A five institution analysis', *American Journal of Education*, **94**, 4, pp. 427–46.

CLIFFORD, G. and GUTHRIE, J. (1988) *Ed School: A Brief for Professional Education*, Chicago, University of Chicago Press.

CUBBERLEY, E. (1909) *Changing Conceptions of Education*, Boston, Houghton Mifflin.

CUSHMAN, M.L. (1977) *The Governance of Teacher Education*, Berkeley, McCutchan Press.

ELSBREE, W.S. (1939) *The American Teacher: Evolution of a Profession in a Democracy*, New York, American Book Company.

GILFORD, D. and TENNENBAUM, E. (1990) *Precollege Science and Math Teachers: Monitoring, Supply, Demand, and Quality*, Washington, DC, National Academic Press.

GITLIN, A. and LABAREE, D.F. (1994) 'The Roots of an unprofession: Notes on the barriers to professionalization in the history of American teachers', Paper presented at the annual meeting of the American Educational Research Association.

HAGSTROM, W.O., DARLING-HAMMOND, L. and GRISSMER, D. (1988) *Assessing Teacher Supply and Demand*, Santa Monica, Rand Corporation.

HERBST, J. (1980) 'Nineteenth-century normal schools in the United States: A fresh look', *History of Education*, **9**, pp. 219–27.

HERBST, J. (1989) *And Sadly Teach: Teacher Education and Professionalization in American Culture*, Madison, University of Wisconsin Press.

HOLMES GROUP (1986) *Tomorrow's Teachers*, East Lansing, MI.

HOLMES GROUP (1990) *Tomorrow's Schools*, East Lansing, MI.

HOWSAM, R., CORRIGAN, D., DENEMARK, G. and NASH, R. (1976) *Educating a Profession*, Washington, DC, American Association of Colleges for Teacher Education.

JUDD, C. (1929) 'Teachers colleges as centers for progressive education', *National Education Association Addresses and Proceedings*, **67**.

KENNEDY, M. (1992) 'The problem of improving teacher quality while balancing supply and demand', in BOE, E. and GILFORD, D. (Eds) *Teacher Supply Demand and Quality*, Washington, DC, National Academy Press, pp. 65–103.

LABAREE, D.F. (1995) 'The lowly status of teacher education in the US: The impact of markets and the implications for reform', in SHIMAHARA, N. and HOLOWINSKY, I.Z. (Eds) *Teacher Education in Industrialized Nations: Issues in Changing Contexts*, New York, Garland, pp. 41–85.

LABAREE, D.F. (1994) 'An unlovely legacy: The disabling impact of the market on American teacher education', *Phi Delta Kappan*, **75**, 8, pp. 591–5.

LANIER, J.E. and LITTLE, J.W. (1986) 'Research on teacher education', in WITTROCK, M. (Ed) *Handbook of Research on Teaching*, 3rd ed., New York, Macmillan, pp. 527–569.

LARSON, M. (1977) *The Rise of Professionalism: A Sociological Analysis*, Berkeley, University of California Press.

NATIONAL CENTER FOR EDUCATIONAL STATISTICS (1991) *Profiles of Faculty in Higher Education*, Washington, DC, Government Printing Office.

NATIONAL CENTER FOR EDUCATIONAL STATISTICS (1993) *Digest of Educational Statistics*, Washington, DC, Government Printing Office.

OAKS, J. (1990) *Multiplying Inequalities: The Effect of Race, Social Class, and Tracking on the Opportunities to Learn Math and Science*, Santa Monica, Rand Corporation.

POWELL, A. (1971) 'Speculations on the early impact of schools of education on educational psychology', *History of Education Quarterly*, **51**, 4, pp. 406–12.

POWELL, A. (1980) *The Uncertain Profession*, Cambridge, Harvard University Press.

RURY, J. (1991) *Education and Women's Work: Female Schooling and the Division of Labour in Urban America, 1870–1930*, New York, State University of New York Press.

RUTKOWSKI, E. (1979) *Wisconsin Normal Schools and Educational Hierarchy*, Ceder Falls, University of Northern Iowa Press.

SCHMIDT, P. (1992) 'Shortage of trained bilingual teachers is focus of both concern and attention', *Education Week*, **12**, 14.

SEDLAK, M.S. (1989) 'Let us go and buy a schoolmaster', in WARREN, D. (Ed) *American Teachers: Histories of a Profession at Work*, New York, Macmillan, pp. 257–90.

SHAFER, A. (1994) 'University academic senate to investigate gender bias in faculty salaries', *The Daily Chronical*, **103**, 120, pp. 1–2.

STEER, H.J. (1931) 'The developmental trends of teachers colleges', *Educational Administration and Supervision*, **57**, 2, pp. 191–4.

TROW, M. (1988) 'American higher education: Past, present, and future', *Educational Researcher*, **17**, 3, pp. 13–23.

TYACK, D.B. (1967) *Turning Points in American Educational History*, Waltham, MA, Blaisdell Publishing Company.

URBAN, W.J. (1990) 'Historical studies of teacher education', in HOUSTON, W.R. (Ed) *Handbook of Research on Teacher Education*, New York, Macmillan, pp. 59–82.

WARREN, D. (1985) 'Learning from experience: History and teacher education', *Educational Researcher*, **14**, 10, pp. 5–12.

WITZ, A. (1992) *Professions and Patriarchy*, London, Routledge.

WOODRING, P. (1958) 'The new look in teacher education', *American Association of Colleges of Teacher Education*, **11**.

WRIGLEY, J. (1982) *Class, Politics and Public Schools*, Brunswick, Rutgers University Press.

Chapter 6

Using Drawings to Interrogate Professional Identity and the Popular Culture of Teaching[1]

Sandra Weber and Claudia Mitchell

Teacher Identity and Image

What are the sources and nature of our earliest images of teachers' work and professional identity? In the ongoing deliberations on teachers' work and on policy changes in education, teacher identity is too often treated as unproblematic and singular in nature. It is usually taken for granted in some a priori way as an outcome of pedagogical skills or as an aftermath or function of classrooom experience (Britzman, 1992, p. 23). Goodson reminds us that this way of viewing the teacher 'represents a subject who is on the one hand depersonalized, that is, essentially interchangeable with other subjects, and on the other hand static, seen as existing outside time or unchanging' (in Elbaz, 1991, p. 7). Britzman (1992) concurs, stating that this static view unproblematically scripts teacher identity as synonymous with the teacher's role and function. But role and function are not synonymous with identity; whereas role can be assigned, the taking up of an identity is a constant social negotiation that can never be permanently settled or fixed, occurring as it necessarily does within the irreconcilable contradictions of situational and historical constraints (Britzman, 1992, p. 42).

There is growing acknowledgment that many aspects of being a teacher are rooted in childhood experiences and culture (Bullough, Knowles and Crow, 1991; Cole and Knowles, 1993; Cole and Knowles, 1994; Connelly and Clandinin, 1988; Feiman-Nemser and Floden, 1986; Goodson and Walker, 1991; Hargreaves and Fullan, 1992). All teachers were once young children engaged consciously or unconsciously in observing and constructing knowledge of teaching both at home and at school (Jackson, 1968; Britzman, 1986). This study is part of a larger investigation into many aspects of children's and teachers' prior knowledge and socialization into teaching (Mitchell and Weber, 1993; Weber and Mitchell, 1993; Weber, 1993). By drawing on data that include visual, oral, and written sources, we investigate the images that children and adults incorporate into their personal views of teaching. We will illustrate how cultural images and childhood experiences linger in the pedagogical notions and orientations of people who choose to become teachers, permeating and shaping in unacknowledged ways teachers' professional identity and work.

It is understandable that the teaching profession would want to distance itself from many of the stereotypes and metaphors of teachers and teaching with which it is saturated (Britzman, 1991; Lawton, 1984; Provenzo *et al.*, 1989). Nevertheless, we contend that by studying these images, and by probing their influence, our understanding of professional development will increase, thus enabling us to play a more conscious and effective role in shaping our own and our society's perceptions of teachers' work.

In the discourse of education, the term 'image' has frequently been used to describe teachers' practical knowledge. According to Calderhead (1989, p. 47), images can be defined at three different levels of abstraction: as powerful metaphors with both affective and moral associations (Clandinin, 1986), as models of teaching (Calderhead and Robson, 1991), and as mental pictures of lessons, for example, pictures of what an arithmetic, spelling, or practical science lesson typically involves (Morine-Dershimer, 1991). Eraut (1985) also uses 'image' to refer to the many visual memories or snapshots of children and situations that enter teachers' minds in the course of everyday teaching. Concepts such as 'image' and 'metaphor' speak particularly to the integrated nature of teachers' knowledge in its simultaneously emotional, evaluative and cognitive nature, and also conveys the personal meanings which permeate this knowledge (Elbaz, 1991, p. 13).

An important link could be made between image and narrative modes of inquiry or life history. The importance of narrative discourse to understanding teachers' professional knowledge has been well-demonstrated by numerous scholars, (Cole, 1991; Connelly and Clandinin, 1988; Egan, 1990; Elbaz, 1991; Goodson, 1992; Goodson and Walker, 1991; Hollingsworth *et al.*, 1993; Raymond *et al.*, 1992, and Weber, 1993, just to name a few). The role and power of images in these narratives needs to be studied further.

Image-making is not only an individual process but also a collective one, part of the sharing that creates a 'we-ness' threaded with the images that permeate a culture. Images can both hide and reveal. They can oversimplify, mislead or elucidate. Their role and contribution to professional knowledge cannot be understood, however, until they are uncovered, recognized, and explored. The importance of studying images lies partly in the fact that much of teachers' background knowledge is tacit. Bullough (1991) suggests that the power of tacit knowledge to shape understanding stems from its situation, embedded in our language and hidden from view. Our work probes a tacit knowledge of teaching which, embedded in the images of our popular culture, is powerful, because it is largely unnoticed by teacher educators and other academics.

Drawings and Images

Drawings are a compelling source of data that has seldom been used in educational research. For adults and children alike, drawing can express that which is not easily put into words: the ineffable (Dienske, 1985), the elusive, the not-yet-thought-through, the subconscious. Much of what we have seen and known slips unbidden into our drawings, which mirror the social images that surround us, especially those portrayed in the media (Wilson and Wilson, 1977). Adler (1982) has shown that as a projective technique, drawings provide people with a good opportunity not only to reflect their personal feelings and their attitudes toward people and situations, but also to express the group values that are prevalent within their cultural environment. Similarly, Dennis (1966, 1970) found that children's drawings were useful for the investigation of group values. An analysis of drawings of teachers could thus reveal much about both the personal and the prevailing cultural images of teaching that have, for the most part, been ignored. Our work focuses on visual images (drawings) as representations and repositories of meaning, as well as mediators of meaning between the social and the personal.

The data we have collected include a sample of 150 elementary-school children's drawings of teachers. These drawings are almost equally representative of boys and girls and of different social classes. Most of the children drew with coloured pencils or crayons on standard blank paper (81/2″ × 11″). They were asked to 'please draw a teacher (any teacher)', and were then either interviewed about their picture ('Tell me about your picture'), were asked to write about their picture, or were invited to join a group discussion about who teachers are and what teachers do.

Our second major data source explored images of teachers held by neophyte and experienced teachers. These data included drawings from three sets of university students enrolled in elementary-education programmes (two undergraduate groups of pre-service teachers and one group of graduate students, most of whom were experienced teachers). As part of a reflective log or journal, the teachers were simply asked to draw a teacher (any teacher, or themselves as a teacher). They were then asked to write about their drawings, indicating any ideas they had about why they had drawn the pictures the way they had. Some of the third-year education students also chose to draw another picture after they had completed their practicum. Consistent with the reality of the gender imbalance in Canadian elementary-school teaching staff, only 2 per cent of the participants were male.

To facilitate comparisons of the drawings, we displayed them on a long wall close to each other in several parallel rows and then repeatedly rearranged them, systematically juxtaposing different sets. Our subsequent analysis is thus a sort of dialogue between children and teachers, between males and females, and between different class sets. The images conveyed by the drawings were further interrogated and clarified in the light of contextual field notes we had written when we visited the children's classes, interviews and written comments provided by many of the children, and excerpts from comments made by teachers on their drawings in their journals and teaching logs.

Although, like any written text, drawings are subject to varied interpretations, certain aspects of the database helped to direct our analysis. For instance, through our classroom visits and interviews with some of the children and teachers about specific drawings, we were able to identify how children intertwined creative or fanciful aspects with more 'realistic' features that directly reflected their actual schooling experience. Even without these visits to schools or interviews, we could see that the drawings had some relationship to real-life experiences. For example drawings from each class set had marked resemblances, reflecting the commonality of the children's classroom experience.

There were some striking similarities between the drawings produced by the children and those drawn by the pre-service teachers, not only in terms of style and form, but also in terms of content (see Fig. 6.1, drawings 1, 2). There seems to be a shared western visual vocabulary, widely used by both children and teachers to portray 'a teacher'. Both groups used almost identical symbols and showed similar preoccupations with elements such as clothes, blackboards, pointers, math and homework. Possible interpretations and implications will be discussed in the next section.

Images of Teaching Portrayed in Teachers' and Children's Drawings

The drawings provided so much material for thought that a book is in progress to provide a more thorough discussion than space allows here. This chapter will therefore focus on three major features of the images that are helpful in understanding the notion of professional identity: models of teaching evoked by the drawings, teacher appearance, and gendered aspects of the images.

Models of Teaching: The Persistence of Symbols and Stereotypes from the Past

Perhaps the most striking finding of our analysis was the pervasive presence of traditional transmission images of teaching in the drawings. Reminiscent of Goodlad's (1984) study of over 1,000 American schools, the typical teacher portrayed in the pictures drawn by both teachers and children was a white woman pointing or expounding in front of a blackboard or desk. We were led to conclude (as Lortie (1975) noted in the 1970s), that traditional stereotypes remain firmly entrenched in today's children (some of whom are tomorrow's teachers) and in today's teachers (all of whom were yesterday's children), despite the common myth that teaching methods nowadays are radically different. Referring to Lortie's work, Britzman (1991) raises the connection between professional identity and stereotypes, saying that,

trapped within these images, teachers come to resemble things or conditions; their identity assumes an essentialist quality and, as such, socially constructed meanings become known as innate and natural. Likewise, the

drawing 1: Self-portrait (female student teacher)

drawing 2: My teacher (boy)

drawing 3: Post student teaching self-portrait (female student teacher)

Figure 6.1: Signs of teaching

backhanded compliment of 'funny, you don't look like a teacher', attempts to disassociate the individual from a social caricature. (Britzman, 1991)

In reflecting and commenting on their pictures, many of the pre-service teachers became aware of the power that past experience and stereotypes seemed to have on them. The following excerpts from their journals will illuminate further:

drawing 1: A teacher (female student teacher)

drawing 2: Self-portrait (female student teacher)

Figure 6.2: Traditional images of 'teacher'

1.1.   I drew my teacher very traditionally with glasses, conservative clothing, in front of a chalkboard, a woman. I don't think I was thinking about myself as a teacher but more what many of my elementary-school teachers looked like. What a stereotype! . . . A picture of a teacher sitting with her class as they are actively involved in their learning be a more appropriate 1990s picture . . . *though it's kind of funny how many of the pictures drawn by my classmates resembled mine. Many other professions don't have such a strong stereotype.* (Fig. 6.2, drawing 1)

1.2.   When asked to either imagine or even draw a picture of a teacher, I still come up with the same figure I used to think of when I was younger . . . the first two things that came to my mind when asked to think of a teacher were a desk and a board. A teacher can't be a teacher without these two. I guess I made the desk quite big because it is that that gives the teacher some power and control . . . *it seems like we can't completely rid ourselves of the traditional ways.* (Fig. 6.2, drawing 2)

1.3.   It's funny how I believe myself to be non-traditional yet here was this teacher standing at the front of the class. I realize there was some factors that made me draw this way but I could have attempted to draw the scene I had wanted to do at first. Maybe this is the true reflection of any teaching — *maybe I want to break away from this traditional role I know so well but for some reason I can't.* (Fig. 6.1, drawing 1)

Stereotypes that are prevalent in the culture and experience of childhood play a formative role in the evolution of a teacher's identity.

Waller (1932) observed that favourable stereotypes represent the community ideal of what a teacher ought to be and that the unfavourable one represents the common opinion of what a teacher actually is. But as Britzman (1991) asserts:

> The persistency of stereotypes does more than caricature the opinions and hopes of a community. Such images tend to subvert a critical discourse about the lived contradictions of teaching and the actual struggles of teachers and students. Stereotypes engender a static and hence repressed notion of identity as something already out there, a stability that can be assumed. (Britzman, 1991, p. 5)

Although most of the beginning teachers' drawings were traditional, some did draw symbolic non-traditional pictures (see Fig. 6.3, drawing 1, 2). Their journal entries suggested that they were using the drawing activity to articulate or recognize their own struggles, stances, or ambivalences in relation to the dominant images of teaching embedded in our culture. Some of them consciously questioned or protested certain stereotypes:

1.4. Why is it that I don't have a board nor alphabet (in my drawing)? It is supposed to be a first grade class. No alphabet? This is where I ask myself questions. There are teachers who put them up and there are others who don't think alphabets are necessary in a classroom. Who is right? (Fig. 6.3, drawing 2)

Others voiced ideals:

1.5. The fear of my first image of 'the teacher' drew me to this drawing (like a rebound I suppose). Middle-aged, polyester-suited, greasy-haired men in green holding a pointer just fill me with fear. This drawing, in contrast is my idealistic view. The teacher is equal to the students and shares with them at their level . . . my drawing, however hokey and unrealistic it my be, is likeable — at least I like it. It has a lot in it of what I hope to be. (Fig. 6.3, drawing 1)

Although these pre-service teachers tried to use the drawings as an opportunity to symbolize the more transformative or child-centred approaches to teaching to which they had been exposed during their teacher preparation, we see how

drawing 1: How I want to teach (female student teacher)

drawing 2: How I want to teach (female student teacher)

drawing 3: My teachers and me (girl)

drawing 4: My teachers and me (girl)

Figure 6.3: Counter images of teaching

problematic it is even for self-aware professionals to forge new identities by modifying images that they have held all their lives — images that are rooted in both the mythology and the reality of teaching. Moreover, many of the third-year education pre-service teachers indicated that their actual practicum experiences only served to reinforce traditional images (see also Liston and Zeichner, 1991; Zeichner and Tabachnik, 1981).

What does this signify? Perhaps that certain stereotypes persist because they still have a firm base, not only in our imaginations, but also in our actual experiences of schooling and of teacher education. Perhaps most people draw a white woman standing in front of a classroom pointing at the board because that still *is* the typical North American elementary-school experience lived by today's children and pre-service teachers. This experience naturally colours perceptions of teacher identity and teaching as a career. One girl, for example, wrote on the back of her traditional portrayal of a teacher:

> This teacher is teaching her class how to measure. Some are eager and some don't understand. I really enjoyed this activity [drawing a teacher] because that's what I would like to be when I grow up.

The direct connection between lived experience and the portrayal of teachers was further supported by a particular grade 1 class-set that stood out markedly from the drawings done by other children (see Fig. 6.3, drawings 3, 4). Of all the classes, these children submitted the highest percentage of non-traditional depictions of a teacher (over 30 per cent) and the highest percentage of 'happy' faces. The teachers in their drawings were consistently portrayed as playing beside, rather than lecturing in front of the children, and were often drawn the same size as the children. A visit to their classroom revealed a non-traditional 'whole language' approach, team teaching, and a general bustling atmosphere much like that portrayed in the drawings. This finding suggests that when children are taught with alternative models, these non-traditional experiences find their way into drawings. There is thus a real possibility that the stereotypes that dominate most of the drawings are not only vestiges of a past visual shorthand to represent teaching, but are also reflections of children's actual schooling experiences.

Our professional rhetoric tends to put a positive value on progress and change: whatever does not change is seen as stagnant and stultified, rather than simply enduring or stable. However, as Elbaz (1991) provocatively suggests, the persistence of images from the past is not necessarily bad:

> The traditions of the school and the culture are a source of authority for what the teacher does and says. I believe that the place of tradition in teacher thinking is a matter we have tended to treat poorly. When a teacher tells us of a particular innovation 'that won't work in my school', we are likely, as educators interested in progress and improvement, to hear this as the voice of teacher conservatism. However, it is just as likely to be the expression of the teacher's tacit understanding of school tradition and culture. I believe our difficulty in finding a place for tradition in our own conceptualizations of teacher thinking has to do with the conceptual maps we have ourselves acquired from liberal theories of education according to which progress and change based on dispassionate criticism of the outmoded ways of the past are unquestioned goods, and the traditional is seen as equivalent to the conservative and the archaic. (Elbaz, 1991, p. 14)

In our deliberations on changes in school policy and practice, it is important to address contradictory interpretations and ambivalences that professionals have towards traditional images and practice. Authentic reform efforts need to consider that which should be conserved as well as that which needs to be discarded.

We Are What We Wear?: The Importance of Teacher Appearance

Both the education students and the children were remarkably preoccupied with fashion and appearance, drawing the teachers' clothes in great detail. Clothes are central to our perceptions of teachers, variously reflecting powerful stereotypes, memories of schooling, actual experience, dreams, and intentions. The following comments from the pre-service teachers' journals highlight the significance of this feature in their drawings:

2.1. My idea of the perfect teacher has pretty much remained the same over the years. The idea is that of a person (male of female) who was always well-dressed, prim and proper with no visible faults. Hair and make-up was always perfect and well applied in women, and men would be in neatly pressed suits, matching ties and always smelling good . . . and were all-knowing. In both the elementary schools I attended, most of the teachers . . . were always so well-dressed and I would think to myself 'Wow, they must be rich for owning all those beautiful clothes'. I suppose this rubbed off on me to some degree because when I did my first practice teaching, I found myself always going in well-dressed and made up.

2.2. Another thing that is important in my drawing is my clothes. I drew myself in my favourite 'first day' outfit. Dress is important as it helps demand respect. I am very nervous about having a grade 5 class. It is important that they respect me as a teacher, and not a babysitter, or older sister. I find that being short, and not looking harmful are two things that work against me, so I must dress and act in a way that demands respect.

Historically, people's choice of clothes and adornments has always been an important mode of expressing their identity, both personally and socially (Cordwell and Schwartz, 1979). Dress can denote power, status, conformity, sense of community or belonging, or, as any parent of an adolescent can testify, rebellion (De Long, 1987; Roach and Eicher, 1973). In this latter vein, some of the pre-service teachers' portrayals of clothing in their drawings seemed to be another way of either examining or fighting a stereotype, reflecting a conscious determination not to be like certain teachers they had known. Drawing a teacher dressed 'differently' was their way of symbolically breaking with tradition or reacting against personal past experience, as the following excerpt from a beginning teacher's log illustrates:

2.3. As I was doing this picture I thought of myself as a teacher. I pictured myself dressed very comfortably and surrounded by all my children. I don't know why, but ever since I was a child, I was always afraid of teachers dressed with suits. That is why I'd like to portray a different image for my children. (Fig. 6.3, drawing 2)

After her field-teaching experience, however, this same beginning teacher drew a second picture which, as the following excerpt from her log illustrates, alerts us to the way in which clothes also signal social or institutional pressures to conform:

2.4.   My second picture was a little different. I'm not with little children. I'm with fifth-graders and I feel as though this is the way I have to look at my practicum school. Maybe this is the idea that I get from this school. I wouldn't say it is terrible, but that is the way they happen to dress in this school, so I also try to look like these teachers as well. But I would like to look like the first picture I drew. I feel more comfortable looking like the first teacher. That's more me. (Fig. 6.1, drawing 3)

Recent work done by Cole and Knowles (1994) suggests that maybe pre-service teachers are simply being realistic in worrying about attire, since this pre-occupation with appearance is not confined to pre-service teachers and children, but is evident in reports and comments made by those who evaluate teachers (e.g., principals and university supervisors). Indeed, the evaluation forms still in use at some teacher-education institutions require comments on teacher appearance.

The children, in their drawings, also showed a preoccupation with the way teachers dress. They often faithfully reproduced a favourite outfit that their teacher actually wore, carefully drawing in every last button and earring. This attention to appearance is not an artifact of the study design. Many teachers remark on the frequency of young children's comments on their appearance. As one teacher put it: 'If I so much as change the colour of my nail polish, they notice.' The majority of children's drawings of teachers illustrate a conservative dress code, which, like the stereotypical teaching styles are probably a reflection of their lived experience. Some children were very much aware of how a 'traditional' or 'normal' teacher should dress, and were sensitive to departures from this norm. For example, one girl in a special-education class wrote of her teacher:

Everyone in the school wants her as their teacher because she is the coolest teacher. He classroom is full of colours and she doesn't wear any dresses on pantsuits — she wears jeans and t-shirts. [spelling and punctuation modified]

Through their drawings, other children liberated their teachers from the pressures to conform to 'normal' teacher dress codes, only to subject them instead to images and stereotypes from the popular culture of childhood (especially television, movies, books, and cartoons). We thus received some carefully executed drawings of teachers as fairytale princesses in long evening gowns or decked in chains and leather as punk rock stars! These young artists, perhaps in a more spontaneous manner than the pre-service teachers who self-consciously tried to 'break' from the norm of teacher attire, allowed their own personalities and popular culture to colour their drawings of a teacher.

Teachers Are Women: Selected Gendered Aspects of the Drawings

The significance of women as teachers has been taken up by feminist scholars such as Walkerdine (1990) and Wheeler (1988) whose work has begun to address what Irigaray (1990) would describe as the 'sexuated' spaces of elementary classrooms, and to suggest the need to further probe the significance of gender in the classroom. As Miller (1992) observes:

> The presence of women and of girls at all levels of education has crucially influenced curriculum, teaching, the organization of school, and the value put on a whole range of educational outcomes. A beginning would be made by acknowledging this, and by acknowledging at the same time that there are serious gender implications in all forms of criticism levelled at education and in all proposals for change. (Miller, 1992, p. 26)

Indeed, the overwhelming majority of teachers in the drawings done by both children and pre-service teachers were female. This is not surprising, given that the majority of primary and elementary teachers in Canada are women (Gaskell and McLaren, 1987). The pre-service teachers (most of them female) noticed and commented on the association they automatically tended to make between 'teacher' and 'woman':

3.1. I drew my teacher like this because she looks like all of the elementary-school teachers I had. Most of my teachers have been women and most of them wore skirts.

3.2. Most of my teachers were female, except for the physical education teacher who was the requisite male.

One of the few men enrolled in a section of the elementary practicum course made the following comment:

3.3. What to draw? What does a teacher look like? Like anybody else, I guess. What sex is a teacher? I might have originally drawn a woman, *since my brain tells me that a teacher is female,* but I wanted also to strike a blow for male equality. I wanted to make a conscious effort to overcome stereotypes (how else are we to get around these except by conscious effort?).

The majority of the teachers portrayed in the pre-service teachers' drawings were not only female, but also a certain 'kind' of female. A significant number were portrayed wearing long skirts, with their hair pinned back in severe buns, evoking the stereotype of an 'old maid' (Fig. 6.4, 1). This image seemed to be strongly rooted in both childhood experience and cultural history, as the following excerpts from their logs indicate:

drawing 1: Typical teacher? (female student teacher)

drawing 2: My teacher (boy)

drawing 3: My teacher (boy)

Figure 6.4: Sterotypes of 'teachers' as female

3.4. I drew my teacher very traditionally with glasses, conservative clothing, in front of a chalkboard, a woman. I don't think I was thinking
about myself as a teacher but more what many of my elementary-
school teachers looked like and what a *stereotype*.

3.5. I must embarrassingly admit that my view is shaded by stereotypes.
It's funny because a part of me still sees a teacher as a woman in
a long prairie dress in a one-room school house somewhere in the
country. She is extremely traditional and proper, as well as warm

and sensitive. This is quite peculiar since it does not match my own liberal education nor my view of my own teaching persona. Now that I think about it, it bothers me that I have this image. (Fig. 6.4, 1)

These images from the past are thus often perceived to be in contradiction with those of the present, creating an uncomfortable dilemma in the student teachers' minds. As many of the comments used throughout this chapter illustrate, many pre-service teachers are making a 'conscious effort' to combat an image which is obviously still very powerful and prevalent within the profession.

Turning now to the children, most of them also drew a woman wearing a dress or skirt, with more varied hairstyles. There were often striking differences between the drawings of teachers done by boys and girls. After looking at just two class-sets, the researchers were able to sort through a third set and accurately predict which drawings were done by boys. Besides a noticeable difference in choice of colours (boys usually opted for browns, blacks, dark greens and blues, while girls more often favoured pinks, purples, and bright colours), there was a great contrast in style (the boys tended to do more hurried and less sophisticated drawings than the girls, see Fig. 6.4, 2). It was as if the boys didn't really *want* to draw a teacher. Perhaps they viewed teachers and teaching as *girl stuff*. Upon examining one of her male students' drawings, a teacher remarked:

He is a terrific artist — if you asked him to draw monsters, snakes, Frankenstein, or blood and gore, he would put a lot more effort into it than just these scribbles.

Britzman (1991), commenting on the social caricatures assigned to teachers, remarked that many of the stereotypes commonly associated with women teachers 'are profoundly sexist and reveal a disdain for the teaching profession's female roots' (p. 5). The boys' attitudes towards the drawing exercise often seemed to suggest such a disdain, an unconscious belittling of a profession and identity that is female, and obviously 'not theirs'. Perhaps, however, they were simply feeling free to 'rebel', to display the teacher in a less flattering light, or to take less seriously a teacher-assigned task, in comparison with the 'please the teacher', compliant attitude often attributed to girls (Robertson, 1992).

The girls, in contrast to the boys, seemed in many cases to identify with their female teachers, incorporating them into their own playworlds. Several of them took the drawing task very seriously, seeming to derive much satisfaction from dressing up their teachers as dolls, paying a lot of attention to 'feminine' detail (earrings, make-up, flowers etc., see Fig. 6.4, 3). Our findings thus support the gender differences in style, manner and identity that have been explored by many scholars (see, for example, Bailey, 1993; Best, 1989; Seiter, 1993).

Conclusion

Both the children and pre-service teachers in our study overwhelmingly portrayed teachers as traditional, usually pleasant, female figures of authority who point out or explain. It's as if for generations, we have been born into these images which shape our expectations of what 'teacher' really means in our culture. Perhaps these images tacitly play a role in the way both children and teachers shape the reality of our schools? Although a lot of university rhetoric and models of teacher education strive to refute or ignore these traditional stereotypes (Zeichner and Tabachnick, 1981; Olson, 1993), the pervasiveness and power of these images cannot be combatted by pre-service teacher education alone. Indeed, perhaps part of the difficulty is that teacher education focuses too much on 'overcoming' or 'unlearning' past experience. It may be more fruitful to work *with* rather than 'undo' prior knowledge.

The way the drawings were collected and used in this study can serve as a basis for developing appropriate methods to further explore people's conceptions of teaching. Our method might prove useful not only in making more explicit the images that influence us, but also in providing a way to evaluate, challenge, or reflect on those images. The drawings can thus provide a strategy not only for research, but also for professional development and self-awareness. Inviting children or colleagues to draw, and then to share their drawings, or to write and talk about them, provides an excellent forum for critical reflection, channelling our attention to the tacit, everyday understandings that, unbeknownst to us, may be colouring or filtering our conceptions of teaching. Our work contributes to the growing body of evidence (e.g., Armaline and Hoover, 1989; Cole and Knowles, 1993, 1994; Elbaz, 1991; Goodson, 1980; Hargreaves and Fullan, 1992; Liston and Zeichner, 1991; Popkewitz, 1987) that suggests that we should take into account, learn from, and use the traces left by certain childhood experiences, in order to more effectively initiate changes in our organization and experience of schooling.

Notes

1   The research on which this chapter is based was funded by the Social Sciences and Humanities Research Council of Canada. We are most grateful for their continued support. We also gratefully acknowledge the expertise and dedicated assistance of Faith Butler, Catherine Lawton, Vanessa Nicolai. Their help was crucial to the data collection, analysis, and preparation of this manuscript.
2   Based partially on a paper presented at The International Conference on Teacher Education: From Practice to Theory, Tel-Aviv, Israel, June 27–July 1, 1993.

References

ADLER, L.L. (1982) 'Children's drawings as an indicator of individual preferences reflecting group values: A programmatic study', in ADLER, L.L. (Ed) *Cross-cultural Research at Issues*, NY, Academic Press, pp. 71–98.

ARMALINE, W. and HOOVER, R. (1989) 'Field experience as a vehicle for transformation: Ideology, education and reflective practice', *Journal of Teacher Education*, **40**, 2, pp. 42–8.

BAILEY, K. (1993) *The Girls Are the Ones with the Pointy Nails*, London, Ontario, The Althouse Press.

BEST, R. (1989) *We've All Got Scars*, Bloomington, IN, Indiana Press.

BRITZMAN, D.P. (1986) 'Cultural myths in the making of a teacher: Biography and social structure in teacher education', *Harvard Educational Review*, **56**, 4, pp. 442–56.

BRITZMAN, D. (1991) *Practice Makes Practice: A Critical Study of Learning to Teach*, Albany, State University Press.

BRITZMAN, D.P. (1992) 'The terrible problem of knowing thyself: Toward a poststructural account of teacher identity', *JCT*, **9**, 3, pp. 23–46.

BULLOUGH, R.V. (1991) 'Exploring personal teaching metaphors in preservice teacher education', *Journal of Teacher Education*, **42**, 1, pp. 43–51.

BULLOUGH, R.V. JR., KNOWLES, J.G. and CROW, N.A. (1991) *Emerging As a Teacher*, NY, Routledge.

CALDERHEAD, J. (1989) 'Reflective teaching and teacher education', *Teacher and Teacher Education*, **5**, 1, pp. 43–51.

CALDERHEAD, J. and ROBSON, M. (1991) 'Images of teaching: Student teachers' early conceptions of classroom practice', *Teaching and Teacher Education*, **7**, 1, pp. 1–8.

CLANDININ, J. (1986) *Classroom Practices: Teachers' Images in Action*, London, Falmer Press.

COLE, A. (1991) 'Interviewing for life history: A process of ongoing negotiation', in GOODSON, I. and MANGAN (Eds) *Qualitative Educational Research Studies: Methodologies in Transition*, RUCCUS Occasional Papers, **1**, London, Ontario, University of Western Ontario.

COLE, A. and KNOWLES, J.G. (1993) 'University supervisors and preservice teachers: Clarifying roles and negotiating relationships', Paper presented at the Annual Conference of the Canadian Society for the Study of Education, Ottawa, Ontario, June.

COLE, A. and KNOWLES, J.G. (1994) *Through Preservice Teachers' Eyes: Exploring Field Experiences through Narrative and Inquiry*, NY, Macmillan.

CONNELLY, F.M. and CLANDININ, J. (1988) *Teachers as Curriculum Planners: Narratives of Experience*, Toronto, OISE Press.

CORDWELL, J.M. and SCHWARZ, R.A. (1979) *The Fabrics of Culture: The Anthropology of Clothing and Adornment*, The Hague, Mouton.

DE LONG, M.R. (1987) *The Way We Look: A Framework for Visual Analysis of Dress*, Ames, Iowa State UP.

DENNIS, W. (1966) *Group Values through Children's Drawings*, NY, Wiley.

DENNIS, W. (1970) 'Good enough scores, art experience and modernization', in AL-ISSA, I. and DENNIS, W. (Eds) *Cross-cultural Studies of Behavior*, NY, Holt, Rinehart and Winston.

DIENSKE, I. (1985) 'Beyond words: On the experience of the ineffable', *Phenomenology and Pedagogy*, **3**, 1, pp. 3–19.

EGAN, K. (1990) *Romantic Understanding: The Development of Rationality and Imagination, Ages 8–15*, New York, Routledge.

ELBAZ, F. (1991) 'Research on teacher's knowledge: The evolution of a discourse', *Journal of Curriculum Studies*, **23**, 1, pp. 1–19.

ERAUT, M. (1985) 'Knowledge creation and knowledge use in professional contexts', *Studies in Higher Education*, **10**, pp. 117–33.

FEIMAN-NEMSER, S. and FLODEN, R. (1986) 'The cultures of teaching', in WITTROCK, M.C. (Ed) *Handbook of Research on Teaching*, 3rd ed., New York, MacMillan.

GASKELL, J. and MCLAREN, A. (1987) *Women and Education: A Canadian Perspective*, Calgary, Detselig.

GOODLAD, J.I. (1984) *A Place Called School*, NY, McGraw-Hill.

GOODSON, I. (1980) 'Life histories and the study of schooling', *Interchange*, **11**, 4, pp. 62–77.

GOODSON, I.F. (1992) 'Sponsoring the teacher's voice: Teachers' lives and teacher development', in HARGREAVES, A. and FULLAN, M.G. (Eds) *Understanding Teacher Development*, NY, Teachers College Press.

GOODSON, I. and WALKER, R. (Eds) (1991) *Biography, Identity and Schooling*, London, Falmer Press.

HARGREAVES, A. and FULLAN, M.G. (Eds) (1992) *Understanding Teacher Development*, NY, Teachers College Press.

HOLLINGSWORTH, S., DYBDAHL, M. and MINAREK, L.T. (1993) 'By chart and chance and passion: The importance of relational knowing in learning to teach', *Curriculum Inquiry*, **23**, 1, pp. 5–35.

HUNT, D. (1987) *Beginning with Ourselves: In Practice, Theory, and Human Affairs*, Cambridge, MA, Brookline.

IRIGARAY, L. (1990) *The Irigaray Reader*, Oxford, Basil Blackwell.

JACKSON, P.W. (1968) *Life in Classrooms*, NY, Holt, Rinehart and Winston.

JOHNSTON, S. (1992) 'Images: A way of understanding the practical knowledge of student teachers', *Teaching and Teacher Education*, **8**, 2, pp. 123–36.

LAWTON, D. (1984) 'Metaphor and the curriculum', in TAYLOR, W. (Ed) *Metaphors of Education*, London, Heinemann Educational Books, pp. 79–88.

LISTON, D.P. and ZEICHNER, K.M. (1991) *Teacher Education and the Social Conditions of Schooling*, NY and London, Routledge.

LORTIE, D. (1975) *Schoolteacher*, Chicago, University of Chicago Press.

MILLER, J. (1992) *More Has Meant Women: The Feminization of Schooling*, London, Tafnell Press.

MILLER, S.I. and FREDERICKS, M. (1988) 'Uses of metaphor: A qualitative case study', *Qualitative Studies in Education*, **1**, 3, pp. 263–72.

MITCHELL, C.A. and WEBER, S.J. (1993) 'Where are you Mr Schwarzenegger?: Children's popular culture as a site of interrogation in teacher education', Paper presented to the Children's Popular Culture 1993 Popular Culture Association Conference, New Orleans, Louisiana.

MORINE-DERSHIMER, G. (1991) 'Learning to think like a teacher', *Teaching and Teacher Education*, **7**, 2, pp. 159–168.

MUNBY, H. (1986) 'Metaphor in the thinking of teachers: An exploratory study', *Journal of Curriculum Studies*, **18**, 2, pp. 197–209.

OLSON, M.R. (1993) 'Knowing what counts in teacher education', Paper presented at the Canadian Association of Teacher Educators section of the Canadian Society of Studies in Education (CSSE) Conference, Ottawa, Ontario, June.

POPKEWITZ, T. (1987) *Critical Studies in Teacher Education: Its Folklore, Theory, and Practice*, London, Falmer Press.

PROVENZO, E.F., JR., MCCLOSKEY, G.N. (1989) 'Metaphor and meaning in the language of teachers', *Teachers College Record*, **90**, 4, pp. 551–73.

RAYMOND, D., BUTT, R. and TOWNSEND, D. (1992) 'Contexts for teacher development: Insights from teachers' stories', in HARGREAVES, A. and FULLAN, M.G. (Eds) *Understanding Teacher Development*, NY, Teachers College Press.

ROACH, M.E. and EICHER, J.B. (1973) *The Visible Self: Perspectives on Dress*, Englewood Cliffs, New Jersey, Prentice-Hall, Inc.

ROBERTSON, H.-J. (1992) 'Teacher development and gender equity', in HARGREAVES, A. and FULLAN, M.G. (Eds) *Understanding Teacher Development*, NY, Teachers College Press.

RUSSELL, T. and JOHNSTON, P. (1988) 'Teachers learning from experiences of teaching: Analyses based on metaphor and reflection', Unpublished paper, Faculty of Education, Queen's University, Kingston, Ontario, Canada.

SEITER, E. (1993) *Sold Separately: Parents and Children in Consumer Culture*, New Brunswick, NY, Rutgers University Press.

WALKERDINE, V. (1990) (Ed) *Schoolgirl Fictions*, London, Verso.

WALLER, W. (1932) *The Sociology of Teaching*, NY, Wiley.

WEBER, S.J. (1993) 'Autobiography, identity and intercultural schooling', in SCHLEIFER, M. and GOHIER, C. (Eds) *La Question d'Identité/The Question of Identity*, Montreal, Les éditions logiques, inc.

Sandra Weber and Claudia Mitchell

WEBER, S.J. and MITCHELL, C. (1993) 'Through the looking glass: How children's views of teachers and teaching can inform teacher education', Paper presented at the International Conference on Teacher Education, Tel-Aviv, Israel, July.

WEILER, K. (1988) *Women Teaching for Change: Gender, Class and Power*, New York, New York, Bergin and Garvey.

WILSON, B. and WILSON, M. (1977) 'An iconoclastic view of the imagery sources in the drawings of young people', *Art Education*, **30**, 19, pp. 5–11.

ZEICHNER, K. and TABACHNICK, R. (1981) 'Are the effects of university teacher education washed out by school experience?', *Journal of Teacher Education*, **32**, 3, pp. 7–11.

Chapter 7

Teacher Professionalism in Local School Contexts

Joan E. Talbert and Milbrey W. McLaughlin

Introduction

Teaching has long been portrayed as lacking both organizational and professional controls, conventionally conceived (Bidwell, 1965; Lortie, 1975; Weick, 1976; Meyer and Rowan, 1977). Neither professional socialization nor organizational policy provides clear definition of teachers' roles and classroom practice; and neither schools nor collegial bodies have much capacity to meaningfully evaluate and sanction teachers. Yet, despite the effective absence of such formal controls, observers of teachers and teaching comment on the regularities in teaching practice (Cuban, 1984; Cohen, 1988) and the appearance of logic and rational management in 'real school' (Meyer and Rowan, 1977; Metz, 1990). Institutional theorists argue that the constancies observed across schools arise largely from teachers' and schools' enactment of institutional rules enforced by public expectations and agencies in the periphery of primary–secondary teaching. In this view, conditions *external* to the school and ultimately to the education-policy system are responsible for the apparent sameness of America's schools.

Yet anyone who has visited schools or who has spent time observing classrooms knows that a school-is-not-a-school and that teachers' classrooms within the same school vary in significant ways — ways that matter enormously to students (and their parents). The differences manifest in such core aspects of classroom life as how much teachers respect and expect of their students and whether they portray subject-matter knowledge as static or dynamic, given or constructed. Such differences, we argue, derive to a significant extent from local norms and standards — the negotiated order of teachers' daily worklives in schools. In the absence of overarching professional, organizational, and institutional mandates and sanctions, teachers' worklives are heavily framed by local school traditions and norms.

This chapter addresses the problem of professionalism and 'standard setting' for teaching in the everyday contexts of schooling. We argue that teachers' professionalism, considered in terms of generic criteria for professional work and authority, is highly variable and contingent upon the strength and character of local teacher community. This claim rests, in part, on the assumption that colleagues are potentially important sources of work norms and sanctions when official or internalized standards for practice are weak or inconsistent.[1] The argument also builds upon prior research on teaching which suggests that privacy norms characteristic of the profession undermine capacity for teacher learning and sustained professional commitment (Little, 1982, 1990; Rosenholtz, 1989). Conversely, teacher communities which promote collegial discourse and collaboration set conditions for shared professional standards to emerge and be enforced.

Over recent decades, educational researchers and reformers have concentrated on technical, economic, and legal strategies for improving education and teachers' claims to professional status, with little attention to the social-normative or moral-ethical dimensions of professional practice (though see Darling-Hammond, 1990; Metz, 1990; Noddings, 1984, 1992; Louis, 1990 for exception). Yet recent research in high schools points to considerable ambiguity and diversity in the norms and relationships that frame teachers' daily worklives, and so the educational experiences of students. Researchers have observed, for example, considerable variation in teachers' commitments to their students and sense of instructional efficacy (LeCompte and Dworkin, 1992; McLaughlin and Talbert, 1993a; Raudenbush *et al.*, 1992). The problematic character of professional standards in schools and the factors that make a difference for the social-normative context of teaching are critical issues for educational research and policy formulation, particularly at a time when teachers face increasingly diverse and challenging student populations (Ward and Anthony, 1992).

This chapter addresses two empirical issues. First, to what extent do particular local contexts of the school system — sector, district, school, and subject-area departments — matter for teacher professionalism? Prior research suggests that *each* of these embedded school contexts can influence the development of teacher community; they may also play a role in promoting or inhibiting professional standards among teachers. Second, to what extent does teacher professionalism appear to be socially negotiated or constructed within school communities? Evidence consistent with our argument would show positive correlations between teacher community, or the level of collegial interaction and support in a school context, and professionalism indicators that persist after adjustments for teacher-background differences across settings.

We first enumerate generic standards for professional work and authority and consider conditions of teaching which inhibit professionalism so construed. Then we review literature on the school-organization contexts of teaching to suggest how strong, local teacher communities might promote professionalism. Data from a multi-year study of secondary-level teachers and schools are analysed to evaluate the argument and to frame issues for further research.

Problematic Bases of Professionalism in Teaching

The technical and moral bases for professional authority in modern society is the subject of a long line of sociological research (Weber, 1947; Parsons, 1954; Wilensky and Lebeaux, 1958; Wilensky, 1964; Scott, 1965; Vollmer and Mills, 1966; Hall,

1968; Montagna, 1968; Etzioni, 1969; Freidson, 1970, 1986; Bendix, 1974; Larson, 1977; Collins, 1979; Abbott, 1988). In recent years, analysts and reformers of teaching have drawn upon this literature to specify standards of professionalism against which to evaluate and improve the profession (Lortie, 1975; Shulman, 1986, 1987; Darling-Hammond, 1990).

Primary among the conditions which distinguish a 'profession' from other occupations are:

- a specialized knowledge base and shared standards of practice
- a strong service ethic, or commitment to meeting clients' needs
- strong personal identity with, and commitment to, the occupation
- collegial versus bureaucratic control over entry, performance evaluations, and retention in the profession.

Primary–secondary teaching is portrayed as relatively weak on each criterion for professional status (Etzioni, 1969; Larson, 1977). Academics have debated whether teaching is a profession or a semi-profession, whether it is an art, a craft or a science. Reformers have sought to engender teacher professionalism through various strategies to strengthen and amplify the specialized knowledge base for teaching, to enhance teachers' economic status and professional commitment, and to increase professional control over performance sanctions.

Challenges to Professionalism in Teaching

Nearly a quarter century ago Dan Lortie (1975) documented teachers' uniform dissatisfaction with their professional socialization and their *limited sense of a shared technical culture*. These conditions still hold, for the most part. Susan Rozenholtz's (1989) research with Tennessee elementary-school teachers provides recent evidence of the occupation's inadequate professional socialization and weak technical culture. Many teachers in her sample felt uncertain about the technical and intellectual bases of their teaching. Available evidence suggests that teachers do not experience their work as employing knowledge and standards for judgment widely shared in the profession. Research on teaching yields divergent conclusions about the potential for a specialized knowledge base for primary–secondary school teachers. While analysts seem to agree that, currently, teachers do not widely share knowledge for practice, some see promise in the growing body of literature on pedagogical content knowledge for teaching (Shulman, 1987; see also Stodolsky, 1988; Stodolsky and Grossman, 1992 for discussion of subject difference in teachers' knowledge and beliefs). Other educational researchers, however, see constraints on the development of specialized knowledge for teaching rooted in institutional traditions and routines (Cuban, 1984) or in the dominance of texts and bureaucratic controls in education (McNeil, 1986; Wise, 1979). Regardless of perspective and prognosis, these analysts tend to locate constraints and enablers of professionalization in temporal or organizational contexts far removed from the daily worklives of teachers. Such macro views of teachers' specialized knowledge base anticipates, at best, a slow and general process of professionalization.

The service ethic, a second dimension of professional standards, *is highly variable among teachers* (at least at the high school level). Teachers' commitment to all students' personal and academic growth cannot be taken for granted. For example, research on tracking and teachers' perceptions of high-school students in their classes reveals that many teachers believe that their students are not capable of learning course material and so water down the curriculum or write off the students (Oakes, 1985; LeCompte and Dworkin, 1992; McLaughlin and Talbert, 1993b; Talbert, 1990). In the interviews that Oakes and colleagues conducted with high-school teachers in the early 1980s and in our interviews in the early 1990s, many teachers stated directly and without apology that their students could not or would not learn course material. The client orientation key to professionalism receives uneven application in schools, depending largely on teachers' assessment of student interests, abilities and motivation. Teachers may subscribe generally to the service ethic, but this standard is transformed and interpreted differently when made explicit in the school or classroom.

The weak *professional commitment and control in teaching*, the remaining standards of professionalism, were also well-documented in Lortie's work (1975). He analysed teachers' limited professional identity and commitment as rooted in the occupation's origins as a 'temporary' line of work and in its wide accessibility and limited socialization. Professional control, Lortie and others have argued, is constrained by the insular character of classroom teaching. Further, Judith Warren Little's research (1982, 1990) revealed the operation of strong privacy norms that effectively prohibit teachers' 'intrusions' into one another's professional space and define as illegitimate a teacher's attempt to promote or enforce collegial standards of any sort. In schools characterized by high norms of privacy, comment on another teacher's classroom was permissible only when aspects of practice, most especially inadequate control or discipline, encroached on another's classroom. 'Bad' teaching, or even harmful classroom practices, typically were noticed silently.

We suspect, further, that public authority and market influences in US education set external limits, or conditions for variability, on each criterion for teachers' professionalism. The fact that conceptions of good teaching are highly permeated by public values and beliefs — parents' and others' opinions about education, child development, and different 'kinds' of students — constrains the development of strong professional standards. For one, the *service ethic* in teaching is vulnerable to negative judgments within the local community about the abilities, character and potential of some of today's students. An atmosphere of distrust or hostility toward new immigrant groups, for example, can foster and legitimize many teachers' negative stance toward the growing proportions of non-traditional students in their classrooms.

The development of a shared *technical culture among teachers* is also inhibited, or even defined as illegitimate, by our nation's strong tradition of local control coupled with divergent definitions of valuable knowledge and good teaching practice among parent communities (Anyon, 1981). The premium placed on specialized school programmes and choice within the current education reform movement furthers the frame of local, versus overarching professional, standards for teaching. The issue of teachers' professionalism, then, may increasingly hinge upon local values and beliefs about 'best practice'.

Such external constraints on educators' authority help to account for the generally weak levels of professionalism reported and observed among teachers. However, they also set conditions for local standard-setting within teaching. In this regard, we know that the extent to which teachers collaborate and experience ongoing professional growth varies dramatically from site to site; this variability may well translate into differential professionalism across local school contexts. Strong teacher communities are likely to engender the technical culture, shared commitment to student clients, and occupational commitment that characterize the prototypic profession.

Multiple Contexts of Teacher Community

A teacher's worklife is conducted within multiple organization settings, each of which influences aspects of the teaching job and delimits a professional community of particular character and strength (Little and McLaughlin, 1993). The contexts for teacher community include school sectors, districts, schools, departments, and, for many teachers, professional associations such as networks, collaboratives, and unions. The multiple communities are, further, embedded in one another and so can be mutually reinforcing or competing in the signals and conditions they set for teachers' professional lives and collegial relationships. In summarizing research on particular teaching contexts, we suggest how each can support or undermine teacher professionalism.

Sector differences in teacher community — the workplace differences associated with teaching in public or private schools — find expression primarily in terms of mission, values and autonomy (see for example, Bryk and Driscoll, 1988; Chubb and Moe, 1990). Independent schools generally have a more coherent and mutually understood sense of school purpose, common norms and values for both teachers and students than public schools do. Teachers working in the private sector say they have greater freedom than their public-school colleagues in terms of what and how they teach and choice of instructional materials. In fact, many independent school teachers give professional autonomy as the reason why they teach in the private sector. Analysts also point to the institutional freedom, or absence of bureaucratic controls, of schools in the private sector as central to teachers' roles — being able to 'act as a professional', free from the rules, regulations, and multiple authorities that operate in the public sector (Chubb and Moe, 1990).

District differences also figure importantly in how teachers think about and enact their professional roles and relations (Rosenholtz, 1989; Louis and Miles, 1990; McLaughlin, 1992). Districts differ in the type and amount of resources available to education, in the expectations of the community for its schools, and in the organizational arrangements that support school administration and management. The messages conveyed to teachers about their professional status, purpose, and value by district activities and choices such as committee structures, professional-development support and opportunities, or governance play a prominent role in framing teachers' worklives. Case comparisons of CRC districts, for example, showed that different levels of respect, trust, and value conveyed to teachers by district administrators generated significantly different district cultures which either bolstered or eroded teachers' sense of professional efficacy (McLaughlin, 1993). The extent of loyalty to the district — the pride or hostility teachers feel about their district — translates to an important degree into their sense of professional worth and of belonging to a community of educators.

School differences in strength of community are much remarked upon by those who have looked inside schools (see Mortimore *et al.*, 1988; Newmann *et al.*, 1989; Bryk and Driscoll, 1988; Little, 1982; Metz, 1990; Rosenholtz, 1989). The extent to which teachers subscribe to norms of ongoing professional growth and development, collegiality and professional interaction contributes powerfully to school culture and community for teachers. Likewise, we found that a strong school mission, which characterizes the independent schools and special public schools in our CRC sample, can be an influential frame for teachers' professional roles and relations (McLaughlin, 1993). Strong school-level community can sustain teachers' sense of professional efficacy even under difficult teaching conditions (Talbert, 1993).

Important differences in the strength of teachers' professional community also exist within the school, at the *department* level (Johnson, 1990; Talbert, 1991; Siskin, 1991). Departments, like schools, differ in the coherence of purpose or mission, norms of collegiality, and goals held for their students. Departments, even within the same school, vary in terms of expectations about teachers' classroom activities, critical examination of practice, and involvement in curriculum development. Some departments comprise strong learning communities for teachers where faculty meet on a regular basis to reflect upon practice, review student accomplishments, or share information about new strategies, resources or ideas. At the other extreme are departments where faculty seldom meet on other than administrative matters, where there is little or no shared information about practice or students, where teachers are isolated from one another in both professional and personal terms. These department community differences lead to important differences in teachers' sense of commitment to the school and their students, and in their willingness to take the risks associated with critical reflection and change.

Networks comprise yet another context for teacher community and one which can significantly influence teachers' professional lives (Little and McLaughlin, 1991; Lichtenstein *et al.*, 1992; Lieberman and McLaughlin, 1992). Subject-area teacher networks (the 'Urban Math Collaboratives', for example) can provide the occasion and support for innovation and change and opportunities for teacher leadership in areas of instructional development and curriculum. Networks engage teachers in discourse about the technology of teaching, exposing them to new content, conceptions of pedagogy, and providing the supportive context essential to serious change. Teacher networks outside the school context sometimes provide the only strong professional community for teachers working in schools or departments with limited collegial interaction.

Research on the multiple contexts of teaching supports the proposition that communities of teachers — based in collegial networks, departments, whole schools, or districts — constitute the meaningful unit and potential for teacher professionalism in US education. Analyses of *each* level or kind of teaching context revealed substantial variation in the strength of teacher community and so in the potential for shared professional standards to develop. We expect that strong teacher communities foster a shared knowledge base or technical culture, shared commitment to meeting the needs of all students, and durable professional identities and commitments.[2] Conversely, without opportunities to acquire new knowledge, to reflect on practice, and to share successes and failures with colleagues, teachers are not likely to develop a sense of professional control and responsibility. With Sarason (1990, p. 145), we believe that schools must be learning communities for teachers as well as students.

Our goal in this chapter is to demonstrate that teachers' professional standards vary significantly across multiple, embedded work contexts and to suggest why that is the case. The analysis uses survey data for a large field sample of high-school teachers and draws upon extensive qualitative data to explicate the survey research findings.

Data and Analyses

The study is part of a multi-year research programme conducted by the Center for Research on the Context of Secondary School Teaching (CRC). Data analysed are from the 1991 survey of approximately 800 teachers in sixteen California and Michigan high schools. We also draw upon three years of interviews and two prior surveys conducted with these teachers to interpret this study's findings (see McLaughlin and Talbert, 1993a for discussion of the CRC database).

We analyse survey measures developed for three of the criteria or dimensions of professionalism: technical culture (shared knowledge and standards), service ethic, and professional commitment. The criterion of professional/collegial controls over teachers' performance evaluations and careers is invariant, since none of the schools in this sample has established formal sanctioning authority for teachers. While we have qualitative evidence that performance norms and informal sanctioning of colleagues evolved within some of the schools and departments in this study, we do not have survey measures of this process and regard it as highly dependent upon the presence of a strong technical culture and/or service ethic in a teacher community.[3]

Our analysis has two stages. First, we examine variation in teacher professionalism and community at different levels of the education system: sector, district, school, and subject department. Here we consider which organizational contexts make a difference for teachers' sense of shared knowledge, commitment to serving student clients, and engagement with the profession.

The second stage of analysis concerns the relationship between an active teacher community — or high levels of collaboration and mutual support for innovation among colleagues — and teacher professionalism. We examine correlational data at the teacher level and at the subject-area department level to assess the general proposition that professionalism among teachers is a product of social interaction and negotiation of norms within collegial work groups or networks. Regression analyses including controls for job satisfaction and for personal characteristics and subject preparation help to rule out the possibilities that relationships are due to survey response bias or to teacher-selection effects. We conduct these analyses for teachers in academic departments (English, mathematics, science, and social studies) of sufficient size to warrant department-level analyses.

Sample and Units of Analysis

The CRC sample of sixteen private and public high schools was constructed within two different metropolitan areas in each of two states (CA and MI). The states were selected to represent different levels of system centralization and reform efforts. The metropolitan areas were chosen to provide contrasts for middle-sized urban districts on local economic conditions, demographics, and recent administrative leadership. For each of the four metro areas, we selected two or three high schools within the core urban district and one school from a nearby suburban district. In California, we also selected three independent schools serving distinctive student populations (one academic élite, one regular college preparatory school, and one for students unsuccessful in traditional school settings).

All teachers in the CRC field sites were surveyed each spring for three years (1989, 1990, 1991). The respondent N of 623 for the most recent, 1991 survey used for this analysis represents a response rate of 74 per cent for the pooled faculty population or 77 per cent average for the CRC schools. The samples appropriate for particular analyses differ as follows. For analyses of variance associated with school sector, the full teacher sample is used (N = 623). Analyses of district versus school variance include only public-school teachers in urban districts with two or three CRC schools (N = 538). Department-level analyses are conducted for the subsample of English, mathematics, science, and social-studies teachers in public high schools for which we have sufficient department-level data (at least four teacher respondents for all four academic departments); eight schools meet these criteria (department N = 32; teacher N = 253).

The sample partitioning required for this study does not affect the nature of variance analysed in different phases of the study and yields the maximum sample size appropriate for any given analysis. As shown in Table 7.1, the means and standard deviations for study variables are comparable for the total, public-school, and academic-department samples. Further, the separate correlation matrices for the three teacher samples show no significant differences in the structure of relationships among variables (available on request).

Table 7.1: Means and Standard Deviations for Teacher Professionalism and Community Variables: Breakdown for Study Subsamples

Variables	All Teachers $(N = 623)^1$	Subsamples Independent $(N = 90)$	Public $(N = 538)$	Public, Academic Teachers only[2] $(N = 253)$
Technical culture	−0.05	0.49	−0.14	−0.28
(Z score)	(1.11)	(1.07)	(1.09)	(1.11)
Service ethic:				
Caring for students	28.9	31.05	28.57	27.58
	(4.23)	(3.44)	(4.25)	(4.57)
Expectations for achievement	23.46	26.66	22.87	22.52
	(5.21)	(5.31)	(4.97)	(4.76)
Professional commitment	24.61	26.86	24.23	23.89
	(3.76)	(2.54)	(3.80)	(3.73)
Teacher community	0.13	0.92	−0.01	−0.10
(Z score)	(1.12)	(0.95)	(1.09)	(1.01)

Note:
1 Standard deviations are reported in parentheses.
2 This subsample is used for analyses of departments: it includes teachers whose primary assignment is in English, mathematics, science, or social sciences.

Measures

The four *dependent variables* for the study correspond to three dimensions of professionalism and are represented by multiple-item survey measures (see Appendix for scale reliabilities and wording of the component items). We developed two indicators of the 'service-ethic' dimension of professionalism to represent different facets of the concept which are important to teaching — the personal or affective and the academic or instrumental aspects of teachers' commitment to serving their student clients.

These variables and brief description of their measures are:

- Technical culture: shared standards for curriculum, subject instruction, relations with students, and school goals;
- Service ethic:
  Caring for students: sense of responsibility and caring for all students as individuals;
  Expectations for students' success: converse of belief that some students are not capable of learning the subject matter and lowered expectation.
- Professional commitment: commitment to teaching, the subject matter, and continued professional growth.
- Teacher community, the *independent variable* for the study, a measure of collaboration and ongoing learning among teachers in a school setting. This variable is an indirect indicator of the process we refer to as social negotiation, since interaction and discourse among teachers in a district,

school, department or network is a necessary condition for the construction of social norms.

Control variables used in the multivariate analyses include:

- Job satisfaction: satisfaction with the the school;
- Personal characteristics, including:
  Gender (Male = 1; female = 0)
  Age (in years)
  Subject preparation: number of college and graduate school courses in subject of primary assignment)
  enrolment in a degree programme (yes = 1; n = 0)

The survey measures of independent- and dependent-study variables tap teachers' perceptions of their work and work environment. Some are subjective reports of work conditions (technical culture and teacher community); others are attitudes and beliefs (caring, expectations, and professional commitment). Since these measures are commonly subject to bias from personality and affective factors, we include the global job-satisfaction measure as a control variable when assessing effects of teacher community on the professionalism variables. The job satisfaction measure is subject to the same personality effects as our study variables and so allows us to adjust for the common source of measurement bias. Controls for job satisfaction yield conservative estimates of teacher-community effects on professionalism variables, since both our independent and dependent variables should have substantively meaningful, positive relationships with teachers' job satisfaction.

Analyses

The first stage of analysis asks which local contexts matter for particular teacher professionalism and community variables of interest in this study. We analyse the total variance among CRC teachers on each variable in relation to embedded teaching contexts: sector, district, school, and subject-area department. While schools are the usual unit for research on teacher community, this analysis makes problematic the proper unit(s) for analysis of professional relations, norms and shared standards.

A series of dummy variable regression analyses are used to address the issue. Each level of school context is represented by a set of dummy variables: sector (private = 1, public = 0); district (a dummy variable for each of the four districts with more than one school in the CRC sample); school (a dummy variable for each of sixteen high schools); and department (dummy variables representing each of four academic departments in the eight CRC schools that meet our sampling criteria for departments (see above)). Another set of dummy variables representing the four academic subjects (English, math, science, and social sciences) is included in the analysis of department effects. The empirical question is whether or not a significant portion of variance in teachers' scores on a given professionalism variable is associated with between-unit differences at a given level of school context, beyond that accounted for by higher-level contexts.

Using a series of dummy variable regression analyses for each set of contexts, we examine and compare the R^2, or explained variance, for each study variable. To assess sector, district and school effects, we compare the R^2 for the three sets of dummy variables. To assess department effects, we compare the R^2 for the model with department dummy variables with that for a model including school and subject dummy variables. Since the set of department dummy variables takes up thirty-two degrees of freedom and may yield unstable estimates with a sample of 253, we also used a nested analysis of variance technique to corroborate regression estimates of department versus school effects.[4]

The second stage of analysis addresses the question of teacher-community effects on professional standards. We first examine individual-level and department-level correlations among the community and professional-standards variables. We then analyse the professionalism variables as a function of teacher community with controls for job satisfaction and for individual background variables. Here we consider whether or not correlations of teacher community and professional standards at the individual level might be due to measurement biases and/or to differences in teachers' personal and professional backgrounds.

Embedded Contexts of Teacher Community and Professionalism

The data reported in Table 7.2 reveal the levels of teaching context that matter for teacher community and specific dimensions of professionalism among teachers in the CRC field sample. Three sets of comparisons are presented, each using the school level as the point of reference. The first two columns of Table 7.2A juxtapose school and sector sources of variance; the second two columns consider school and district sources. Table 7.2B allows one to separate department sources of variance from school and subject differences.

Consistent with our own and others' prior research, the data indicate that each level of school context matters for teacher community. Teacher-reported levels of community vary significantly and independently by sector, district, school, and department. Together these contexts account for about one-third of the variance among CRC teachers on the 'Teacher community' index (this estimate combines the public school department R^2 (.28) and the sector R^2 (.06)).

Levels of school context appear to differ, however, in their importance for specific dimensions of professional standards. Sector differences account for a small but significant portion of variance on each indicator of professionalism, as was the case for 'Teacher community'. School differences, on the other hand, account for no teacher variance on the professionalism variables that are independent of estimated sector- or district-context effects. School-related variance on 'Technical culture' and 'Caring for students' shown in the first column of Table 7.2A can be accounted for by sector differences. Public-school differences on 'Expectations' and on 'Professional commitment' shown in the third column of Table 7.2A can be explained by district differences.

High-school departments appear to matter, independently of their school/

Table 7.2: *Embedded Contexts of Teacher Professionalism and Community: Estimated Variance at Sector, District, School, and Department Levels*

A. Sector and District vs. School Sources of Variance

| | All Teachers (N = 623) | | Public School Teachers (N = 538) | |
	School	Sector	School	District
Technical culture	.06***	.03***	.02	.01
Service ethic				
Caring for students	.07***	.03***	.03	.01
Expectations for				
achievement	.14***	.06***	.07***	.05***
Professional				
commitment	.12***	.05***	.06***	.03**
Teacher community	.25***	.06***	.18***	.05***

B. Department vs. School and Subject Sources of Variance
Public School Academic Teachers (N = 253)

	School	Subject	School and Subject	Department
Technical culture	.04	.04*	.08	.31**
Service ethic				
Caring for students	.02	.01	.03	.11
Expectations for				
achievement	.07*	.01	.09*	.21*
Professional				
commitment	.04	.03	.07	.18
Teacher community	.13***	.03*	.16***	.28**

Note:
Estimates are based on regression models including dummy variables for all units at each level, e.g., the set of dummy variables representing CRC schools is used to estimate variance associated with the school level. The table reports the R^2, or percent variance explained, for each model.

*** $p < = .001$
** $p < = .01$
* $p < = .05$

district contexts and of their subject-matter contexts, for three dimensions of teacher professionalism — 'Technical culture', 'Expectations for achievement' and, to a lesser extent, 'Professional commitment'. As shown in Table 7.2B, the between-department variance in teacher scores on these measures substantially exceeds that of the school and subject combined.[5]

This analysis says nothing about *why* sector, district, or department contexts matter for the teacher-professionalism variables of interest in this study nor whether or not they covary with teacher community. It does illustrate, however, the import-ance of attending to the multiple, embedded contexts of teaching in educational research. While school effects show up in the CRC sample (per Table 7.2), they can all be accounted for by apparent conditions in higher levels of the system; and conditions at lower levels of high-school organization matter in ways that do not show up at the school (or higher) levels.

We next explore the issue of teacher-community effects on professionalism at both department and individual levels of analysis. Our data indicate that the

Table 7.3: Correlations of Teacher Community with Professionalism Variables: Academic Teachers in Public Schools

	Teacher Community	Technical Culture	Caring	Expectations	Professional Commitment
Teacher community	1	.53***	.02	.08	.52***
Technical culture	.43***	1	−.10	.00	.34**
Service ethic: Caring	.34***	.05	1	.39**	.29*
Service ethic: Expectations	.32***	.12*	.42***	1	−.06
Professional commitment	.47***	.16*	.41***	.29***	1

Note:
Individual-level correlations are reported below the diagonal (N = 253); Department-level correlations are shown above the diagonal (N = 36).

*** p < = .01
** p < = .05
* p < = .10

department is an important context for understanding differences in both teacher community and professional standards. However, considerable individual variation in reported participation in teacher community and in professional standards exists within departments, and part of this variation is due to the existence of teacher networks within subject departments, across departments in a school, and beyond the school.[6]

Teacher Community Effects on Professional Standards

The correlational data reported in Table 7.3 are mostly consistent with the proposition that professional standards evolve within the context of strong teacher communities. At both the individual level (shown below the diagonal) and department level (shown above the diagonal), teacher community is strongly related to shared conceptions of teaching practices (Technical culture) and to teachers' professional commitment. On the other hand, expected relationships of community to the service ethic indicators appear only at the individual level.

The pattern of correlations among professionalism variables helps to account for the weak association of department community with the caring and expectations dimensions of a strong service ethic. Specifically, the department's technical culture appears to mediate this weak relationship. While teacher community is strongly related to technical culture, the latter variable is essentially uncorrelated with caring and expectations for students. In fact, the technical culture variable is least coherent within the set of professionalism variables. Additional survey and interview data provide interpretation of this pattern and, especially, the lack of a positive association between the technical culture and service-ethic indicators.

It appears that qualitative differences between academic departments' technical cultures make problematic teachers' commitment to all of their students. In

Table 7.4: Regression Effects of Teacher Community on Professionalism Variables: Academic Teachers in Public Schools

Professionalism Variables

Teacher Community and Control Variables	Technical Culture			Service Ethic — Caring			Service Ethic — Expectations			Professional Commitment		
	I	II	III	I	II	III	I	II	III	I	II	III
Teacher community	.47*** (.43)	.48*** (.44)	.51*** (.46)	1.56*** (.34)	.97** (.21)	1.50*** (.32)	1.50*** (.32)	1.12** (.24)	1.45*** (.31)	1.76*** (.47)	.80*** (.22)	1.70*** (.47)
Control variables:												
A. Job satisfaction (Affect)		-.02 (-.02)			1.05*** (.24)			.70* (.15)			1.77 (.50)	
B. Personal characteristics												
Gender (M = 1)			-.06 (-.02)			.65 (.07)			.51 (.05)			-1.01* (-.13)
Age			.00 (.03)			.00 (.01)			-.01 (-.01)			-.05 (-.11)
Subject preparation (#courses)			-.08* (-.15)			.08 (.03)			.10 (.04)			-.03 (-.02)
Enrolled in degree programme (yes = 1)			-.23 (-.07)			.53 (.04)			1.47 (.10)			-.72 (-.11)
Intercept	-.25	-.24	.16	27.84	27.95	27.49	22.71	22.80	21.52	24.14	24.40	26.34
R^2	.19***	.19***	.21***	.11***	.15***	.11***	.10***	.12***	.12***	.22***	.40***	.26***
N	224	217	185	227	221	187	224	218	186	226	219	188

Note:
Model II controls for Job Satisfaction; Model III controls for teachers' personal characteristics. Unstandardized and standardized (in parentheses) coefficients are reported. Ns vary for the models due to missing values for control variables.

*** $p <= .001$
** $p <= .01$
* $p <= .05$

some cases, teacher communities develop strong commitments to 'upholding tradi-tional standards' in the face of widespread student failure; a strong service ethic is inconsistent with the beliefs and commitments of these teachers' technical culture.[7] In other cases, teacher communities embrace the service ethic and collaborate to forge new conceptions of subject matter and approaches to teaching adaptive to their non-traditional students.

Our data suggest that strong teacher communities promote shared norms of prac-tice, or a technical culture, and enhance teachers' professional commitments — two conditions identified with professionalism. However, the substance of the culture and commitments, the normative character of the department or school work-place, vary significantly in ways that matter for students' learning opportunities and educational equity. Shared beliefs and norms among teachers in a high-school department may promote or actively undermine a strong service ethic. A case of the latter in our sample of schools was a math department united in the belief that the majority of their students were neither very bright nor motivated. In this department context, the failure of more than half of the students enrolled in math-ematics courses was both expected and approved. In contrast to this department-specific client orientation was the ethic of the social-studies department in the same school, where standards of practice were defined in terms of 'success for all stu-dents'. (See McLaughlin and Talbert, 1993b for further discussion of teachers' alternative adaptations to challenging students; see also Davidson, 1992; Phelan, Cao and Davidson, 1992.)

The fact that individual-level data show substantial positive correlations be-tween teacher community and service ethic (though not between the latter and technical culture) could be interpreted in various ways. One possibility which fol-lows from our general argument, is that a teacher's participation in a strong pro-fessional community outside the department engenders or sustains a service ethic among teachers. Another possibility is that the relationship is an artifact of person-ality or professional-background differences. For example, teachers with a relat-ively positive and caring nature are likely to see and report more support and collaboration from colleagues, i.e., to have inflated scores on the 'Teacher com-munity', and to score high on the 'Service ethic' scales. Another possibility is that teachers relatively well-prepared in their subject matter are over-represented in strong teacher communities and are better able to sustain students' success — in which case their participation in a strong community is coincidental with their high levels of professionalism.

Analyses reported in Table 7.4 shed light on this issue. For each profes-sionalism variable, we examine the regression effect of teacher community with controls for a global measure of job satisfaction (Model II) and for personal char-acteristics of gender, age, subject preparation, and programme enrolment (Model III). Results do not support the claim that the community effects are artifactual due to either personality bias or background variables. Effects of community are essen-tially unaffected by controls for the background variables; indeed, a teacher's sub-ject preparation appears unrelated to the professionalism indicators. Controls for job satisfaction reduce the estimated regression effects of teacher community on service ethic and commitment variables, but the adjusted coefficients remain significant. Also, the community and professionalism variables are likely to promote job satisfaction, so this strategy which assumes that correlations among them are due to personality factors yields conservative estimates of the community effect.

Conclusion

This study supports the proposition that teacher professionalism depends, to a significant degree, on the extent and character of local teacher community. Consistent with this claim are data showing systematic variation in high-school teachers' adherence to particular professional standards between the multiple, embedded local contexts of teaching: subject-area departments, schools (private versus public), and public-school districts. Were standards among teachers largely a matter of bureaucratic controls over requirements for professional credentials and licenses, for example, then we might see sector differences (favouring public schools) but no systematic variation across lower levels of the system. Or, were standards among teachers largely a matter of individuals' professional socialization and values, then we might see district and school differences associated with their differential ability to attract highly 'professional' teachers, but random variation in teaching standards within schools. Our finding that high-school departments vary substantially on professionalism indicators, after school and subject effects are taken into account, supports the argument that norms of teaching practice are socially negotiated within the everyday contexts of schooling.[8]

Further, our data reveal that teachers who participate in strong professional communities within their subject-area departments or other teacher networks have higher levels of professionalism, as measured in this study, than teachers in less collegial settings. On average, they report higher levels of shared standards for curriculum and instruction, evidence a stronger service ethic in their relations with students, and show stronger commitment to the teaching profession.

We find, however, that teacher professionalism is somewhat contingent upon the substance of the department's technical culture. Specifically, we observe some tension between strong community and technical culture and the service ethic across the academic departments in our field sample. We suspect that qualitative differences in the beliefs teachers hold about subject matter, instruction, and students underlie the ambiguous relationship between department community and service ethic. In other words, the *substance* of teachers' shared technical standards can either promote or undermine their adherence to a service ethic. The math department mentioned earlier held strong standards of practice: flunk the students.[9] In such cases, the department community embraces traditional conceptions of teaching and learning — emphasizing text-and-lecture-based instruction and absolute, grade-level academic standards for student evaluation — which compete with teachers' commitment to meeting the needs of growing proportions of non-traditional students who often are unprepared to learn, or even to survive academically, under these circumstances.

Issues for Further Research

Our survey data for a large field sample illustrate local variation in professionalism among US high-school teachers that is related to collegial relations. Given limitations of the sample, however, further research should be designed to replicate and extend these findings. Specifically, both our district sample and school-within-district samples are small; and variance estimates are therefore imprecise. A much larger nested sample of teachers, schools, and districts would yield better estimates of variance in professionalism associated with different levels of the public-school system. The sampling design we call for is costly — population samples of teachers at the school level (needed to estimate department versus school variance) and multiple school samples within a large number of districts (needed to estimate school versus district variance). The state level would be a valuable addition to such a design. Unfortunately, none of the national survey programmes uses such a nested sampling design, and the survey we envision would require a major investment.

Despite its crude statistical estimates, this study calls for further research on the development of teacher communities and on the negotiation of professional standards within them. Our survey data do not shed light on key issues of *how* teacher community develops in the local contexts of teaching nor the *nature* of technical cultures that promote all standards of professionalism simultaneously. Such lines of research would require in-depth longitudinal studies, or retrospective analyses, of the development of teacher communities and their technical cultures.

Research on teacher-community building would extend the social-system perspective on teaching standards and professionalization and inform educational reform policy. At least two core problems frame this line of analysis. First, through what stages do teacher communities evolve? Or, what is the process by which a high-school department or a subject network, for example, moves from teacher isolation and norms of privacy to dialogue about teaching and collaboration? Are the stages common across kinds of settings? Do they begin with new beliefs and principles, as often assumed in current reform models, or do they begin with discussions of practice and evolve toward new, shared beliefs?

Second, what division of functions and roles is played in building teacher communities by the different levels of the system analysed in this chapter? How does department leadership work to promote collegial trust and collective problem solving, for example; what essential support is provided by district versus school administrators and staff? Further, can state policy and programmes set the stage for, or facilitate, the development of local professional communities? What about outside organizations and networks? Answers to such questions will provide substance to this study's observation that each level of the embedded school context helps to account for variation among teachers' community and professional standards.

A second line of research concerns the norms and beliefs around which teacher community develops. Our research points to tension between some teaching cultures and the service ethic. It calls for in-depth qualitative studies of different communities of teachers in, say, mathematics to determine the substance of this tension. What elements of teaching in a content area are most negotiable; what norms for teaching compete with commitment to the learner?

Especially, this work would aim to identify technical cultures that embrace both strong subject standards and the service ethic. How do teachers in such communities construe their subject matter and student learners in ways that avoid conflict between the two professional standards? Answers to such questions promise to inform theory on teaching and professionalism — specifically, as suggested below, to extend the analysis from social processes in organizational settings to the broader institutional environment. We suspect that such research can, further, help to promote teacher professionalism by contributing models of strong professional communities of teachers effective with all students.

Implications for Theory on Schools and Teaching

This chapter's social-system perspective on the problem and potential of teacher professionalism seems well-suited to current conditions in US education. Conventional conceptions of professionalism as rooted in codified knowledge and legal controls over entry and careers point to constraints on teacher professionalism in the US context. Among the constraints are: a highly diverse and shifting knowledge base for teaching, wide recruitment and minimal preparation of teachers, the strong tradition of local control, and the movement toward school specialization and parental choice. The prospects for wide consensus and centralized authority among American educators are slim for practical and political reasons.

The challenge of enhancing teacher professionalism is, then, significantly a local matter. The prospects can be framed in social-system terms — as colleagues coming to share standards for educational practice, including strong commitments to students and the profession. In this view, local communities of teachers are the vehicles for enhanced professionalism in teaching. Dan Lortie entertained this notion of teacher professionalization, suggesting that collegiality would be a possible, albeit unlikely, route to teachers' enhanced professional authority (1975, pp. 235–40).

Nevertheless, we believe that organizational and institutional perspectives on US education provide critical complement to our social-system view of teacher professionalism. They explicate the contexts and substance of teachers' professional communities. Our research shows, for example, that district administrations can promote or undermine teacher community and, in turn, professional commitments and expectations for students. It appears, too, that the different technical cultures which emerge within teacher communities derive from the institutional environment: the various local cultures appear to be rooted in alternative, legitimate goals for education and prescriptions for teaching practice. To understand teacher professionalism in the everyday context of schooling requires the multiple lenses of organizational, institutional, and social-system theory.

An organizational perspective highlights the diversity among US schools, particularly in student composition, which has important implications for differences in the work of teachers and in the substance of their local professional communities. For example, the educational challenges for teachers in poor inner-city schools differ from those for teachers in private schools or suburban public schools and so present different problems for teacher collaboration. Both the local-community context and the technical challenges of teacher communities are delimited by school-organization boundaries. School organizations also establish varying capacities for building teacher community, by virtue of resources and leadership. School administrators and staff can enable or constrain teacher community in ways such as providing more or less space and time for collegial interaction, signalling and authorizing more or less teacher responsibility for good professional practice, establishing more or less meaningful opportunities for teachers to continue learning.

Institutional theory also sheds light on the diversity of educational cultures we have seen among academic departments in our field sample of high schools. The theory's principle of isomorphism is pivotal. Accordingly, classroom teachers and schools obtain legitimacy for their practices and support by conforming to the norms of 'real school'. Generally the case is made with regard to structural regularities of school organization (Meyer and Rowan, 1977); but the principle can also apply to technical rationality and modal teaching practices.

Given a wide variety of 'theories' about effective education and good teaching in US education, teachers and schools can obtain legitimacy by embracing any one of the alternatives. In this view, the various educational theories, programmes, values, and norms expressed in the broad arena of American education find local markets or niches. The problem posed by institutional theory regarding the character of teachers' technical cultures and the problem of professionalism is: 'isomorphic with what?' Which public values for education, notions of effective practice, conceptions of students and their differences, educational tastes does a community of teachers embrace to make sense of — and gain legitimacy for — their professional decisions?

Institutional theory can help interpret the tensions we detect in our research between the service ethic and technical-culture dimensions of professionalism. In most general terms, the tension is rooted in competing priorities in American education of promoting equal opportunity versus sorting students according to academic performance, of developing the 'whole person' versus promulgating subject-matter knowledge. These competing priorities can become sources of deep conflict among teachers and of differences between strong teacher communities.

A recent analysis of teacher beliefs (Prawat, 1992) reveals how institutionalized tension between commitment to students and enforcement of subject-matter standards manifests in individual teachers' beliefs and internal conflicts. Prawat and others have found that most (traditional) teachers compartmentalize these core components of teaching and so experience an ongoing struggle between the priorities of the curriculum and learners' needs (1992, p. 361). It is not surprising, then, that teacher communities often develop norms favouring one or the other priority.

We suggest that an integrative theoretical framework — combining social system, organizational, and institutional perspectives on American education and the teaching occupation — is essential for understanding the problems and potentials of enhanced teacher professionalism. Any one framework, alone, cannot explain the variability, boundaries, and substance of teachers' professional communities and standards. The prospect and process of teacher professionalism appear to be in the dialectic of local and institutional constructions of education standards within teacher communities.[10]

Appendix: Teacher Community, Professionalism, and Job Satisfaction Scales[11]

I. Teacher Community (Independent variable)

Teacher Community Index (8 items; Alpha = .85)

CRC 18. Please indicate how strongly you agree or disagree with each of the following statements regarding your current feelings about teaching in general and your present job.

    a. I feel that I have many opportunities to learn new things in my present job.
    b. I feel supported by colleagues to try out new ideas.

CRC 29 (ATS 19) Using the scale provided, please indicate the extent to which you agree or disagree with each of the following statements about working conditions in your school.

    e. In this school we solve problems, we don't just talk about them.
    i. My job provides me continuing professional stimulation and growth.
    k. The staff seldom evaluates its programmes and activities. (Reverse coded)
    t. In this school, I am encouraged to experiment with my teaching.
    w. Teachers in this school are constantly learning and seeking new ideas.
    ee. The principal is interested in innovations and new ideas.

II. Professionalism Variables (Dependent variables)

A. Technical Culture (6-items; Alpha = .73)

CRC 14. To what extent does each of the following statements describe relationships among the teachers *in your primary subject area* in this school?

    b. We have very different ideas about what we should emphasize in the curriculum. (Reverse coded)
    h. We have little idea of each other's teaching goals and classroom practices. (Reverse coded)

i.   There is little disagreement about what should be taught in our subject area.

m.   There is a lot of disagreement among us about how to teach the subject. (Reverse coded)

n.   We share views of students and how to relate to them CRC 29 (ATS 19). Using the scale provided, please indicate the extent to which you agree to disagree with each of the following statements:

b(e).   Most of my colleagues share my beliefs and values about what the central mission of the school should be.

B. Service Ethic

1. *Caring for Students* (6 items; Alpha = .74)
CRC 6. The statements below concern goals for educational outcomes and for relationships with students. Please indicate how strongly you agree or disagree with each statement as it applies to your own teaching philosophy and practice.

f.   I try very hard to show my students that I care about them.

i.   I feel that I should be accessible to students even if it means meeting with them before or after school, during my prep or free period, etc.

m.   It is important for me that my students enjoy learning and become independent learners.

CRC 7 (NELS: 88 First Followup Item IV.5). On the scale below, indicate the extent to which you agree or disagree with each of the following statements:

a.   If I try really hard, I can get through to even the most difficult or unmotivated students.

b.   I feel that it's part of my responsibility to keep students from dropping out of school.

f.   I am certain I am making a difference in the lives of my students.

2. *High Expectations for Student Achievement* (6 items; Alpha = .60)
CRC 5. Now consider each of the statements below concerning instruction in your subject area. Indicate the extent to which you agree or disagree with each statement.

j.   No matter how hard they try, some students will not be able to learn aspects of my subject matter. (Reverse coded)

CRC 6. The statements below concern goals for educational outcomes and for relationships with students. Please indicate how strongly you agree or disagree with each statement *as it applies to your own teaching philosophy and practice.*

   c. My expectations about how much students should learn are not as high as they used to be. (Reverse coded)

   g. Students who work hard and do well deserve more of my time than those who do not. (Reverse coded)

CRC 7 (NELS: 88 item IV.5). On the scale below, indicate the extent to which you agree or disagree with each of the following statements:

   e. There is really very little I can do to insure that most of my students achieve at a high level. (Reverse coded)

CRC 27. (ATS 19) Indicate how much you agree or disagree with each of these statements about students in your classes this year.

   d. The attitudes and habits students bring to my classes greatly reduce their chances for academic success. (Reverse coded)

   f. Most of the students I teach are not capable of learning the material I should be teaching them. (Reverse coded)

      C. Professional Commitment *(6 items; Alpha = .71)*

CRC 18. Please indicate how strongly you agree or disagree with each of the following statements regarding your current feelings about teaching in general and your present job.

   d. I am willing to put in a great deal of effort beyond that usually expected of teachers.

   g. I feel that I am improving each year as a teacher.

   h. I don't seem to have as much enthusiasm now as I did when I began teaching. (Reverse coded)

   i. I really love the subject I teach most frequently.

   k. I am always eager to hear about ways to improve my teaching.

   l. I feel little loyalty to the teaching profession. (Reverse coded)

III.   Job Satisfaction (Control variable)

Job Satisfaction Index (2-items; Alpha = .73)
CRC 30 (ATS 32). How much of the time do you feel satisfied with your job in this school?

   1. Almost never
   2. Some of the time
   3. Most of the time
   4. All the time

CRC 29 (ATS 19). Using the scale provided, please indicate the extent to which you agree to disagree with each of the following statements:

aa (ff)   I usually look forward to each working day at this school.

Notes

1   Sociological research on work in a variety of occupational and organizational settings demonstrates the power of work groups to set standards for occupational roles and productivity (most notably, Homans, 1950; Gouldner, 1954; Whyte, 1959; see Scott, 1988, for review of more recent research).

2   While in some cases the norms which emerge in a strong teacher community may actively undermine one or another professional standard, we will take up the issue of qualitative differences among teacher communities after evaluating the general proposition.

3   One school in our sample, for example, established by faculty vote a committee of five elected teachers to serve as a jury and sanctioning body for colleagues alleged to have complained about students — thus formalizing the strong service ethic that characterizes this school community.

4   This analysis treats school as the top level and subjects (English, math, science, and social studies) as the lower level; given uneven numbers of cases within the subject cells across schools, statistical tests of significance are not computed. Results of this corroborating analysis are not reported but may be obtained upon request.

5   These results are replicated by a nested analysis of variance (separating school and department variance) for the professionalism variables. For our sample of public comprehensive high schools, variance in 'Technical culture' and 'Professional commitment' is associated with departments but not schools; 'Expectations' and 'Teacher community' vary at both department and school levels; and neither level accounts for variation in the 'Caring' variable.

6   We currently are investigating networks as contexts for professional community and standards among CRC mathematics and science teachers. Clearly, some of variance unexplained by formal school-organization contexts in this study can be accounted for by informal networks of teachers. The individual-level analysis of teacher-community effects on professionalism assumes such informal or out-of-school contexts of teachers' worklives.

7   CRC survey data show that, on average, teachers' technical cultures tend toward the traditional side of this dichotomy. This is illustrated by the positive, though weak, correlation between 'Technical culture' and indicators of static conceptions of subject matter and routine views of the teaching job (both of which are negatively related to the service ethic and professional-commitment variables).

8   We note, however, that substantial variation among individuals within departments remains. In particular, the standards of caring for students and overall professional commitment are not well explained by context differences represented in this field sample. Neither are these dimensions of professionalism accounted for by individual preparation and personal variables; even a likely relationship between teacher gender and caring for students is not shown by these data. Of course, it may still be the case that unmeasured background variables are important, such as different emphases in teacher-preparation programmes on normative standards for the profession.

9   This department scored relatively high on our measures of teacher community and technical culture but low on the service ethic indicators.

10   Principal components factor analyses of CRC survey data for approximately 650

teachers were used to define the scales; alpha coefficients indicate the internal consistency of scale items.

Some of the CRC teacher-questionnaire items replicate items from the 'High School and Beyond programme's 1984 Administrator and Teacher Survey (ATS)' or from the NELS:88 First Follow-up Teacher Survey. In these cases, the questionnaire item number from the relevant national teacher survey is reported (in parentheses) along with the item number from the CRC 1991 Teacher Survey.

11 An earlier version of this chapter was presented at the American Educational Research Association meetings, San Francisco, April, 1992. The research was supported by funding from the US Department of Education, Office of Educational Research and Improvement to the Center for Research on the Context of Secondary School Teaching (CRC) at Stanford University (Grant G0087C0235) and from the National Science Foundation (Grant RED-9253068). We thank Marian Eaton, Shur-er Tsai, and Rebecca Perry for help in analysing the survey data and Renee Hoch and Julie Cummer for preparing the tables for this chapter. We are grateful to two anonymous reviewers for helpful comments on an earlier version of the chapter.
(Forthcoming in *American Journal of Education.*)

References

ABBOTT, A. (1988) *The System of Professions: An Essay on the Division of Expert Labor*, Chicago, University of Chicago Press.

ANYON, J. (1981) 'Social class and school knowledge', *Curriculum Inquiry*, **11**, pp. 3–42.

BENDIX, R. (1974) *Work and Authority in Industry*, Berkeley, University of California Press.

BIDWELL, C.E. (1965) 'The school as a formal organization', in *The Handbook of Organizations*, MARCH, J.E. (Ed), Chicago, Rand McNally.

BRYK, A. and DRISCOLL, M.E. (1988) *An Empirical Investigation of the School as a Community*, Chicago, University of Chicago School of Education.

CHUBB, J.E. and MOE, T.M. (1990) *Politics, Markets, and America's Schools*, Washington, DC, The Brookings Institution.

COHEN, D.K. (1988) 'Teaching practice, plus ça change...', in *Contributing to Educational Change*, JACKSON, P.W. (Ed), Berkeley, McCutchan Publishing Corporation, pp. 27–84.

COLLINS, R. (1979) *The Credential Society*, New York, Academic Press.

CUBAN, L. (1984) *How Teachers Taught: Constancy and Change in American Classrooms 1890–1980*, New York, Longman.

DARLING-HAMMOND, L. (1990) Teacher Professionalism: Why and How? *Schools as Collaborative Cultures: Creating the Future Now*, Ann Lieberman (Ed), London, New York and Philadelphia, Falmer Press.

DAVIDSON, A.L. (1992) *Border Curricula and the Construction of Identity: Implications for Multicultural Theorists*, Stanford University, Center for Research on the Context of Secondary School Teaching, pp. 92–145.

ETZIONI, A. (1969) *The Semi-professions and their Organization*, New York, Free Press.

FREIDSON, E. (1970) *Profession of Medicine*, New York, Dodd, Mead.

FREIDSON, E. (1986) *Professional Powers: A Study of the Institutionalization of Formal Knowledge*, Chicago, University of Chicago Press.

GOULDNER, A.W. (1954) *Patterns of Industrial Democracy*, Glencoe, IL, The Free Press.

HALL, R.H. (1968) 'Professionalization and bureaucratization', in *American Sociological Review*, **33**, pp. 92–104.

HOMANS, G.C. (1950) *The Human Group*, New York, Harcourt Brace.

JOHNSON, S.M. (1990) *Teachers at Work: Achieving Success in Our Schools*, New York, Basic Books, Inc.

LARSON, M.S. (1977) *The Rise of Professionalism*, Berkeley, The University of California Press.

LeCOMPTE, M.D. and DWORKIN, A.G. (1992) *Giving Up on School: Student Dropouts and Teacher Burnouts*, Newbury Park, CA, Corwin Press.

LICHTENSTEIN, G., McLAUGHLIN, M.W. and KNUDSEN, J.L. (1992) 'Teacher empowerment and professional knowledge', in *The Changing Contexts of Teaching. National Society for the Study of Education 91st Yearbook, Part I*, LIEBERMAN, A. (Ed), Chicago, University of Chicago Press, pp. 37–58.

LIEBERMAN, A. and McLAUGHLIN, M.W. (1992) 'Networks for educational change: Powerful and problematic', *Phi Delta Kappan*, **73**, 9, pp. 673–7.

LITTLE, J.W. (1982) 'Norms of collegiality and experimentation: Workplace conditions of school success', *American Educational Research Journal*, **19**, pp. 325–40.

LITTLE, J.W. (1990) 'Conditions of professional development in secondary schools', in *The Contexts of Teaching in Secondary Schools: Teachers' Realities*, McLAUGHLIN, M.W., TALBERT, J.E. and BASCIA, N. (Eds), New York, Teachers College Press, Columbia University, pp. 187–223.

LITTLE, J.W. and McLAUGHLIN, M.W. (1991) *Urban Math Collaboratives: As Teachers Tell It* (Draft report), Stanford University, Stanford CA, Center for Research on the Context of Secondary School Teaching.

LITTLE, J.W. and McLAUGHLIN, M.W. (1993) (Eds) *Teachers' Work: Individuals, Colleagues, and Contexts*, New York, Teachers College Press.

LORTIE, D.C. (1975) *Schoolteacher: A Sociological Study*, Chicago, University of Chicago Press.

LOUIS, K.S. (1990) 'Social and community values and the quality of teachers' work life', in *The Contexts of Teaching in Secondary Schools: Teachers' Realities*, McLAUGHLIN, M.W., TALBERT, J.E. and BASCIA, N. (Eds), New York, Teachers College Press, Columbia University, pp. 17–39.

LOUIS, K.S. and MILES, M.B. (1990) *Improving the Urban High School*, New York, Teachers College Press, Columbia University.

McLAUGHLIN, M.W. (1992) 'How district communities do and do not foster teacher pride', *Educational Leadership*, **50**, 1, pp. 33–5.

McLAUGHLIN, M.W. (1993) 'What matters most in teachers' workplace context?', in *Teachers' Work: Individuals, Colleagues and Contexts*, LITTLE, J.W. and McLAUGHLIN, M.W. (Eds), New York, Teachers College Press, pp. 79–103.

McLAUGHLIN, M.W. (forthcoming) 'Strategic sites for teachers' professional development', in *The Struggle for Authenticity: Teacher Development in a Changing Educational Context*, GRIMMETT, P. and NEUFELD, J.P. (Eds), New York, Teachers College Press.

McLAUGHLIN, M.W. and TALBERT, J.E. (1993a) *Contexts that Matter for Teaching and Learning*, Stanford, CA, Center for Research on the Context of Secondary School Teaching.

McLAUGHLIN, M.W. and TALBERT, J.E. (1993b) 'How the world of students and teachers challenges policy coherence', in *Designing Coherent Educational Policy: Improving the System*, FUHRMAN, S.H. (Ed), San Francisco, Jossey-Bass, pp. 220–49.

McNEIL, L. (1986) *Contradictions of Control: School Structure and School Knowledge*, New York, Routledge and Kegan Paul.

METZ, M.H. (1990) 'How social class differences shape teachers' work', in *The Contexts of Teaching in Secondary Schools: Teachers' Realities*, McLAUGHLIN, M.W., TALBERT, J.E. and BASCIA, N. (Eds), New York, Teachers College Press, Columbia University, pp. 40–107.

MEYER, J.W. and ROWAN, B. (1977) 'Institutionalized organizations: Formal structure as myth and ceremony', *American Journal of Sociology*, **83**, pp. 340–63, September.

MONTAGNA, P. (1968) 'Professionalization and bureaucratization in large professional organizations', *American Journal of Sociology*, **74**, pp. 138–45.

MORTIMORE, P., SAMMONS, P., STOLL, L., LEWIS, D. and ECOB, R. (1988) *School Matters*, Berkeley, University of California Press.

NEWMANN, F.M., RUTTER, R.A. and SMITH, M.S. (1989) 'Organizational factors affecting school sense of efficacy, community, and expectations', *Sociology of Education*, **64**, pp. 221–38.

NODDINGS, N. (1984) *Awakening the Inner Eye: Intuition in Education*, New York, Teachers College, Columbia University.

NODDINGS, N. (1992) *The Challenge to Care in Schools*, New York, Teachers College Press.

OAKES, J. (1985) *Keeping Track: How Schools Structure Inequality*, New Haven, Yale University Press.

PARSONS, T. (1954) *The Professions and Social Structure: Essays in Sociological Theory*, New York, Free Press, pp. 34–49.

PHELAN, P., CAO, H.T. and DAVIDSON, A.L. (1992) *Navigating the Psycho/Social Pressures of Adolescence: The Voices and Experiences of High School Youth*, Stanford University, Center for Research on the Context of Secondary School Teaching, pp. 92–144.

PRAWAT, R.S. (1992) 'Teachers' beliefs about teaching and learning: A constructivist perspective', *American Journal of Education*, **100**, 3, pp. 354–95, May.

RAUDENBUSH, S.W., ROWAN, B. and CHEONG, Y.F. (1992) 'Contextual effects on the self-perceived efficacy of high school teachers', *Sociology of Education*, **65**, 2, pp. 150–67.

ROSENHOLTZ, S.J. (1989) *Teachers' Workplace: The Social Organization of Schools*, New York, Longman.

SARASON, S.B. (1990) *The Predictable Failure of Educational Reform*, San Francisco, Jossey-Bass.

SCOTT, W.R. (1965) 'Reactions to supervision in heteronomous professional organization', *Administrative Science Quarterly*, **10**, pp. 65–81.

SCOTT, W.R. (1988) *Work Units in Organizations: Ransacking the Literature*, Stanford University, CA, Center for Research on the Context of Secondary School Teaching, pp. 88–104.

SHULMAN, L.S. (1986) 'Those who understand: Knowledge growth in teaching', *Educational Researcher*, **15**, pp. 4–14.

SHULMAN, L.S. (1987) 'Knowledge and teaching: Foundations of the new reform', *Harvard Educational Review*, **57**, 1, pp. 1–22.

SISKIN, L.S. (1991) 'Departments as different worlds: Subject subcultures in secondary schools', *Educational Administration Quarterly*, **27**, 2, pp. 134–60.

STODOLSKY, S. (1988) *The Subject Matters: Classroom Activity in Math and Social Studies*, Chicago, University of Chicago Press.

STODOLSKY, S.S. and GROSSMAN, P.L. (1992) 'Subject matter as context', *American Educational Research Association meeting*, San Francisco.

TALBERT, J.E. (1990) *Teacher Tracking: Exacerbating Inequalities in the High School*, Stanford University, Center for Research on the Context of Secondary School Teaching, pp. 90–121.

TALBERT, J.E. (1991) *Boundaries of Teachers' Professional Communities in U.S. High Schools*, Stanford University, Center for Research on the Context of Secondary School Teaching, pp. 91–130.

TALBERT, J.E. (1993) 'Constructing a school-wide professional community: The negotiated order of a performing arts school', in *Teachers' Work*, LITTLE, J.W. and MCLAUGHLIN, M.W. (Eds), New York, Teachers College Press, pp. 164–84.

VOLLMER, H.W. and MILLS, D.J. (1966) (Eds) *Professionalization*, Englewood Cliffs, NJ, Prentice-Hall.

WARD, J.G. and ANTHONY, P. (1992) (Eds) *Who Pays for Student Diversity?: Population Changes and Educational Policy*, Newbury Park, CA, Corwin Press.

WEBER, M. (1947) *The Theory of Social and Economic Organization*, Glencoe, IL, Free Press.

WEICK, K.E. (1976) 'Educational organizations as loosely coupled systems', *Administrative Science Quarterly*, **21**, pp. 1–18.

WHYTE, W.F. (1959) *Man and Organization*, Homework, IL, Richard D. Irwin.

WILENSKY, H.L. (1964) 'The professionalization of everyone', *American Journal of Sociology*, **70**, pp. 137–58.

WILENSKY, H.L. and LEBEAUX, C.W. (1958) 'The professionalization of everyone', *American Journal of Sociology*, **70,** pp. 137–58.

WISE, A. (1979) *Legislated Learning: The Bureaucratization of the American Classroom*, Berkeley, University of California Press.

Chapter 8

Student Teachers' Lay Theories: Implications for Professional Development

Ciaran Sugrue

Introduction

This chapter provides a detailed analysis of student teachers' lay theories of teaching. The deconstruction of fifteen student teachers' 'voices' establishes the degree of continuity and change between their lay theories, their apprenticeship of observation, (which future students serve while they are themselves students), and culturally embedded archetypes of teaching. Understanding the critically formative influences in student teachers' lives and the extent to which these are reinforced, reproduced and recast in, and through, student teachers' lay theories has major significance for initial teacher education and ongoing professional development of teachers. The cultural context of this analysis is Ireland. The analysis begins by identifying the male and female cultural archetypes in the setting and these become an essential touchstone for the deconstruction of student teachers' lay theories. The chapter concludes with some comments on initial teacher education and teachers' professional development which are grounded in the voices of student teachers.

The analysis takes for granted the importance of personal narrative, metaphor and experienced knowledge as having significance for student teachers' lay theories (Elbaz, 1983; Clandinin, 1986; Connelly and Clandinin, 1988; Hunt, 1987; Johnson, 1992; Holt-Reynolds, 1992; Calderhead, 1987; Pollard and Tann, 1987; Calderhead and Gates, 1993; Russell and Munby, 1992; Clift, Houston and Pugach, 1990; Day, Pope and Denicolo, 1990). It also seeks to situate these theories within the more broadly based historically and socially situated literature on life history and biography because of its significance for shaping the beliefs and professional behaviours of teachers (Woods, 1985; Sikes, Measor and Woods, 1985; Ball and Goodson, 1985; Goodson and Walker, 1991; Goodson, 1992). A contextualized analysis of this nature is warranted because 'the traditions through which particular practices are transmitted and reshaped never exist in isolation from larger social traditions' (Goodson, 1992, p. 242). Due to the absence of life history and teacher biographical inquiry in the setting, I have turned to Irish literary sources to identify the archetypal contours of the 'Master' and the 'Mistress': both of whom have assumed the status of 'cultural *myths* in teaching [in the Irish context] which provide a set of "ideal" images, definitions, justifications and measures for thought and activity in schools' (Day, 1993, p. 12). My analysis assumes that these archetypes have significance for popular perceptions of primary-school teachers. Consequently, in addition to their apprenticeships of observation, these archetypes are a subterranean influence also on student teachers' orientation towards teaching as a career and their personal constructions of themselves as intending teachers. The personal and the wider socio-historical context of their schooling and socialization shape their reconstructions of these archetypes of teaching.

Holt-Reynolds (1992) describes lay theories as:

> . . . beliefs developed naturally over time without the influence of instruc-
> tion. Pre-service teachers do not consciously learn them at an announced,
> recognised moment from a formal teaching/learning episode. Rather, lay
> theories represent tacit knowledge lying dormant and unexamined by the
> student (see Barclay and Wellman, 1986). Developed over long years of
> participation in and observation of classrooms (Lortie, 1975) and teaching/
> learning incidents occurring in schools, homes or the larger community
> (Measor, 1985; Sikes, 1987), lay theories are based on untutored inter-
> pretations of personal, lived experiences. (Holt-Reynolds, 1992, p. 326)

The personal experiences of these student teachers form a nexus between their apprenticeship of observation and the embedded cultural archetypes of teaching. By deconstructing student teachers' lay theories, therefore, insights are gained into the most formative personal and social influences on their professional identities. These insights are critical to the process and substance of initial teacher education and subsequent professional growth.

Method

The data for this analysis are derived from fifteen interviews with nine regular (late adolescent) and six mature (aged 28–42) entrants to a Bachelor of Education pro-gramme.[1] These audio-taped, in-depth interviews were completed during the first five months of the programme and prior to the interviewees' first school experi-ence. The interviews were semi-structured and open-ended. Their length varied from forty to ninety minutes. The discrepancy in length is accounted for by the mature student teachers having much more biographical material to provide. The interviews with the nine regular student teachers were completed during February and March of 1992 while those with the mature student teachers were completed a year later (1993). By focusing on two distinct groups of students it is possible to lend further breadth to the analysis by indicating how personal experience resonates with the cultural archetypes, and how particular features continue to be reproduced with subtle variation. Repeated analysis of interview transcripts yielded three cul-tural themes which crystallized around the following issues. The first of these — personal identity and teaching archetypes — explores the motivation of individuals to become primary-school teachers and how their personal identities are shaped by a combination of apprenticeship of observation and the comments of significant others who suggest they are personally suited to teaching.

The second theme deals with the student teachers' archetypal metaphors for teaching which are derived from their apprenticeships of observation and more broadly based cultural influences.

The third theme focuses on what regular and mature student teachers identify (from their apprenticeships of observation) as the hallmarks of 'good teaching'. These perceptions are analysed for continuity and change in relation to cultural archetypes. As these cultural archetypes provide the 'key' whereby the student teachers' lay theories are deconstructed, it is first necessary to identify these archetypes in the Irish context. Description of the 'master' and the 'mistress' is confined to two brief cameos.[2]

'The Master': A Cultural Archetype of Teaching

The terms master and mistress share identical origins in the Latin word *dominus*: to be head of a household and servants, including slaves. Archetypal teachers are, therefore, likely to dominate classrooms and students and, their teaching styles, to dictate the learning process through a transmission mode of teaching.

The octogenarian writer, Bryan MacMahon (1992) in his appropriately titled biographical text *The Master* describes the social conditions during the first half of this century which shaped Irish primary teachers' perceptions of themselves and circumscribed their role when he says:

> It was enjoined upon us by the State to undertake the revival of Irish as a spoken language[3], . . . and it was also enjoined upon us by the Catholic Church,[4] which, to put it at its mildest, was powerful at the time, to transfer from one generation to the next the corpus of Catholic belief . . .
> (MacMahon, 1992, p. 89)

Church and State combined to determine a centrally prescribed curriculum for delivery by teachers. John Banville's *Mefisto* (1986) provides a moving if disturbing, account of the dominant pedagogy of the period. The description of his first day in school is testimony to the domination of students by teachers by means of corporal punishment so that the former would know their place while the classroom atmosphere and curriculum content were frequently alienating and disengaged from students' cultural experience.[5] He says:

> I think of . . . a sense of enclosure, of faces averted from the world in holy fright. On my first day there I sat with the other boys in solemn silence while a red-haired master reached into an immensely deep pocket and brought out lovingly a leather strap. Say hello, he said, to teacher's pet.
> (Banville, 1986, pp. 20–1)

When 'teacher's pet' was rained indiscriminately on an unfortunate student 'the rest of the class averted its gaze from the victim slumped at his desk, hiccuping softly and knuckling his eyes' (p. 21). Students bore silent witness: a matrix of protest against, and collusion with, this archetypal mode of teaching. While teachers demanded subservience from learners, they too were 'stiffly polite to the manager [local clergyman] and overanxious with inspectors' (Friel, 1983, p. 92). There is little doubt that such an approach is essentially 'teaching as telling' (Bullough, 1992, p. 242) or 'teaching as transmission of knowledge' (Samuelowicz and Bain, 1992, p. 242). This archetypal teaching was teacher-driven and its corollaries were obedience and passivity. These archetypal axioms were embodied in the 'master' to produce a didactic pedagogic cocktail which paid scant attention to the personal, social and/or cognitive development of learners.[6]

'The Mistress': A Female Archetype of Teaching

In a recent publication *Excursions in the Real World* William Trevor (1993) gives a vivid account of his teacher who, despite her youth, wore the mantle of the village school mistress. He says of Miss Willoughby:[7]

> [she] was stern and young, . . . she was Methodist and there burnt in her breast an evangelical spirit which stated that we, her pupils, except for her chosen few, must somehow be made less wicked than we were. Her chosen few were angels of a kind, their handwriting blessed, their compositions a gift from God, I was not among them.
>
> . . . I vividly recall Miss Willoughby. Terribly she appears. Severe and beautiful. . . . 'Someone laughed during prayers,' her stern voice accuses, and you feel at once that it was you, although you know it wasn't. V. *poor* she writes in your headline book when you've done your best to reproduce, four times, perfectly, *Pride goeth before destruction*. (Trevor, 1993, p. 7)

Being strict, presenting a stern face, being distant from learners, insisting on strict adherence to rules, sticking to the letter in relation to prescribed curriculum content and demanding accuracy without taking the learners' perspective into account are very dominant features of the female archetype of teaching. Many contemporaries of mine, both male and female, can attest to frequent use of corporal punishment also as a means of 'teaching' respect, subservience and, very often also, a hatred of school, books and learning through an overly didactic transmission mode of teaching.

Social Change and Educational Reform in Ireland

It is generally accepted that Irish society has changed rapidly and radically during the past twenty-five years. These changes have been reflected in Government policy through it's espousal of child-centred education since 1971: a policy which was advocated and enthusiastically endorsed by primary teachers (Sugrue, 1990). Many might be inclined to the view, therefore, that in recovering these teaching archetypes, I am simply raking over old coals that have long since ceased to glow in classrooms. However, I endorse the view expressed by Kearney (1985, p. 37) that: 'to ignore our past is, ironically, to remain in corrosive collusion with it.' I am not suggesting that these archetypes are the reality in schools today. Rather, their dominant characteristics provide important cultural benchmarks against which the continuity, complexity and variation of student teachers' lay theories can be analysed.

Identity, Lay Theories and Cultural Archetypes

Identification with teaching as a profession is an important first step for intending student teachers. Such identification is particularly important in the Irish context where primary teachers continue to enjoy social status and respect within the community, particularly in rural areas. Despite significant diversification of career opportunities in recent years, the primary teaching profession continues to attract some of 'the brightest and the best'.[8]

The construction of self-as-teacher is the foundation stone of student teachers' lay theories which are built upon their apprenticeship of observation of their own teachers, and reinforced by family and close friends who draw on their own culturally embedded images of teachers and teaching. The first of three cultural themes to emerge from analysis of the fifteen interview transcripts: the construction of self-as-teacher, is the initial lens through which the complex dialectic between student teachers, their apprenticeship of observation, and culturally embedded archetypes of teachers and teaching are deconstructed. In the interest of clarity and comparison, the data from each of the two groups of interviewees are presented separately. As already indicated, nine of the fifteen interviewees were regular (late adolescent) entrants to teacher education while the remainder (six) ranged in age from 28 to 42.

Regular Student Teachers

Six of the regular student teachers remarked: 'I always wanted to be a teacher' while they had difficulty articulating why. Morag's comments were typical: 'I can't really say why, it's just always been there in my head, it's what I wanted to do' (Tr. 4). While Celia stated that she 'didn't really want to be a teacher' in the sense that she 'never thought of it', nevertheless, she had no doubt that she would 'do something with kids' (Tr. 5). The apparent contradiction in Celia's not wanting to be a teacher while regarding work with kids as inevitable, suggests an unconscious resistance to the teaching archetype.[9] When at the age of 15 or 16 Mona had to make subject choices for her Leaving Certificate Examination, she began to think: '...maybe I'd like to be a teacher, and then it sort of stuck with me' (Tr. 1).

Margo, though not committed to teaching herself, found that her sister (who was about to complete a BEd.) 'was actually a major influence because she always wanted to be a teacher and she loved it.' Additional reinforcement came from her mother who 'was always interested in me being a teacher as well' because she thought it was a respectable position (Tr. 3). Margo's farming background reinforces the perspective that identification with teaching is shaped by respect for, and the acknowledged status of, teachers within the community. This interpretation also lends further legitimacy to the socially constructed nature of identity where the influence of immediate family was crucial to Margo's decision to enter teacher education. However, the critical issue seems to be that suitability for teaching is assumed to be 'born' so that these students see themselves, and are regarded by others, as 'natural teachers' (Britzman, 1986, p. 451).

Nikki had similar formative experiences that shaped her identification with teaching. She commented: '. . . as I was growing up everyone used to always say, Nikki you'd be a good teacher and all this kind of thing' (Tr. 7). This perception of herself as a natural teacher was reinforced by adults who offered advice when she was choosing between a degree in science and a Bachelor of Education. Significant others suggested: 'you'd be wasted in a laboratory . . . I always thought you should have been a teacher, you've this way with people.' Nikki herself thought that because she 'was kind of interested in music' it would be lost if she pursued a science degree and, anyway, her own preference was 'to be dealing with people' (Tr. 7). Similarly, Kirsti, who has 'always' wanted to be a teacher (though she briefly entertained the notion of pursuing a commerce degree) was influenced by those who said: 'you're more suited to teaching than being stuck in an office . . .' and she too was 'into music a lot' (Tr. 6). It is clear from these comments that aspects of the cultural archetypes of teaching inform the advice proffered to intending student teachers. For instance, those with science or commerce degrees work in laboratories or offices while those who are academically bright with additional talents such as music, and who are people oriented, are best suited to teaching. Traditional requirements for female entrants to the primary teaching profession in Ireland reinforce this perspective.

Until very recently, it was necessary for female entrants to 'have singing' while this was optional for males. Traditionally the 'mistress' took responsibility for playing the organ in church and for marshalling the voices in the parish choir. While this is no longer axiomatic, it is a commonplace in Irish primary schools that musically talented teachers are assigned to classes of pupils who will receive the sacraments of Penance, Communion and Confirmation during the school year.[10] This archetypal factor: being musically talented, may be an invisible influence in shaping the perceptions of females and their families when constructing identities around teaching as a career.

A more subtle and less obvious influence on the identification of self with teaching is provided by atypical teaching episodes. These encounters take the form of helping younger siblings with homework, teaching music, giving tuition to less able peers in school, looking after the reception class during recess and babysitting.[11] What each of these isolated and sporadic quasi-teaching episodes have in common is that they lack the complexity of classroom teaching which places heavy demands on pedagogical and organizational skills as well as on expert knowledge of subject-matter content. In many instances also they are one-on-one encounters where help has been solicited which suggests that there is a willingness to learn on the part of the solicitor. Such episodes have the capacity to confer power on the providers through the cultural connections which are frequently made between knowledge and control. Being the helpful type is frequently reinforced by greater demands to provide assistance.

The six regular interviewees who felt they had always wanted to be teachers, also made reference to their experiences of helping with homework and babysitting as enabling them to construct themselves as teachers, in many instances, long before entry to teacher education. Mary's comments are typical:

> Well I always thought that I would like to be a teacher and being the eldest in the family I have helped my brothers and sisters to do their homework most of the time. And I've done house-keeping jobs for my relations and I have also helped my cousins to do their homework and I've taught the piano during the Summer holidays. I really get on well with children so I thought teaching would be a good option. (Tr. 2)

Perhaps part of the vicarious reinforcement which these intending teachers receive from the quasi-teaching roles they play periodically is that they can be trusted to be in charge: they have a capacity to control. Helping with homework or problem-solving reinforces individuals' perceptions of themselves as having expert knowledge. While knowledge and control in these circumstances are far removed from the complexities of classroom life, nevertheless, they may be sufficient to strengthen a student's construction of self around teaching. This socially constructed nature of identity in relation to teaching suggests that there is a particular kind of personality which is ideally suited to teaching. Consequently, having a 'teaching personality' is privileged over cognitive skills or pedagogical and subject-matter knowledge.

Mature Student Teachers

The formative influences on mature student teachers lay theories, and in particular their atypical teaching encounters which help to mould identification of self with teaching, are remarkably consistent with those of their younger colleagues. Susan declared: 'teaching . . . was what I wanted to do originally' (Tr. 11) and Gert echoed this refrain when she said: 'I used to always want to be a teacher in national [primary, elementary] school' (Tr. 13). The influence of an immediate relative played a decisive role in David's decision to apply for primary teaching. Significant others who influenced his identification with teaching appear to suggest that he has the necessary teaching personality, thus perpetuating the cultural axiom that teachers are born, not made. David's brother, himself a successful teacher, according to David, 'mentioned' teaching to him as being particularly suited to his needs because of 'the lifestyle' he wanted and, he added: 'you get on well with kids, you've got a pretty even manner for teaching . . .' (Tr. 12). Former teachers reinforced this perspective when they said: 'this will suit you down to the ground. This is you, you should definitely follow this.' Subsequently, as David tried this new identity for size, he went on: 'everybody that I spoke to was saying, that you will make a good teacher, you have the qualities that it would take to be a good teacher' (Tr. 12). While there is undoubtedly an element of telling David what he wants to hear in these conversations, the central archetypal message being conveyed is that he has what it takes: namely the essential 'teaching personality'. Consequently, David is reinforced in the belief that: 'I probably have . . . the qualities' necessary to be a good teacher, though he is less certain about his 'commitment' (Tr. 12). His ambivalence in relation to committing conclusively to identification with teaching suggests that part of his difficulty is related to the essential, yet highly ambiguous, cultural pronouncement that he possesses the appropriate 'teaching personality' though the archetype does not elaborate on 'the qualities' inherent in the born teacher. He is left to conclude that being in possession of a teaching personality is more important than a range of skills or qualities. The very essentialist pronouncement within the culturally embedded archetype which decrees that there is an ideal teaching personality at once suggests that some are born teachers: they are 'called' to teaching, while the cultural axiom itself is reproduced and remains unchallenged.[12]

Maud feels that as a mature student she has come to primary teacher education 'fully committed' though when she left school she 'definitely thought that, yes, I'd love to do teaching'. However, she wanted 'to do more with her life' before committing herself to the classroom. In many respects, therefore, she too like Susan and Gert was realizing a long-time ambition. A number of disparate atypical teaching encounters reinforced her initial identification with teaching. As university students, she and her husband were keen windsurfers with at least one significant difference.

> I did a lot of windsurfing and I found that . . . people were really getting what I was talking about, so easily. My husband was a great windsurfer, but he couldn't teach for nuts. He just could not get it through. He was too technical, he couldn't break it down. Whereas, I wasn't as good at all but I could teach. (Tr. 14)

Similarly, when dealing with individual clients in an office environment, she was reinforced in her belief that she would 'be a good teacher' and that she would 'like an actual one-to-one relationship with children and help them to learn' (Tr. 14). Satisfying individual customer needs and tutoring fellow students on the finer points of windsurfing are the atypical non-classroom quasi-teaching scenarios which reinforce Maud's basic identification with teaching thus legitimizing the culturally embedded axiom that teachers are indeed born.

Vernon's experience of being a trouble-shooter in the financial services sector brought him to the realization that he was people-oriented as much of his work involved solving programming problems for individual colleagues. Like many of the other interviewees, he found reinforcement among his peers for his orientation towards teaching.

> ... this progression that we're talking about ... it did come about in fact because having left computers to go into social work and then into teaching, and it's funny, when I talk to all the mates that I had in computers, even to-day, they say it's a wonder I didn't do it a long time before ... because apparently, unawares to myself I suppose at some stage I was in fact a teacher then. (Tr. 15)

Similarly, after a chequered military career with several overseas postings, Kevin found that he had played a variety of teaching roles without being conscious of it. However, much of this teaching experience was outside the normal structures and routines of classroom teaching. For example, when the peace and tranquillity of his own suburban garden was overrun by pre-school children, like many of his regular and mature student colleagues, he found this atypical teaching encounter strengthened his identification with teaching.

> ... I'd just come back from the Lebanon. ... I was digging the garden and I was sowing some spring bulbs and these two kids came to the gate, and they said 'What are you doing?' They were about 4 or 5. And I said 'I'm digging the garden, I'm going to sow some bulbs.' All of a sudden I found myself in the situation where I was explaining to them about bulbs and daffodils, irises and crocuses and that sort of stuff. And all of a sudden they were in, and they were down and they were placing the bulbs in the ground, and I was standing looking at them. And, then there were more kids, and then there were more kids, and the whole garden was infested with these small children who were very busily scraping holes with their hands and laying out the bulbs and pouring the bulb fibre over them and covering it in with their hands. And, I was saying to myself, Jesus, I really like this, you know, I really like this. This is enjoyable. To see the tension on their faces as they were doing it. This focus on their faces and that, I discover, is teaching. (Tr. 1)

These non-classroom, and therefore atypical, teaching encounters of mature student teachers have striking parallels with the babysitting and homework assistance provided by their younger colleagues. These experiences are critical to how intending student teachers construct personal identities around teaching. These identities include important dimensions of cultural archetypes of teachers and teaching in the setting and in particular the central axiom that teachers are born: a definitive teaching personality is the single most important prerequisite for being a teacher.[13]

Johnston, (1992, p. 125) relying on arguments advanced by Britzman (1989) and Eisner (1988), makes the point that it is necessary to hear the voices of pre-service teachers 'in an effort to understand the process of teaching and learning from their perspectives'. Such an approach avoids the twin errors of 'superimposing potentially inappropriate theoretical frameworks derived either from the knowledge of researchers or from experienced teachers'. Because there is so much investment on the part of the interviewees in personal identification with teaching, an identification which is reinforced by family and community, they are already predisposed towards resisting theoretical frameworks which are commonplace in initial teacher education. Their apprenticeships of observation, general socialization and atypical teaching episodes which support and encourage their identification with teaching, implicitly suggest that they are 'born' teachers. Consequently, they are predisposed to the view that they have little to learn from teacher education. This deeply held cultural belief suggests that student teachers are predisposed also to perpetuating a 'culture of individualism' which many researchers have identified as pervasive in schools and classrooms (Hargreaves, 1994, 1992). If student teachers are 'to the manner born' there is little need for collaboration or interactive professionalism as everything revolves around the personality of the teacher, thus reinforcing isolation, rugged individualism and the pervasive 'cellular' classroom (Lortie, 1975). Their very personal identification with teaching helps to perpetuate 'the misconception . . . that any smart person can teach' (Fullan, 1993, p. 111) and this has implications throughout the teaching career.

Metaphors, Lay Theories and Cultural Archetypes

The cultural archetypes outlined above, and recent research on teaching suggest that the realities of 'teaching as transmission' are pervasive (Samuelowicz and Bain, 1992; Biggs, 1990; Dall'Alba, 1990; Martin and Balla, 1990). These researchers indicate that there are a number of conceptions of teaching which are arrayed on a continuum from 'information presentation to facilitation of student learning' (Samuelowicz and Bain, 1992, p. 94). Dunkin (1990) also identifies four dimensions which can be used to describe teaching. These range from structuring learning, motivating learning, encouraging activity and independence in learning to establishing interpersonal relations conducive to learning. Additionally, he suggests that individuals' theories may be uni- or multi-dimensional, thus embracing combinations of all four elements (Samuelowicz and Bain, 1992).

During the interview process, the student teachers were invited to provide their own personal metaphors for teaching and/or to complete the sentence 'for me, teaching is. . . .' Their responses emerged as important elements within their lay theories of teaching. My analysis assumes that the more uni-dimensional their chosen metaphors, the more likely they are to resonate with archetypal notions of teaching as telling or teaching as transmission. This interpretation is supported by the suggestion made by Lakoff and Johnson (1980, p. 156) that metaphors lend 'coherence' to our experience by serving as 'a guide to future action'. These student teachers' metaphors, therefore, serve to indicate their basic pedagogical orientation. Such metaphors are a complex matrix of the students' personal identification with teaching, their socialization and, in particular, their apprenticeships of observation.

Regular Student Teachers

Five of the nine late adolescent entrants to primary teacher education described a metaphor of teaching which is close to being uni-dimensional as well as being focused on transmission of information, thus resonating in basic outline with the cultural archetype.

For Freda teaching is centrally concerned with 'communicating your knowledge to them' and 'to a certain extent you could fashion their personalities as well' (Tr. 9). Though Monica protests that 'there's no ideal teacher' and 'everybody's a different teacher', thus highlighting the centrality of personality and the idiosyncratic nature of teaching style, she is very much in agreement with Freda when she declares that teaching is 'a way of passing on traditions'. She elaborates on this when she says that it is 'giving them . . . an opportunity to have . . . the right . . . grades for what they want to do in later life'. It is important to give them a 'good basis' as well as 'an interest in work'. This portrays a transmission mode of teaching which also reflects the dominance of the examination system over students' lives and the constraint it imposes on teachers. Kirsti expresses some difficulty with articulating an appropriate metaphor though she says that teaching is a matter of 'give and take'. Central to this, however, is that 'you have to put stuff in to get results'. She continues, teaching is 'like an injection'. When doctors provide medical aid the intention is to 'help you . . . improve'. She qualifies the analogy by saying that it is not her intention 'to drill everything into them' but 'if you put something in you get results, you get something from it' (Tr. 6). Likewise, Margo understands teaching to be centrally concerned with 'getting across information to children' while this is intended to 'broaden their knowledge' (Tr. 3).

Mona has particular difficulty in articulating a metaphor for her model of teaching which reinforces the view that student teachers may require support and encouragement in this process (Bullough, 1992; Johnston, 1992; Russell and Mumby, 1992). Nevertheless, when asked to identify her anxieties in relation to impending school experience, she articulates three central concerns that will inform her actions. Mona expresses these concerns as rhetorical questions:

a. Will you be after imparting something to them?
b. Will they actually . . . grasp what you're trying to teach? and
c. Will you [be able] to keep track [meaning can she retain control]?

Her perspective remains very close to 'teaching as telling'. Celia began from a negative position when she declared: 'I definitely don't want to be the aggressive type', because these teachers had 'no control over you or anything'. Some teachers whom she encountered through her apprenticeship of observation indulged in 'giving out too much' or 'shouting' as a means of exerting control (Tr. 5). Her comments suggest that control is important while teachers who resorted to overt aggressive behaviour such as verbal abuse and shouting, were not the most successful in maintaining discipline. In a tacit, unarticulated manner, by attempting to distance herself from overt control of pupils by what she regards as unacceptable aggressive behaviour, she is seeking to resist aspects of the cultural archetype while searching for her own voice. Teacher education should enable student teachers to surface these tensions and facilitate their resolution rather than to provide general prescriptions for classroom discipline and control that continue to deny them a voice.

Nikki had difficulty articulating a personal metaphor for teaching. She spoke of it in general terms as being distinct from 'working . . . in an office where . . . you go home and switch off. . . .' By comparison, teaching is 'practically . . . life really' because 'you have to prepare stuff for the following day and . . . something could have happened that day in school and it'll be bothering you.' She sees teaching as essentially dealing with 'people' rather than 'figures and invoices' (Tr. 7). Nikki gave implicit recognition to the need for relationship in the teaching process. Research evidence suggests, however, that when peoples' personal metaphors have not been systematically articulated, student teachers (or practitioners) are easy prey to the vicissitudes of school and classroom culture where they can experience a great deal of frustration and personal dissatisfaction without knowing why (Johnston, 1992; Calderhead, 1991; Bullough, 1992).

Two other interviewees build on Nikki's vague notion of teaching being a people oriented activity. Morag declares: '. . . my image of teaching is to help, just to help people to learn easier' and this belief is firmly rooted in her own experience. Because she 'always liked school' she 'couldn't understand people who didn't'. Consequently, she would approach teaching so that 'they [pupils] would like school' (Tr. 4). There is a degree of naivety about this aspiration which is particularly problematic in the Irish context. She liked school because, as a bright student, she did not encounter any difficulties. However, as a teacher with this experience of learning she, and many of her colleagues, may have little empathy with, or understanding of, less able learners or those with learning difficulties. Mary, alone among the nine interviewees, appears firmly committed to a relationship with the learners while wishing to remain in control. She 'would like to be somebody that the children felt they got on well with, and that she could explain things well and keep good control' (Tr. 2). It is generally accepted that student teachers and beginning teachers are preoccupied initially with fear of being unable to maintain 'proper order' in classrooms. However, unless these anxieties are dealt with constructively during their most formative years in initial teacher education and as beginning teachers, then dominant aspects of school culture such as control and transmission of information are likely to be privileged over developing more sophisticated teaching methodologies. Such strong personal identification with teaching on the part of the interviewees leaves them vulnerable to the received wisdom that it is tantamount to personal failure if students cannot be properly controlled. Consequently, they are encouraged to look within themselves as teachers for sustenance and succour when closer scrutiny of curricula, institutional structures and the cultivation of more collaborative working relationships might be more beneficial.

Mature Student Teachers

Three of the six mature student teachers indicated that they were quite definitely oriented towards 'teaching as telling', while the others recognized the importance of individual difference and of creating an enabling environment.

Kevin's comments are illustrative of his apprenticeship of observation. He says of his own schooling: 'we did Irish, English and maths' and 'that was it.' Consequently, the essence of teaching requires that 'a child should be taught to read and to express themselves properly and some numeracy skills' (Tr. 10). Similarly, Susan wishes to be 'someone who is able to give information to the children' (Tr. 11). Gert had spent some months as a temporary teacher in her former school prior to entering teacher education. She found the movement of pupils around the room 'difficult to cope with', as her preference was for 'a little bit more order'. She commented further: 'the discipline thing is harder now' and she 'found children much more questioning your authority, whereas when I went to school you just didn't do that.' Central to her internal conflict are issues of passivity and control. Though her own teachers used corporal punishment and one was vindictive, strong identification with the pedagogy is retained when she says: 'you didn't really like them [the teachers] at the time but, when you look back with hindsight, you know that they were good teachers' (Tr. 4).

David gave some thought to an appropriate metaphor before settling for 'the carpenter', drawing on his experience of working on North American building sites. His analogy was that this craftsman 'takes in different types of woods, different standards of woods and comes up with a final product.' Similarly, he suggests 'a horse trainer . . . takes in horses of different standards, puts different amounts of training into each horse on an individual basis and comes up with winners' (Tr. 12). David's awareness of individual difference is obvious though his metaphor suggests a significant shaping and moulding of learners rather than developing potential. By comparison, Maud's guiding metaphor includes a more explicit awareness of individual difference.

> For me, teaching would be like creating a situation where a child can really develop and come out of themselves fully and I would just help them to do that. Not just me giving them information but helping them to learn it themselves. (Tr. 14)

The most apt metaphor for teaching that springs to mind for Vernon further acknowledges the importance of individual difference. He thinks of himself as 'the gardener' who will nurture learners and help them to 'bloom'. Central to this is 'a relationship of trust' where there is mutual respect and 'you can start from there' (Tr. 15). It is significant that Maud and Vernon have had success in teaching adult learners on a one-to-one basis. However, in a classroom context they could encounter significant difficulty realising this principle. Both are conscious of this and Maud admits that her 'greatest fear' is 'being able to keep everyone going, and everyone challenged at the same time' (Tr. 14). While their recognition of individual difference is laudable, in the absence of a more multi-dimensional approach to teaching and a teacher-education programme that encourages its articulation, and fosters appropriate pedagogical skills for its actualization, a school culture which continues to emphasize class teaching and places a premium on mastery of content, may frustrate these teaching intentions (Morgan and Kellaghan, forthcoming).

In general, therefore, the metaphors of most regular and mature student teachers reflect prominent features of teaching archetypes in the setting, while a minority recognize the importance of individual difference. There is little evidence of multi-dimensionality in all interviewees' approaches to teaching. If these deeply held archetypal concepts, (which are primarily rooted in the students' experience through their apprenticeships of observation) are not articulated and confronted in initial teacher education, they are much more likely to be perpetuated in schools.

'Good' Teaching, Lay Theories and Cultural Archetypes

The third theme of this analysis becomes an important means of putting some flesh on the bones of these basic metaphors. From their own apprenticeships of observation the fifteen student teachers were asked to describe what they regarded as the salient features of 'good' teaching.

The characteristics which each of the interviewees identified were rooted in the personalities and behaviours of individual teachers whom they regarded as being particularly good. What they characterize as good teaching is influenced significantly, though not exclusively, by teachers with whom they came in contact. In virtually all cases, the characteristics of good teaching which they identified were attributed to the influence of teachers whom they encountered in junior classes. This may suggest that lay theories could be formed rather early during schooling. It may also be the case that teachers encountered in junior classes are almost always female. Consequently, at this level, students have more identification with teachers as being in *loco parentis*, or more accurately in *loco matris* than at any other period of schooling, leading to strong identification with their perceived personal traits.

Regular Students

From their apprenticeships of observation, seven of the nine regular student teachers used one of the following words to describe a good teacher whom they had encountered — 'discipline', 'control', and 'very strict'. As an extension of being in control, they suggested also that these 'good' teachers were 'really fair'. While this typically meant that the teacher did not have 'pets' it also included a more coercive element so that such teachers 'never let anybody away without doing their work' (Tr. 2) and ensured that everyone, without exception, completed assigned homework.[14] These teachers were focused on curriculum as content which was reflected in such comments as 'she taught us stuff' (Tr. 6), and 'we had to have our work done' (Tr. 3). In classrooms where a premium is placed on getting work done, those who come to school with cultural capital (which would include the vast majority of entrants to primary teacher education in Ireland) may manage particularly well and, thus, have little appreciation of the effects on less able learners of a content-driven teacher-dominated approach to teaching.

The interviewees also attached importance to getting work done. They valued being task-oriented and setting moderate or significant amounts of homework. Again, higher achieving pupils are more likely to thrive in such circumstances and thereby endear themselves to their teachers. Both teachers' and pupils' behaviours therefore tend to mirror each other in mutually reinforcing ways. Perhaps the price which more able pupils pay for such an apparently comfortable arrangement is a degree of conformity which does not encourage or tolerate challenging questions or taking significant initiatives which would allow for individual flair or particular interest. Becker, Geer and Hughes (1968, p. 65) suggest that good students: those who get the highest grades, are those who are most astute at identifying the nature of the 'classroom bargain' which primarily requires conformity to teachers' expectations. This interpretation is supported by recent international comparative research which indicates that Irish pupils are above average in basic skills but score significantly lower when it comes to problem solving and higher cognitive processes. These results are consistent across mathematics, language and science (Morgan and Kellaghan, forthcoming).[15] Many educators argue on the contestable premise that, if the approach to teaching implicit in these student teachers' comments was appropriate at any time, it is particularly unsuited to a post-industrial, post-modern society (Hargreaves, 1994; Purpel, 1989; Aronowitz and Giroux, 1991, 1985; Giroux and Simon, 1989; Grumet, 1988).

Beyond these issues of control, domination and the creation of a business-like atmosphere in the classroom, the personal traits of 'good' teachers assumed particular significance. Phrases such as 'very kind', 'very gentle' and 'very nice and kind' came readily to mind when describing good teachers. Margo recalls that the teacher she had in mind 'had a lovely way about her' (Tr. 3) and for Morag 'it's her personality more so than her teaching' that she remembers (Tr. 4). Within this framework, the routines of teaching and curriculum are predictable and consistent. These qualities of fairness, kindness and consistency could just as easily be employed to describe a good parent. Nevertheless, they harmonize with the interviewees' specific beliefs that having a teaching personality is an important prerequisite for the task of teaching. This perception of good teachers serves to down-play the importance of pedagogical skill and, thus also, diminishes student teachers' expectations of teacher education as offering a worthwhile and workable preparation for practice. It behoves teacher educators, therefore, to demonstrate in practical ways that they can build on the foundation of student teachers' lay theories. As Fullan (1993, p. 114) suggests: 'Faculties of education should not be advocating things for teachers or schools that they are not capable of practising themselves.' The present analysis suggests that student teachers, at least in the initial phase of their professional education, attach more importance to personality than to having an elaborate understanding of the teaching process and a sophisticated pedagogical repertoire. When concepts such as control and having deep-seated personal characteristics form part of the package of being a 'good' teacher, it is not surprising that when pupils cease to be as compliant and biddable as previous generations, guilt, frustration and burnout may become the lot of the individual teacher (Hargreaves, 1994; forthcoming). Failure to maintain standards in these circumstances suggests that the personal traits and control capabilities of the individual teacher may be wanting, while the policies and structures which constrain practitioners remain unexamined.

Celia, alone among the interviewees, suggests that good teachers are those who are unpredictable: 'the stuff they used to do was totally different . . . you wouldn't be sure what they're going to do next' (Tr. 5). The evidence of all the other regular interviewees suggests that deviation from well-established norms is relatively rare, even among those whom they regarded as good teachers. The characteristics of predictability and consistency identified above suggest that a prescribed curriculum is a necessary requisite for good teaching. As long as it is pursued with dedication, enthusiasm, fairness and friendliness, and in ways that make it interesting, it is automatically assumed to be relevant to the needs of learners. Yet because of their own biographies as successful students, the 'good teaching' that the interviewees describe may well perpetuate pedagogies and curricula in their own teaching which have benefited them in the past, while alternative styles of teaching and learning may be precluded or excluded as a result. Being a good pupil, therefore, may paradoxically hinder student teachers' abilities and willingness to expand their own lay theories of teaching. Because these student teachers regard themselves as having personality traits that equip them to be 'good teachers', this perception may create a disposition which suggests that they are already empowered to teach. Consequently, teacher education and the research-based theories which it seeks to communicate, may be seen as at best intellectually stimulating and interesting, but ultimately dispensable or irrelevant to good practice.

Some interviewees were aware that respecting and encouraging individual difference contributed to good teaching, where being valued by the teacher is made concrete through having difficulties explained on a one-to-one basis. While the rhetoric of authority, submission and subservience, characteristic of the cultural archetypes of teaching in Ireland, have been replaced by terms such as 'discipline', 'control', and 'firm but fair', collectively the impact of the interviewees' professed beliefs suggest that teaching is teacher directed. It is within this framework alone, that the needs of individual learners can be accommodated. However, altering the rhetoric is no guarantee that pro-active classroom-management strategies, so revered in much of school-effectiveness literature, are not merely the current means of inducing submissiveness and passivity as a substitute for the blunt instrument of corporal punishment (Mortimore *et al.*, 1988; Alexander, Willcocks and Kinder, 1989; Alexander, 1992). In a social and economic climate which privileges accountability, efficiency and managerialism, there is a real danger that teaching will become retrenched in ways that reflect outmoded cultural archetypes rather than educating for responsible citizenship (Purpel, 1989; Barth, 1991; Sarason, 1990; Shedd and Bacharach, 1990; Elmore *et al.*, 1990).

Deviation from the prescribed curriculum in ways that generate excitement and enthusiasm among students or facilating pursuit of their own interests are scarcely mentioned by the interviewees. Consequently, the norm, even for exemplars of good teaching, is embodied by those who teach what is prescribed but do so in interesting ways. If a prescribed curriculum and a teaching personality are the major prerequisites for good teaching, there is little, it appears, to be gained from collaboration with colleagues. Consequently, the central tenets of these student teachers' lay theories of teaching carry within them the hallmarks of conservatism, isolation, self-reliance and autonomy (Hargreaves, 1992; Nias, 1989; Lortie, 1975). They are, therefore, already predisposed towards perpetuating a 'culture of individualism' in schools. Though there is some evidence of a multi-dimensional framework of teaching embedded in the lay theories of the regular student teachers who were interviewed, there is much also that resonates with attributes of the archetypes, while this is expressed in less trenchant terms than heretofore. Privileging personality over skills and expertise enables school cultures, and through them cultural archetypes, to be perpetuated in the autonomous and isolated beginning teacher.

Mature Student Teachers

The mature student teachers in this inquiry completed their apprenticeship of observation in Irish primary schools during the 1960s and early 1970s. Their experience, for the most part, was of a system which pre-dated a policy of child-centredness.[16] Kevin's early experience resonates with key aspects of the cultural archetype when he says that his 'good' teacher used 'a lot of punishment' and, while she was 'big into control', she was also 'very effusive . . . and the whole classroom was filled with her'. To his impressionable mind she 'was intimidating' and she appeared to 'know everything'. There was much learning by rote yet he liked this teacher because she would take time to explain things to him. By contrast, Susan served her apprenticeship of observation in the company of a teacher who never raised her voice or gave punishment exercises. Susan was a good student and 'everything just seemed to flow.' However, the end product of this flow was that she 'got into the A stream in secondary school. . . .' Consequently, the teacher 'was good' (Tr. 11). In a somewhat different manner, David's archetypal teacher was 'very good at telling stories' thus perpetuating the notion of 'teaching as telling' (Tr. 12). Similarly, Gert's apprenticeship of observation in a three-teacher school provided an experience of teaching as transmission of information: 'we knew our stuff for those teachers'. She is suspicious of modern teaching methods also: 'we had to learn our tables [by heart] and I don't think it was any loss having to do it. The methods were different but I think they were just as good as today' (Tr. 13). These mature student teachers provide overwhelming evidence that they equate 'good' teaching with 'social control' the primary function of which is to 'instil knowledge rather than to engage learners' (Britzman, 1986, p. 449).

The personal characteristics ascribed to these 'good' teachers are identical to those identified by their younger colleagues. This reinforces the deeply embedded cultural beliefs that teachers are born and those who are successful teachers can stamp their authority on the learners in their classrooms. A combination of personality traits and subject-matter knowledge transforms individuals into autonomous professionals who operate and succeed independently of institutional constraints (Britzman, 1986). A broadly-based curriculum is mentioned by one interviewee only and he acknowledges that his own teacher was probably a 'pioneer' because he included drama, PE, art, music and project work in the curriculum which enabled pupils to work on their own initiative in a very positive atmosphere (Tr. 15). The most significant disparity between characteristics identified by both groups are references to corporal punishment and punishment exercises by the older students. The degree of congruence between characteristics of 'good' teaching cited by both groups strongly suggests that dominant characteristics of cultural archetypes of teaching have remained remarkably consistent in Ireland during the past twenty-five years, despite significant policy shifts.

Implications for Professional Development

At a recent convocation ceremony at Dublin City University, its president stated that:

> . . . a narrowly based education system like the Irish one can serve well only a minority of those that pass through it. It educates an élite, who then go on to perpetuate the system because they are the ones who get to control it. The rest, who are in the majority, leave the system condemned as second-raters or outright failures. (O'Hare, 1994, p. 12)

Entrants to primary teacher education are the successful products of this narrow élitist curriculum (Greaney, Burke and McCann, 1987). It is more than apparent from the foregoing analysis that 'preservice teachers' . . . [lay theories] are well established, tenacious and powerful' (Holt-Reynolds, 1992, p. 344) and these are developed through an 'apprenticeship of observation' (Lortie, 1975). Consequently, entrants to teacher-education programmes, unlike many entrants to other professional schools, are 'insiders' who already possess a very strong sense of what it means to be a teacher (Pajares, 1992; Britzman, 1986). While there have been significant, if isolated, efforts in teacher education to take cognisance of this fact, little has changed in twenty years (Kagan, 1992). Consequently, many teacher-education programmes persist with what Johnston (1992, p. 134) describes as a 'deficit view of the student' rather than 'acknowledging the understandings that the learner brings to the situation.' This point is reiterated by Eisenhart, Behm and Romagnamo (1991, p. 67) when they say that 'it seems more productive to think about ways to address and then to build on students needs' than to 'mandate some other needs just because the program proponents think them more appropriate or sophisticated . . .' (quoted by Kagan, 1992, p. 162). The present analysis supports Holt-Reynold's (1992, p. 345) conclusion that we must 'probe preservice teachers' rationales rather than assess their abilities to apply our rationales.' Consequently, she specifies the agenda for teacher educators as follows:

> Acknowledging the power of personal history-based beliefs and con-
> ceptualizations about teaching and accepting these as coherent, cohesive,
> and therefore legitimate premises from which preservice teachers begin
> their formal, professional studies means assuming that our role as teacher
> educators centers more around fostering the professionalization of those
> existing rationales rather than around generating professional rationales
> and behaviours from scratch. Helping our colleagues discover, under-
> stand, challenge, enlarge inform, and consider changing, reprioritizing, or
> reforming the premises upon which they base their arguments can become
> our primary and legitimate concern. (Holt-Reynolds, 1992, p. 344)

Such an agenda does not suggest, however, that the practical must be privileged over the technical, critical, emancipatory or theoretical. MacKinnon and Erickson (1992, p. 208) argue that, from their experience of repairing the institutional rift between theory and practice, it is necessary to 'embed foundation knowledge in reflective practice in schools.' It is necessary to create an 'interdependency culture' (Day, 1993) by engaging in 'interactive professionalism' (Fullan, 1993) with stu-dents, practitioners, teacher educators being drawn into a critically reflective con-versation 'to continue to develop our practical knowledge by personal reflection and interaction with others rather than alone' (Day, 1993, p. 40) see also (Grossman, 1992; OECD, 1991).

It is not sufficient, therefore, to focus exclusively on initial teacher education as a means of confronting archetypes of teaching. My analysis indicates that the general social milieu as well as apprenticeships of observation tend to reinforce the myth of the 'natural teacher' (Britzman, 1986) and initial teacher education and school cultures frequently reinforce the isolation of the teacher by privileging individual capacity to control and deliver the curriculum over more collegial approaches which are vital to subsequent school-based attempts to promote and sustain renewal and professional growth (Hargreaves, 1992; Lortie, 1975; Fullan, 1993). Critical consideration must, therefore, be given to 'what happens when the student's biography or cumulative social experience, becomes part of the implicit context of teacher education' (Britzman, 1986, p. 443). This project needs to be broadened to include teacher educators and teacher mentors in an ongoing inter-rogation of their own biographies and the often invisible power structures and constraints that operate within schools. Unless this challenging task is taken up in a collaborative manner, cultural archetypes of teaching will continue to be repro-duced through an apprenticeship of observation among successful students in ways that continue to give pride of place to a teaching personality and teaching as telling over more sophisticated conceptions of teaching and learning with appropriately elaborate pedagogical repertoires.

Notes

1   The Bachelor of Education is a three-year concurrent programme. Students take one academic subject to degree level and graduates are qualified to teach in primary school only.

2   I have provided a more extensive account of the 'master' and the 'mistress', from an extensive range of Irish literary sources, in Sugrue, 1993.

3   It is compulsory for each child on entry to primary schools in Ireland, which typically commences on reaching the age of 4, to begin to learn the Irish language.

4   The vast majority of primary schools in Ireland are denominational in nature and they are managed by boards of management which are chaired by a local clergyman and the composition of these boards are such that the particular denomination has an in-built majority. Teachers are employed by individual boards of management and their salaries are paid by the State.

5   This would have been Banville's first day in 'the boys' school' having served a three-year apprenticeship in the 'infant school' in the company of female teachers, where boys and girls were frequently educated together. The account he provides would be of his first encounter with the male/macho culture characteristic of boys' schools of the period.

6   I have had many conversations with elderly Irish people during the past decade, all of whom were very willing to describe the fear and oppression visited on them by their former teachers. Physical assault was commonplace during my own primary and, more particularly, my secondary education. In a very recent conversation with an 81-year-old grandmother, she spoke of the fear she had of 'the master' who made his pupils recite large chunks of the Bible by heart, in preparation for confirmation, while he stood over them wielding a fishing rod. She said: 'I feared him 'till the day he died, and 'twasn't that long since he died.'

7   One of the more fascinating aspects of this account is that it has led to correspondence between Trevor and Willoughby. She has suggested to him that she was oblivious to the fact that he perceived her in such a negative light. Trevor's rejoinder suggests that his image of her is not quite as negative as his text seems to convey. However, this reinforces the deep-seatedness of Lay theories and cultural stereotypes and their uncon-scious reproduction by generations of teachers. (I am grateful to Clíona Uí Thuama for bringing this correspondence to my attention).

8   90 per cent of entrants to primary teaching are now female. These entrants score consistently above the 77th percentile as measured by the State Leaving Certificate Examination.

9   Very recently, (March 1994), I supervised Celia during her final teaching practice and, by common consent among three supervisors and the collaborating teacher, she was completely at home in the role. Her 'natural' aptitude for the teaching role reinforces her own, much earlier, perception that she would inevitably end up working with kids.

10   The age at which pupils receive the sacraments of First Communion and Penance has been changed recently from 7 to 8 and this normally occurs in the second grade. Confirmation is typically received in sixth grade at the age of 12. Preparation for the sacraments is regarded as a very onerous task by the class teachers who teach the necessary doctrine in addition to appropriate hymns and prayers. The burden has increased in recent years as there are meetings (typically six) with parents in advance of the actual church ceremony.

11   Our 13-year-old daughter, Caragh, is extremely fond of children and enjoys looking

after them (baby-sitting) etc. It is very interesting to note that as adults in the extended family become more aware of this, they increasingly suggest teaching as a likely career for her. The popular notion seems to suggest that being fond of children equips the individual to be a good teacher. By comparison, I have never heard it suggested that being fond of children automatically qualifies one to be a paediatrician!

12   In rural Ireland of the 1950s and 1960s, getting 'the call to training' (being awarded a place in one of the primary teacher-training colleges) was very highly prized. The only higher calling was to 'have a vocation': to be 'called' to a life in the Church. In the absence of an industrial base, the alternatives for high achievers, who could not afford a university education, were the banks and the civil service. One of the attractions of primary teacher training was that college fees could be paid by the State and repaid subsequently during the first five years of teaching. 'Permanent and pensionable' was extremely attractive to communities where 50 per cent, or more, of the population emigrated.

13   Until 1992, there had been a comprehensive interview process for intending student teachers in Ireland. This process included music, an oral Irish examination and an interview. While there are many reasons why this process should be retained, it did have the effect of perpetuating and reinforcing the notion of *the* teaching personality.

14   It is common for pupils in 5th and 6th grade (11- and 12-year-olds) in Irish primary schools to be assigned homework regularly which teachers anticipate will take them ninety minutes to complete. For further details see Burke, Dobrich and Sugrue, 1991.

15   A number of recent international comparative studies have included data generated by Irish researchers. Elley (1992) focused on reading while La Pointe, Mead and Askew (1992) focused on mathematics and science respectively. In a comprehensive review of this and smaller-scale Irish research, Morgan and Kellaghan (forthcoming) found that: 'With some exceptions the studies reviewed . . . suggest that . . . while the performance of Irish children on basic skills is quite good, they do relatively less well on tasks that demand higher cognitive capacities. In addition, the evidence is even stronger that Irish schools emphasize basic skills to a relatively greater extent than do their counterparts in other countries.'

16   Child-centred education became official policy in Irish primary schools in 1971.

References

ALEXANDER, R. (1992) *Policy and Practice in Primary Education*, London, Routledge and Kegan Paul.

ALEXANDER, R., WILLCOCKS, J. and KINDER, K. (Eds) (1989) *Changing Primary Practice*, London, Falmer Press.

ARONOWITZ, S. and GIROUX, H. (1985) *Education Under Siege: The Conservative, Liberal and Radical Debate over Schooling*, Massachusetts, Bergin and Garvey Publishers.

ARONOWITZ, S. and GIROUX, H. (1991) *Postmodern Education: Politics, Culture, and Social Criticism*, Oxford, University of Minnesota Press.

BALL, S. and GOODSON, I. (Eds) (1985) *Teachers' Lives and Careers*, London, Falmer Press.

BANVILLE, J. (1986) *Mefisto*, London, Secker and Warburg.

BARCLAY, C. and WELLMAN, H. (1986) 'Accuracies and inaccuracies in autobiographical memories', *Journal of Memory and Languages*, **25**, pp. 93–103.

BARTH, R. (1991) *Improving Schools from Within*, Oxford, Jossey-Bass.

BECKER, H., GEER, B. and HUGHES, E. (Eds) (1968) *Making the Grade*, London, John Wiley and Sons.

BIGGS, J. (1990) 'Teaching design for learning: A keynote discussion', A paper presented at the annual conference of the Higher Education Research and Development Society of Australia, Griffith University Brisbane.

BRITZMAN, D. (1986) 'Cultural myths in the making of a teacher: Biography and social structure in teacher education', *Harvard Educational Review*, **56**, 4, pp. 442–56.

BRITZMAN, D. (1989) 'Who has the floor?: Curriculum teaching and the English teachers struggle for voice', *Curriculum Inquiry*, **19**, pp. 143–62.

BULLOUGH, R. (1992) 'Beginning teacher curriculum decision making, personal teaching metaphors and teacher education', *Teaching and Teacher Education*, **8**, 3, pp. 239–52.

BURKE, A., DOBRICH, P. and SUGRUE, C. (1991) *Time for School*, Frankfurt am main, Deutsches Institut fur Internationale Pädagogische Forschung.

CALDERHEAD, J. (1987) *Exploring Teachers' Thinking*, London, Cassell.

CALDERHEAD, J. (1991) 'Images of teaching: Student teachers' early conceptions of classroom practice', *Teaching and Teacher Education*, **7**, pp. 1–8.

CALDERHEAD, J. and GATES, P. (Eds) (1993) *Conceptualizing Reflections in Teacher Development*, London, Falmer Press.

CLANDININ, D. (1986) *Classroom Practice: Teacher Images in Action*, London, Falmer Press.

CLIFT, R., HOUSTON, W. and PUGACH, M. (Eds) (1990) *Encouraging Reflective Practice in Education: An Analysis of Issues and Programs*, New York, Teachers College Press.

CONNELLY, M. and CLANDININ, J. (1988) *Teachers as Curriculum Planners: Narratives of Experience*, Toronto, OISE Press.

DALL'ABBA, G. (1990) 'Foreshadowing conceptions of teaching', A paper presented at the annual conference of the Higher Education Research and Development Society of Australia, Griffith University, Brisbane.

DAY, C. (1993) 'Research and the continuing professional development of teachers', An Inaugural Lecture delivered at The University of Nottingham School of Education on 19 November.

DAY, C., POPE, M. and DENICOLO, P. (Eds) (1990) *Insight into Teachers' Thinking and Practice*, London, Falmer Press.

DUNKIN, M. (1990) 'The induction of academic staff to a university: Process and product', *Higher Education*, **20**, pp. 47–66.

EISENHART, M., BEHM, L. and ROMAGNANO, L. (1991) 'Learning to teach: Developing expertise or rite of passage?', *Journal of Education for Teaching*, **17**, pp. 51–71.

EISNER, E. (1988) 'The primacy of experience', *Educational Researcher*, **17**, 5, pp. 15–20.

ELBAZ, F. (1983) *Teacher Thinking: A Study of Practical Knowledge*, London, Croom Helm.

ELLEY, W. (1992) *How in the World Do Students Read?*, Hamburg, International Association for Evaluation of Educational Achievement.

ELMORE, R. and ASSOCIATES (1990) *Restructuring Schools: The Next Generation of Educational Reform*, Oxford, Jossey-Bass.

FRIEL, B. (1983) *The Diviner: The Best Stories of Brian Friel* (introduction by Seamus Deane), Dublin, The O'Brien Press.

FULLAN, M. (1993) *Change Forces: Probing the Depths of Educational Reform*, London, Falmer Press.

GIROUX, H., SIMON, R. and CONTRIBUTORS (1989) *Popular Culture, Schooling, and Everyday Life*, Massachusetts, Bergin and Garvey Publishers.

GOODSON, I. (Ed) (1992) *Studying Teachers' Lives*, London, Routledge.

GOODSON, I. and WALKER, R. (1991) *Biography, Identity and Schooling: Episodes in Educational Research*, London, Falmer Press.

GREANEY, V., BURKE, A. and McCANN, J. (1987) 'Entrants to primary teacher education in Ireland', *European Journal of Teacher Education*, **10**, 2, pp. 127–40.

GROSSMAN, P. (1992) 'Why models matter: An alternative view on professional growth in teaching', *Review of Educational Research*, **62**, 2, pp. 171–9, Summer.

GRUMET, M. (1988) *Bitter Milk: Women and Teaching*, Boston, University of Massachusetts Press.

HARGREAVES, A. (1992) 'Cultures of teaching: A focus for change', in HARGREAVES, A. and FULLAN, M. (Eds) *Understanding Teacher Development*, London, Cassell, pp. 216–40.

HARGREAVES, A. (1994) *Changing Teachers, Changing Times: Teachers' Work and Culture in the Postmodern Age*, London, Cassell.

HARGREAVES, A. (forthcoming) 'Development and desire: A postmodern perspective', in GUSKEY, T. and HUBERMAN, M. (Eds) *New Paradigms and Practices in Professional Development*, New York, Teachers' College Press.

HOLT-REYNOLDS, D. (1992) 'Personal history-based beliefs as relevant prior knowledge in course work', *American Educational Research Journal*, **29**, 2, pp. 325–49, Summer.

HUNT, D. (1987) *Beginning with Ourselves in Practice, Theory and Human Affairs*, Toronto, OISE Press.

JOHNSTON, S. (1992) 'Images: A way of understanding the practical knowledge of student teachers', *Teaching and Teacher Education*, **8**, 2, pp. 123–36.

KAGAN, D. (1992) 'Professional growth among preservice and beginning teachers', *Review of Educational Research*, **62**, 2, pp. 129–69, Summer.

KEARNEY, R. (1985) *The Irish Mind: Exploring Intellectual Traditions*, Dublin, Wolfhound Press.

LAKOFF, G. and JOHNSON, M. (1980) *Metaphors We Live By*, London, The University of Chicago Press.

LA POINTE, A., ASKEW, J. and MEAD, N. (1992) *Learning Science*, Princeton, NJ, IAEP/Educational Testing Service.

LA POINTE, A., MEAD, N. and ASKEW, J. (1992) *Learning Mathematics*, Princeton, NJ, IAEP/Educational Testing Service.

LORTIE, D. (1975) *Schoolteacher: A Sociological Study*, London, The University of Chicago Press.

MACMAHON, B. (1992) *The Master*, Dublin, Poolbeg Press.

MACKINNON, A. and ERICKSON, G. (1992) 'The roles of reflective practice and foundational disciplines in teacher education', in RUSSELL, H. and MUMBY, H. (Eds) *Teachers and Teaching: From Classroom to Reflection*, London, Falmer Press, pp. 192–210.

MARTIN, E. and BALLA, M. (1990) 'Conceptions of teaching and implications for learning', A paper presented at the annual conference of the Higher Education Research and Development Society of Australia, Griffith University, Brisbane.

MEASOR, L. (1985) 'Critical incidents in the classroom: Identities, choices and careers', in BALL, S. and GOODSON, I. (Eds) *Teachers' Lives and Careers*, London, Falmer Press, pp. 61–77.

MORGAN, M. and KELLAGHAN, T. (forthcoming) 'Higher-order cognitive performance of Irish children: A review', *Irish Journal of Education*.

MORTIMORE, P., SAMMONS, P., STOLL, L., LEWIS, D. and ECOB, R. (1988) *School Matters: The Junior Years*, England, Open Books.

NIAS, J. (1989) *Primary Teachers Talking: A Study of Teaching as Work*, London, Routledge.

O'HARE, D. (1994) 'Fostering and "enterprising spirit" in education of the future', *Irish Times*, p. 12, 28 March.

ORGANISATION FOR ECONOMIC CO-OPERATION AND DEVELOPMENT (OECD) (1991) *Reviews of National Policies for Education: Ireland*, Paris, OECD.

PAJARES, M. (1992) 'Teachers' beliefs and educational research: Cleaning up a messy construct', *Review of Educational Research*, **62**, 3, pp. 307–32, Fall.

POLLARD, A. and TANN, S. (1987) *Reflective Teaching in the Primary School*, London, Cassell.

PURPEL, D. (1989) *The Moral and Spiritual Crisis in Education: A Curriculum for Justice and Compassion in Education*, Massachusetts, Bergin and Garvey Publishers.

RUSSELL, T. and MUMBY, H. (Eds) (1992) *Teachers and Teaching: From Classroom to Reflection*, London, Falmer Press.

SAMUELOWICZ, K. and BAIN, J. (1992) 'Conceptions of teaching held by academic teachers', *Higher Education*, **24**, 1, pp. 93–111.

SARASON, S. (1990) *The Predictable Failure of Educational Reform*, Oxford, Jossey-Bass.

SHEDD, J. and BACHARACH, S. (1991) *Tangled Hierarchies: Teachers as Professionals and the Management of Schools*, Oxford, Jossey-Bass.

SIKES, P., MEASOR, L. and WOODS, P. (1985) *Teacher Careers: Crises and Continuities*, London, Falmer Press.

SIKES, P. (1987) 'A Life History Approach to Initial Teacher Education', unpublished manuscript, Coventry, University of Warwick.

SUGRUE, C. (1990) 'Child-centred education in Ireland since 1971', *Oideas*, **35**, pp. 5–21, Spring.

SUGRUE, C. (1993) 'Confronting student teachers' lay theories and culturally embedded images of teaching: Implications for teacher education and research', A paper presented at the International Invitational Symposium, St. Patrick's College, Drumcondra, Eire.

TREVOR, W. (1993) *Excursions in the Real World*, London, Hutchinson.

WOODS, P. (1985) 'Conversations with teachers: Some aspects of life-history method', *British Educational Research Journal*, **11**, 1, pp. 13–26.

Chapter 9

Women as Teachers: Teachers as Women

Miriam Ben-Peretz

The professional lives of teachers may be viewed from different aspects. One important aspect is gender. Women play a major role in schools, as most element-ary and many high-school teachers are women. Much has been written on gender issues in teaching. Acker (1988), for instance, states that 'many studies in the gender and education literature imply teachers play an important part in the thwart-ing of girls' potential' (p. 307). Acker claims that the teacher himself or herself is less often studied, though 'an interesting line of work is beginning to locate teachers' attitudes and actions in their own biographies and life situations' (Acker, 1988, p. 314).

Teachers' narratives allow us to grasp some crucial aspects of teaching viewed from a gender aspect. This chapter is based on recollections of professional events in the lives of retired teachers which serve as vivid examples of the role gender plays in their professional lives. Forty-three retired teachers participated in a study of the transformation of experience into professional wisdom and the role of memory in this process. The participating teachers were asked for accounts of their former practice. Retired teachers could look back over many years of practice and their recollections of past events provide a view of changing educational situations. (Ben-Peretz, 1995). In the following parts of this chapter some of these recalled episodes are analysed from a gender viewpoint.

Women as Teachers

Let us listen now to the voices of the retired teachers:

> I had a student called Avischai. His parents were divorced and his mother raised him as a single parent. Each day she travelled to another, nearby city where she worked. When the child became ill he stayed by himself the whole day. I used to visit him every day after school, preparing tea and warming his meal. I pitied the child and his mother. Two years later, I had moved to teach in a different location. I returned to my previous school for the graduation ceremony. Avischai's mother approached me and said: 'Avischai has grown a plant for you for two years. The flower pot is heavy

and I could not carry it with me. Please, as you have your car with you, pass near our home and Avischai will give you the plant.' I was extremely moved. This was a very special present for me. The child grew the plant for two years and kept it for me. The present represents the child's attitude and the depth of his feeling. (Elementary school teacher, heterogeneous population, years of practice at the time of the event: 23, overall years of teaching: 35, years since retirement: 1)

It is interesting to note that this event did not occur early in the teacher's career. At the time it happened she was an experienced and well-established teacher. Her story portrays mature self-assurance and responsibility. In a few sentences the teacher managed to draw the background and to share with her listeners her compassion concerning the circumstances of her student's life. Describing her own actions in helping the family she sounds matter-of-fact and not overly self-congratulatory. Then comes the emotional and surprising ending. The student did not forget his teacher's help. For two years he tended a plant, waiting for the right opportunity to present it. The teacher seems quite overwhelmed by the perseverance of her former student in his expression of gratitude.

The teacher recounting this event took it for granted that the teaching profession entails caring for the emotional and physical well-being of one's students. She did not hesitate to become involved in attending to the needs of a sick child whose mother was unable to be home during the day. What are the roots of such 'caring' behaviour of women as teachers? Noddings (1984) approaches practical ethics and the caring relation from a feminine view, and claims that 'it is necessary to give appropriate attention and credit to the affective foundation of existence.' (p. 3). Noddings calls one party of the caring relation the 'one-caring' and the second the 'cared-for'. Stating that 'as human beings we want to care and to be cared for' (p. 7), Noddings concluded that this longing for caring provides the motivation for being moral. According to Noddings women 'define themselves in terms of caring and work their way through moral problems from the position of one-caring.' (p. 8). Caring is obviously immensely important to the cared-for. 'To the cared-for no act in his behalf is quite as important or influential as the attitude of the one-caring.' (Noddings, ibid., pp. 19–20). Noddings stresses the need for reciprocity in caring, and the dependence of the one-caring on the cared-for. Avischai's story may serve as an example for the caring quality of women as teachers, and for their dependence on the responses of the cared-for, even long after the act of caring. The teacher who chose to recount and share this event with us may be perceived as having defined herself and her profession in terms of caring. Her own attitude and feelings were reciprocated by Avischai's attitude and depth of feeling. The fact that she found out about his response only at a later time served to strengthen the impact of his act. 'I was extremely moved. This was a very special present for me.' These words reveal how meaningful this event had been for the teacher, and may explain its recall thirteen years after it occurred.

Sometimes a teacher will deal explicitly with issues of caring and empathy as reflected in the following event:

Teachers can strengthen and enhance the abilities of their students, but they can also destroy them completely. In the first elementary grades teachers' knowledge is less important than their character and empathy with students. For instance: In my twelfth year of teaching I was the homeroom teacher of a third grade. One of the students had great difficulties in learning to read. His former homeroom teacher, in the second grade, referred to him as 'a piece of furniture in the classroom'. I was shocked by her words. I devoted special attention to this student and tried to encourage him. After the other students had read aloud from the posters around the room, I told this student to read them again which he succeeded in doing. Sometimes I gave him extra time to prepare himself ahead of the other students to read a portion of text. The next day he would be able to read it fluently. In this manner I encouraged him over the whole year and even raised his status among the other children. I engaged him in various class activities; handing out learning materials, being responsible for the classroom cupboard etc. After many years I met him and he reminded me of encouraging him and asking him to fulfil different functions in class. He told me that he would never forget these experiences. I was very happy to hear his words. They gave meaning to my life, they made my day. It is important to note that even in the higher grades he was not considered to be a weak student. He was an average student. (Female elementary school teacher, heterogeneous population, years of practice at the time of the event: 12, overall years of teaching: 30, years since retirement: 7)

The narrator here focuses on an educational principle: she considers the crucial major role that teachers' actions play in determining the academic and social development of their students. The intensity with which she recalls the details of her own practice concerning one third-grade student shows that this principle constitutes her guiding educational philosophy. The elaboration of activities enables her audience to understand explicitly what she meant by her opening general statement. Moreover, the story has a happy ending. The teacher is confirmed in her belief and shares this validation with us. It is as if the narrator had searched her professional memories to find the one event which captures the whole story of her practice, its guiding principle, the appropriate details of classroom actions, and the evidence for the validity of her approach.

As in the previous story, the teacher acted as the caring one for a significant period of time and was rewarded many years later by her student's response. 'He told me that he would never forget these experiences. I was very happy to hear his words. They gave meaning to my life.' In retrospect the work of this teacher gained its meaning from the caring relationships she succeeded in creating.

Other persons, besides the teachers and their students, may become involved in the caring relationships. The following event serves as an example:

I had a student in Kindergarten called Nava, who had a bad limp. She was very intelligent and capable. At the end of the year I gave her the main part in a play. Nava's mother approached me and complained that because of the performance everyone will become aware of Nava's limp. After a long conversation the mother accepted my decision. I told her: 'Don't make the child feel inferior, let her express her abilities.' The girl grew and at the end of her elementary school studies she performed the main part in the graduation play. I sat beside her mother and both of us cried throughout the performance. Nava had grown, was very successful, and ready to appear in a main part in spite of her limp. (Female Kindergarten teacher, heterogeneous population, years of practice at the time of the event: 5, overall years of teaching: 25, years since retirement: 5)

The story reflects the conflicts and dilemmas which may accompany any act of caring. How sure can a teacher be that her decisions are appropriate? What is the weight of responsibilities she may bear? An inner voice tells her that Nava will benefit from her decision, but Nava's mother, who is the major one-caring in Nava's life has a different view. In teaching we may often find several opposing points of view expressed by different persons who are in a caring relationship with a student. The outcome of their conflicts may not always be as satisfying as in the story of Nava. Women who are caring teachers may have to accept the sometimes negative outcomes of their caring actions, yet these acts are an essential component of the work of many teachers.

Teachers as Women

The recollection of professional events that were presented by retired teachers provided insight into a second role that gender plays in the professional lives of teachers. The following story may serve as an example:

In my fifth year of teaching I was transferred to Kiryat-Yam (a small town). I was homeroom teacher of the third grade. Some of the children had not yet mastered reading and writing. I paid special attention to these students and they showed progress. At the end of the year the results were highly satisfactory. The classes in this school were crowded, forty students in each class. The students came from different backgrounds. Some were children of new immigrants, and others came from well-established homes. This was the first time in my life that I had problems with classroom management and discipline. My confidence in myself was shaken. I was not used to such a situation. I had never before experienced disciplinary problems. It was extremely difficult for me. On top of that the principal had very specific demands. He used to come into my class to evaluate the use of the blackboard. The school climate was competitive instead of cooperative. Maybe because of the principal's manner it turned out to be a case of 'each person for herself.' (Female elementary school teacher, heterogeneous population, years of practice at the time of the event: 5, overall years of teaching: 30, years since retirement: 7)

This teacher's story concerns several factors in the professional lives of teachers which are bound to cause difficulties. The teacher was moved to a new school, she found herself teaching a highly heterogeneous class in which some of the students had not yet mastered the basics. She perceived the school climate as non-supportive and highly competitive, and considered herself to be under constant scrutiny by the principal. Her previous successes may have depended to a large extent on a supportive school climate and a less demanding student population. She did not give up, her story tells us that she did succeed with the slower students. And still, the overall tone of the story is sad, almost resigned. The teacher seems to say to herself and to us: 'I may not be such a good teacher as I have thought myself to be. This is not wholly my fault, I worked in difficult circumstances.' Seven years after her retirement she recalled this event, though it had happened at a fairly early stage of her career.

This story exemplifies the gender discrimination experienced by women in the workforce. Casey and Apple (1989) discuss gender and the conditions of teachers' work and stress the uses of gender stereotypes for social control of teachers by male administrators. The principal in this recalled event created a competitive climate in his school and managed to undermine the professional confidence of the narrator through his constant supervision and withdrawing of her instructional autonomy. ('He used to come into my class to evaluate my use of the blackboard.') This experience coloured the teacher's view of her past practice and its impact on her was so great that she recalled and narrated this event. Two aspects of her story are worth noting. One is the apparent discrepancy between the positive, tangible out-comes of her work ('at the end of the year the results were highly satisfactory'), and her feeling of inadequacy. The other point concerns her resignation and sense of dependency and vulnerability. She does not report any attempt to change the school climate and to rebel against the oppressive acts of her principal, but deplores the lack of collegiality and community spirit ('each person for herself'). Casey and Apple (1989) have commented on 'the potential for antagonism between (female) teachers and (male) administrators' (p. 182). The story of this teacher reflects such antagonism. It is interesting to compare this event with one recalled by a male teacher:

Our school, like all schools, maintained certain regulations. It was forbidden to bring penknives to school. One student, his name was Schmueli, was found to have a penknife and was sent to the principal's office. The principal reprimanded Schmueli who happened to be a good student and a good kid. He was told that if he ever brought his penknife to school he would be sent home and would have to return with his parents. Since then the boy had not brought the penknife with him. At the end-of-term teachers' meeting concerning grades (in Israel all class teachers meet to discuss their student's term grades) the principal claimed that the student deserved a poor grade in classroom behaviour. The principal managed to enforce his opinion in spite of the opposition of the homeroom teacher and the other teachers of this class. The same scenario repeated itself in the second term. The principal continued to argue that such a misdemeanour had to receive appropriate punishment in the form of a low grade. In a former teachers' meeting it had been decided that the principal would have no veto rights on grades. A compromise was reached and the student received an average grade. In one of the next meetings teachers wanted to reopen the issue but the principal refused to discuss the topic. I believe that the reason for his stubbornness was that he lacked jurisdiction over grades in subject-matter areas, like math or physical education, therefore he wanted to have powers of decisions concerning grades in students' behaviour. There were many confrontations with the principal over this matter. I am still angry about this incident. All teachers expressed great anger. (Male high-school teacher, heterogeneous population, years of practice at the time of the event: 28, overall years of teaching: 30, years since retirement: 3)

This story reflects the power structure and the power struggles in school. It is a recollection of a fairly recent event that still causes feelings of great anger. One gets a picture of a school which is divided between teachers and principal, with the teachers defending their students against an overly strict disciplinarian. It may well be that the narrator found the overall school climate to be disturbing and unpleasant, similar to the situation in the previous story, his story reflects such feelings. It is interesting that of the many possible recollections this teacher chose to tell a story of interpersonal strife in school. The specific story tells us implicitly about his more liberal pedagogical beliefs and about his views concerning teacher autonomy versus the decision-making power of principals.

A different picture of power struggles in schools emerges from this story. This is a case of strong and lasting resistance of teachers who confronted their principal concerning actions perceived as unjust and uncalled for. It is clearly a case of trying to maintain teachers' professional autonomy versus the hegemony of the principal. Women were obviously involved in this instance of resistance, but the narrator of the event is a male teacher who voices their discontent. Apparently the story of resistance is highly meaningful for this teacher, whose view of school life includes strife and anger. Acker (1988) argues that teachers appear to make relatively little effort to change the power structure in schools, and to challenge the male hegemony. The event narrated by the male teacher represents resistance and challenge. Still, this is a contrasting voice among the voices of other, female, teachers who sound resigned to the sexual division of labour in the schools. As Oram (1989) states: 'Major differences of status and position have divided men and women teachers throughout the twentieth century.' (p. 21).

Acker (1989) points out that the very existence of hierarchies in schools tends to favour men. She explains the relative scarcity of women in high-level administrative positions as being based on 'women's socialization and satisfying experience of alternative values and forms of organization, together with a kind of "situational adjustment" — coming to terms with a situation unlikely to be changed by wishing it so.' (p. 14).

The following episode, recalled by a retired Kindergarten teacher, exemplifies the difficulties of such adjustments, though in this case the supervisor is a woman.

> After three years, in 1972, I was working in Tira. The supervisor there was a very harsh and frightening woman. She used to appear in my dreams like a witch. She admired my work but begrudged me my success. Once she arrived at my Kindergarten with a whole group of visitors.
>
> I held a tray with apples in my hands. When I saw her the tray slipped out of my hands and apples scattered on the floor. Once she screamed at me demanding why I did not have a full list of attendance in my diary. She made me cry. I went to another supervisor in order to resign. I put the keys of the Kindergarten on his desk and told him: 'I resign.' I burst out crying: 'I can not stand this evil supervisor any longer.' Sometime later a new supervisor arrived. She was wonderful, supported me greatly, helped me with good advice and warm friendship thus restoring the supervisor–Kindergarten teacher relationship. All new projects were implemented in my Kindergarten. Over may years student-teachers and visitors from abroad used to visit my Kindergarten. (Female Kindergarten teacher, low socio-economic level population, years of practice at the time of the event: 4, overall years of teaching: 12, years since retirement: 10)

The utter confusion experienced by the teacher when confronted by the supervisor ('when I saw her the tray slipped out of my hands') and her emotional reactions (I burst out crying) reflect some of the difficulties of adjustment to the harsh reality of oppressive hierarchies. The situation may be exacerbated when gender issues are involved. The impulse to resign and leave teaching altogether may be extremely powerful in such cases.

The last event to be presented herewith may be interpreted as related to the two-sided expression of gender issues in schools, the caring inclinations of women as teachers, as well as the dependency syndrome of teachers as women.

> In the third year of my work I taught a non-graded elementary class in a camp of new immigrants. The students ranged from age 7–12. I tried very hard but lacked the necessary knowledge. All teachers were devoted to their work. We collected one teaspoon of oil and one spoon of flour from each family. I brought a stove from home, we made dough and prepared patties. All the children sat around and I was in the centre, baking the patties. My father who happened to visit me and saw me in this situation burst out crying for me. (Female elementary school teacher low socio-economic population, years of practice at the time of the event: 3, overall years of teaching: 30, years since retirement: 7)

A number of difficulties are reflected in this story. The teacher mentions her lack of adequate knowledge in the face of a difficult situation, a non-graded class of new immigrant students. Devotion to one's task is perceived as compensating, at least partially, for the lack of professional knowledge. The narrating teacher chose to focus on a case of home-like activities which may be read as reflecting her caring behaviour. The most fascinating aspect of this event is the apparent close tie of the teacher with her parents. Her father visited her class and was appalled by the classroom scene. The crying-father scene, whether a reconstruction or an authentic incident, reveals dependence on family involvement, support and approval, which may be natural for a young woman thrust into a difficult and alien situation. The story raises interesting gender issues, concerning the special status and self-image of female teachers in a traditional society.

Conclusion

Teachers speak in many voices. The retired teachers whose recollections were presented above emphasized two aspects of gender in schools, their caring relationships to students, on one hand, and the power relationships between themselves and their, mainly male, supervisors on the other hand. These are authentic stories, still imprinted on the memory of teachers many years after the events had taken place, signifying the importance assigned to them by the narrators. The stories are characterized by their high level of emotionality and intensity, reflecting their centrality in the professional lives of women teachers. It is interesting to note that the stories presented above lack expressions of social critique. The retired teachers don't look back with anger; they seem to accept the situations described so vividly as unavoidable, at least in the distant past in which their stories unfolded. The quality Noddings (1991) calls 'interpersonal reasoning' dominates in their narratives. Interpersonal relations are at the centre of their professional lives and are accorded a major role in their recollections. It would seem appropriate to include stories like these in teacher-education programmes, creating opportunities for future teachers to reflect on these issues, possibly from a more critical and transformative standpoint. A fruitful avenue on further research on teachers' perceptions of gender concerns would be on comparative lines. It would be interesting to study teachers' stories and recollections in different cultures, different subject-matter areas, as well as in different periods.

References

ACKER, S. (1988) 'Teachers, gender and resistance', *British Journal of Sociology of Education*, **9**, 3, pp. 307–22.

ACKER, S. (1989) *Rethinking the Teacher's Careers: Researchers, Gender and Careers*, London, New York and Philadelphia, Falmer Press, pp. 7–20.

BEN-PERETZ, M. (1995) *Learning from Experience: Memory and the Teacher's Account of Teaching*, Albany, Suny Press.

CASEY, K. and APPLE, M.W. (1989) 'Gender and the conditions of teachers' work: The development of understanding in America', in ACKER, S. (Ed) *Teacher, Gender and Careers*, London, New York and Philadelphia, Falmer Press.

NODDINGS, N. (1984) *Caring: A Feminine Approach to Ethics and Moral Education*, Berkeley, University of California Press.

ORAM, A. (1989) 'A master should not serve under a mistress: Women and men teachers 1900–1970', in ACKER, S. (Ed) *Teaching, Gender and Careers*, London, New York and Philadelphia, Falmer Press, pp. 7–34.

Chapter 10

Knowledge, Teacher Development and Change[1]

*Marvin F. Wideen, Jolie A. Mayer-Smith and
Barbara J. Moon*

Introduction

The importance of applying what we know to the resolution of social problems has long been a concern to social scientists (Love, 1975). Glasser (cited in Love, 1975) once remarked that civilization was a race between catastrophe and knowledge utilization. Others like Love, see a strong need for applying what social scientists know to the field of education. As he puts it:

> ... most would agree that knowledge utilization, transferring it to a setting where it can be applied, and using that knowledge in some form is a worthwhile aim for social scientists concerned with improving education. (Love, 1975, p. 337)

Despite this interest in knowledge utilization in the social sciences, researchers in education have not dealt with the issue of professional knowledge and the way teachers use it to inform their practice. The literature which has sought to identify the characteristics of effective schools, for example, typically fails to cite knowledge and the way teachers use it as a factor either in creating or defining such schools. Nor is knowledge use generally mentioned when implementation and change are discussed.

In this chapter, we examine two prevailing views of professional knowledge and its use, and describe the assumptions frequently made about how it informs the work of teachers. We will illustrate some of the shortcomings that arise when one takes an uncritical and unproblematic view of knowledge. We then draw on an empirical base of a five-year case study of school change to examine how teachers use professional knowledge. The data imply that knowledge of various forms was used in different ways within the school. We will show that the use teachers made of these different forms of knowledge did not support either a traditional view of knowledge utilization, or arguments made by the proponents of personal, practical knowledge and teacher story. We argue that it is dangerous to accept, without critical scrutiny, any single view of knowledge utilization.

The work leading to this chapter was framed using the concept of teacher development which involves change and improvement in one's practice over a period of time. Central to this concept lies the notion that changing one's teaching is a learning process which involves, in part, building upon and changing prior beliefs and actions about teaching. The concept of teacher development has been evident in the educational literature for several decades. During the 1970s and 1980s teacher-development ideas were based on stage theory, from Fullar and Brown's (1975) early work with pre-service teachers. Developmental stage theories sought to identify concerns, problems, or tasks common to most teachers at various times in their professional lives (Burden, 1990). The task of professional development experts would then be to provide the knowledge appropriate to teachers at each stage. As Fullar and Brown argued, the important question in teacher education was: 'What kinds of interventions by what kinds of interveners in what contexts elicit what responses from subjects?' (p. 26). It was believed that a better understanding of the stages through which teachers pass would enable outside experts to know better what type of knowledge would be most beneficial at a certain period in a teacher's development.

At about the same time, another outlook was emerging which took a more interpretive approach to teacher development. Stenhouse writing in 1984 and reflecting upon his twenty years' experience in the Humanities Curriculum Project, argued that the way to better schools lay in increasing the number of teachers who were not continually frustrated by the system (Hopkins and Wideen, 1984). In the United States this trend began with Corey's work in action research and has grown considerably in recent years (Cochran-Smith and Lytle, 1990). This view takes a more teacher-centred approach and recognizes the limitations of outside experts who mandate change through programmes such as supervision or staff development (Grimmett and MacKinnon, 1992). Development from this perspective focuses on the dilemmas and meanings surrounding the changes that teachers find important (Hargreaves and Dawe, 1990; Lieberman, 1984). The role of the researcher shifts from being one outside the school who advises teachers on their development, to that of one who attempts to understand and interpret developmental change, and who engages in the joint construction of knowledge with teachers. Such knowledge comes through a narrative discourse that occurs within a research interview.

Our view of teacher development, what it means to develop as a teacher, who should steer that development, and how, therefore colour our views of teachers' professional knowledge as something that teachers learn from researchers on the one hand, or clarify or construct themselves with the assistance of researchers on the other. Before examining our specific school case study, we want to examine these two different models of teachers' professional knowledge and knowledge utilization more closely.

Two Views of Knowledge and its Use[2]

The concept of knowledge utilization has traditionally been seen and described from a 'producer-user' perspective. 'Producers' develop knowledge and 'users' implement it. This concept has had a long-standing tradition in the social sciences beginning with studies in rural sociology of how people adopted innovations such as radio and television (Louis, 1981). Early studies of innovation in education focused on patterns of adoption by users (e.g., House, 1974). Such work sought to identify factors associated with the adoption of innovations, and why certain people adopted innovations sooner than others. This view of knowledge utilization under-pinned the development of curriculum materials in the 1960s during what has come to be called the 'period of curriculum reform'. Concerned over the need for more scientists and mathematicians shortly after the Second World War, substantial funding was made available to improve school curricula in those areas. Experts, seeking to provide curriculum materials that could be readily implemented by teachers, con-ducted extensive research and development, followed by field-testing (Havelock, 1969). Such models of curriculum tended to be linear, beginning with theory and proceeding to student outcomes thought to occur if teachers took appropriate actions in their classrooms (Elbaz, 1983). Implementation then became a process of putting into practice the ideas and activities in those curriculum packages that would change teaching practice and thereby improve it in ways such that the desired student outcomes would occur. Knowledge from the 'producer-user' per-spective became a set of propositions that directed the teacher in what to teach and how to teach it. Fenstermacher (1994) refers to such knowledge on teaching that used conventional scientific methods as 'formal knowledge'.

The experience of that period showed that despite the elegance of the curric-ulum design, and despite the enthusiasm of those who had been involved in its development, the much heralded curriculum materials that were to reform the schools generally stopped at the classroom door (Goodlad, von Steophasius and Klein, 1974). Those curriculum materials that did make it into the classroom became a cause for concern, because of the lack of fidelity between what the developers intended and the way teachers implemented them in their classroom. There was much talk about 'mutual adaptation', a concept which seemed designed to soften the 'top–down' character of the curriculum reforms, creating the aura of reciprocity between developers and users. The final result, however, was that after a decade of curriculum activity based on a producer-user notion of knowledge utilization, little was accomplished.

Another example of the traditional knowledge utilization paradigm is seen in the process–product research on teaching which had its beginnings in the 1960s. This research aimed at producing context-free generalizations about the links be-tween teachers' and students' behaviours and measurable student outcomes (Doyle, 1990; Tom and Valli, 1990). It emulated the methods and forms of research in natural science (Soltis, 1984). The process–product research paradigm, viewed teaching as the cause of student achievement, and research questions focused on what sorts of teacher behaviours generated the best student achievement (Macmillan and Garrison, 1984). Such process–product research has become an important foun-dation for school and educational reform. The findings of this research paradigm have met with considerable acceptance and have been converted into applications for teachers to follow. They have been adopted in numerous programmes of pre-service and in-service education (Doyle, 1990).

The knowledge produced during the period of curriculum reform in the 1960s came in the form of curriculum packages, while the process–product research on teaching in the 1970s produced a set of imperatives for teaching that were expected to increase student achievement. The knowledge produced within these two research areas was very different in some respects, but very similar in others. The main similarity was the view proponents held about the implementation of the knowledge produced. They assumed that the knowledge produced by outside experts would be implemented by teachers. In effect, teachers were seen as conduits through which ideas developed outside the classroom would be put into effect inside the classroom. However, such knowledge about curriculum and about teaching, often so painstakingly put together by outsiders, frequently bore little relevance to the day-to-day work and problems faced by teachers. According to Goodlad (1984) the curriculum-reform movement became a solution in search of a problem. A deficit model lay behind these notions: teachers were lacking something in their practice that needed to be fixed. Despite what has now come to be seen as the major failure of the producer-user concept of knowledge in education, it still underpins much of the reform agenda for our schools. In a report produced in the United States in 1983 *A Nation at Risk* which offered a template for improving schools, teachers were still regarded as instruments of school policy not participants.

The social science community increasingly questions this positivist approach to educational research and its technical application to practice (Eisner, 1983; Phillips, 1983; Smith, 1983). Such questioning has paralleled a re-examination of research paradigms in the scientific community (Cleminson, 1990). Many writers doubt that the search for context-free generalizations is suitable for research that focuses on social systems, or that such generalizations are even attainable. Social interactions constructed by individuals with multiple intentions become very complex. Even statistically significant findings from large, randomly-selected samples cannot be applied directly to specific individuals in particular situations (Donmoyer, 1990). Research that focuses on central tendencies reduces complexity, masks contradictions, and downplays human agency (Zeichner and Gore, 1990). Many critics argue that a more interpretive approach to research in the social sciences is needed.

In the last few years we have seen a changing view of what constitutes knowledge and how knowledge is used by those in schools. Based on an interpretive paradigm, this research focuses on the interpersonal and social aspects of human life from the point of view of the participant rather than the observer. Erickson (1986) suggests that interpretive research leads to

> ... questions of a fundamentally different sort from those posed by standard research on teaching. Rather than ask which behaviors by teachers are positively correlated with student gains on test achievement, the interpretive researcher asks 'What are the conditions of meaning that students and teachers create together, as some students appear to learn and others don't?' (Erickson, 1986, p. 127)

When viewed from this perspective, knowledge is no longer seen as non-problematic, external, and independent of the knower, or reducible to lawlike statements about teaching strategies. The interpretive conception defines knowledge as being actively constructed within the unstable, uncertain, conflict-filled world of practice. The resulting knowledge is an idiosyncratic, situated knowledge, made powerful by the contexts in which it is acquired and used.

As a result, many different traditions and ways of thinking about knowledge have developed. These include practical knowledge (Elbaz, 1983), pedagogical content knowledge (e.g., Ball, 1988; Shulman, 1987), knowledge as craft (Grimmett and MacKinnon, 1992), personal practical knowledge (Connelly and Clandinin, 1990), and knowing-in-action (Schön, 1983). Others such as Lindblom and Cohen (1979) use the term 'ordinary knowledge', which stems from common sense or thoughtful speculation and analysis. We use Fenstermacher's (1994) term 'personal and practical knowledge' to subsume these multiple constructions of personally situated knowledge. This view of knowledge brings the producer and the user (in the traditional use of those terms) together. The person developing the knowledge is now also the one who makes use of it.

At present the educational research community appears to be polarized between the two views of knowledge just outlined. In many faculties of education, teacher preparation and in-service continue as though truths derived from formal knowledge are the only reliable sources of knowledge about teaching. The logical extension of this view is that school reform will come as teachers become clearer on the ideas generated by outside experts. For these people, the traditional view of knowledge utilization lives on. However, others hold a different view of knowledge, which, as von Glasersfeld (1985) puts it:

> ... differs from the old one in that it deliberately discards the notion that knowledge could or should be a representation of an observer-independent world-in-itself and replaces it with the demand that the conceptual constructs we call knowledge be viable in the experiential world of the knowing subject. (von Glasersfeld, 1985, p. 122)

Taking an exclusive view of either perspective on knowledge limits our understanding of how teachers actually use knowledge. A total reliance on personal and practical knowledge ignores the richness of ideas generated by research which has taken an outsider's perspective. Furthermore, Carter (1993) cautions us about uncritically accepting the personal and practical knowledge that is conveyed in narrative. She writes, '... an extreme view of teachers' voice endows their stories with an authenticity that is simply unwarranted' (p. 8). Furthermore, she states that this extreme view ultimately can lead to the total rejection of all generalizations about teaching as distortions of teachers 'real' stories. On the other hand, little evidence exists to suggest that formal knowledge generated by outsiders can or will be applied readily by teachers. The road to better schools may well rest on our understanding of how best to combine decades of formal knowledge with the personal and practical knowledge that teachers develop themselves. Because teachers have regular access to formal knowledge, through courses and workshops, which interacts with their personal knowledge and practice, it becomes difficult to determine which form of knowledge is most influential in driving subsequent change.

This has important implications for how we view teachers' professional knowledge. Professional knowledge, we contend, is that combination of formal and personal practical knowledge on which teachers base their practice. Such knowledge is also grounded in teachers' beliefs about what constitutes good teaching. Understanding what makes the learning of specific topics easy or difficult, knowing the misconceptions pupils bring with them to the learning of topics, and finding the most useful ways of representing content are among those things that the professional teacher knows better than anyone else in regard to the content they teach (Shulman, 1986). However, these beliefs are not fixed or invariant among teachers because what counts as good teaching will vary among teachers and so too, therefore, will what counts as professional knowledge.

In the section that follows, we examine a case study of a single school to illustrate how a group of teachers drew on both traditions to support their change effort and examine what this implies for our understanding of teacher professional knowledge.

Knowledge Use at Lakeview Elementary[3]: Case Study

A new principal and several new staff members arrived at Lakeview School in the Fall of 1985; their arrival saw the beginning of the change that was to be the subject of this case study. The perceptions they brought with them provided fertile ground for the school-improvement project that was to develop.

The curriculum change that occurred at Lakeview Elementary involved the staff adopting a series of innovations which included among others reading across the curriculum, whole language, and theme days.[4] For each of the first three years the staff selected and implemented a different set of innovations for the school. These selections appeared to be based on the staff's evolving vision for teaching and improving their school.

This change must be seen in the context of the school prior to the arrival of the new staff. Both parents and teachers described the situation at the school as a 'little shop of horrors'. Teachers kept their distance from each other and from the principal. Those parents that were interviewed indicated that they would send their children elsewhere had they a choice. Language arts were taught using basal readers. Teachers were expected to follow the reading programme that had been selected, and specifically set out, by the principal. This approach to curriculum implementation was based upon a producer–user model of knowledge utilization.

It became apparent to us very early that knowledge and information use played key roles in the thinking of the teachers and the principal at Lakeview. The staff drew on, and used, traditional knowledge in ways that might not have been predicted from a reading of the literature. The knowledge that came into the school, in whatever form, provided an agenda for an ongoing collaborative effort that characterized the change at Lakeview. The chairperson for that collaboration was often the principal, but not always. The manner in which the teachers and principal used knowledge did not completely support either traditional notions of knowledge transfer and utilization, nor the more recent notions of personal and practical knowledge. In some instances knowledge was used in fairly direct ways; on other occasions its use came in ways that one might not expect.

The changes at Lakeview occurred within an information-rich environment where knowledge came in a variety of forms. Reading became an important source of information as the principal started a practice that was to encourage academic reading by the staff. One teacher describes how she saw the practice introduced within the context of discussing language arts:

> That first year, when we talked about language arts Charlie started getting references for us. He started doing things like photocopying articles that related to our topic. They would arrive in our boxes so people who were interested could read them and discuss them at our next meeting.

But reading provided only one source of information. Other sources came through the numerous workshops at the district and school level that became an ongoing part of the school activity during the first three years. Many of these workshops involved the much maligned, 'one-shot' efforts. Another source of knowledge and information came through the connections that a significant number of staff maintained with people within and outside the district. For example, the principal sought to maintain contact with the universities whenever he could, and teachers regularly gained information from university courses. The principal and teachers visited other schools where teachers were working to change their practice. And, the teachers began to set up networks with individuals outside the school that provided additional sources of ideas.

One of the factors that drove the innovation at Lakeview was the staff's commitment to knowledge and the use they made of it. In this setting, knowledge served several purposes. It legitimized the change process; it provided a catalyst for discussion of issues and support for collaboration with peers; and it provided a vision for better teaching.

Legitimization of Change

One of the books frequently mentioned as important by staff was Illich's (1971) *Deschooling Society*. During a meeting with teachers, we asked what a book of this nature could do for teachers engaged in changing their language arts programme. The answer suggested that Illich's book had legitimized their challenge of the system. In short, teachers who had concerns about the system now saw their concerns echoed in print, and therefore, felt legitimized and motivated to continue steps to change the system in which they were working. One teacher identified this quotation from Illich's book:

> Schools are designed on the assumption that there is a secret to everything in life; that the quality of life depends on knowing the secret; that secrets

can be known only in orderly successions; and that only teachers can properly reveal those secrets. (Illich, 1971)

In response to this quotation she made this comment:

Writing allows teachers as facilitators to guide students toward finding and sharing their own secrets to allow them to become confident, autonomous learners and teachers. Teachers too need to be learners. We need to listen and observe carefully as students discover and respond to, and celebrate, their learning. They have lots to teach us.

The reading of Schön's (1983) *The Reflective Practitioner* produced a similar type of legitimization. In it the teachers saw 'permission' to reflect and discuss their experience.

Outsider Knowledge as a Catalyst and Support for Collaboration

In a talk given to a group of primary (elementary) teachers in Britain, David Hawkins used the title *I, Thou, It* to describe the essentials of a useful and product-ive relationship (Hawkins, 1967). Drawing on philosophical traditions, he argued that discussions between people do not amount to much unless they deal with issues outside and beyond the participants. He further asserted that we cannot gain competence and knowledge except through communication with others. 'Without a *Thou*, there is no *I* evolving. Without an *It* there is no content for the context. . . .' (p. 47). Hawkins made this argument with regards to science teaching where the teacher and the pupil comprise the *I* and the *Thou*, respectively. But he contended that teaching of science must include the introduction of materials that are the content that represents the *It* in the *I–Thou–It* relationship.

Hawkins' reference to pupils, teachers, and materials has currency for thinking about the way knowledge became a part of the ongoing relationship and commun-ication between teachers at Lakeview. The collaboration that developed produced the *I–Thou* relationship. While communication and interaction were essential to the change, reading and workshop activity greatly enhanced the substance and content of that communication. The knowledge from these activities produced the *It* in this three-way relationship. This information provided a means by which teachers and principal could move beyond themselves to explore other areas. It produced frames within which they could think about and re-evaluate their practice.

The processing and implementing of information and new knowledge were not necessarily straightforward; teachers struggled to understand and deal with new ideas and techniques. One teacher describes her initial confusion like this:

[A workshop leader] spoke to us, in terms of some of the concepts . . . I didn't really have a background or a real idea of where she was coming from at the time. So when she left I was sort of still in a state of confusion. And at that point she spoke of a one-year unit, a one-year theme, and take off from that into other [ones]. And, she was talking about the whole unit going from a January to June or something. I can't recall exactly when. Anyway, it was at that point that I was thinking, you know, 'this is just ridiculous'. I mean, how can you do that with that group of kids with one general topic area?

This quotation characterizes the struggle that typically occurred as teachers were presented with new information. This teacher initially dismissed the information introduced by the experts, but after considerable discussion with peers, eventually accepted and worked with the information presented. This workshop and others led to discussion, reflection and interaction as teachers struggled to construct an understanding of the new ideas. In this setting all incoming information provided the basis for discourse. The adaptation of new ideas occurred and developed partly through dialogue and partly through trial and error, but often from some sense of struggle.

Outsider Knowledge as a Source of New Ideas

Throughout the change process it appeared to be important for teachers to find ideas that would improve their teaching. The reading and workshops in which they participated served the important function of providing information they could use in their classrooms. In some cases it was the workshop that stimulated teachers to revise their practice. In another case it was a workshop leader's demonstration that a teacher applied directly. One teacher described how reading and interaction with colleagues affected her work in the school in this way:

> . . . I think [change] mostly [came] through my own professional reading and from observing different things that are happening. I have to use Barb [another teacher] as my counterpart here, because I learned a lot from her. But I would say mostly, I have always been interested in actively pursuing new ideas and new strategies and continually doing a lot of professional reading. And so I would always be changing or modifying whatever I was doing, trying to find a better way. I don't think that I am ever perfect and there is certainly a lot more room for improvement.

The valuable combination of reading and contact with other teachers is apparent in this teacher's comments. And, while the interviews indicated that not all teachers were equally enthusiastic about reading, this seemed unimportant because of the intense interaction that continually took place on staff; what one teacher read would generally reach the others through talk.

The findings from this case appear to us discrepant from what one might be led to believe from a reading of literature produced by those who have down-played and indeed criticized the role of traditional forms of knowledge in a school. The traditional forms of knowledge that these teachers drew upon were not imposed upon them. Nor did they use such knowledge and information as perfect templates for their own practice. Rather, they created a context in which they transformed traditional forms of knowledge into something they could either use or simply think about. Our findings in this respect relate to the work of Brown, Collins and Duguid (1989) who use the term 'situated cognition' to argue that when knowledge is abstracted from situations in which it is learned and used, learning of that knowledge is limited. They suggest people learn best when their knowledge develops in authentic situations which they describe as 'ordinary practices of the culture'. The forms of traditional knowledge that we saw teachers learn from at Lakeview were anything but 'ordinary practices of the culture'. In fact, they were often discrepant with the existing culture. This staff through discussion, trial, and more discussion transformed outsiders' knowledge into their new cultural practices.

Creating a Vision for Better Teaching

Social scientists see progress taking place when people demonstrate an ongoing process of seeking to attain a vision that lies beyond their current practice. The figure below illustrates what this might entail. This representation conceptualizes the improvement of teaching in terms of moving from the reality of teaching towards the ideal.

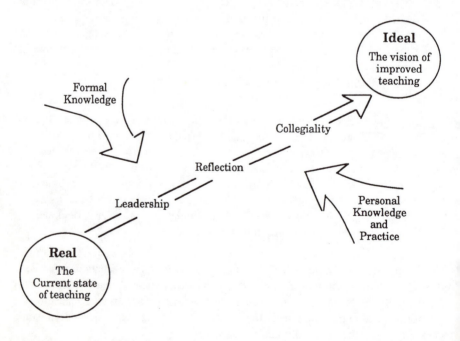

Figure 10.1: Improving teaching

For this process an individual requires some vision of good teaching (the ideal), and some understanding of one's current state of teaching (the real). Progress occurs as one moves from the real towards the ideal.

The Lakeview experience showed that outside input, often in the form of traditional forms of knowledge, helped the teachers and principal to contemplate, and in time develop, such a vision of the ideal for their teaching in language arts. For example, outsiders' knowledge helped the teachers at Lakeview develop a concept of the writing process and whole language which helped them move away from basal readers during the first year. Discussions with the principal indicated that this vision for the teaching of language arts through whole language was nested within a broader vision of what the school could do for children. He spoke about the broad aim of the innovation that was occurring in the school:

> Our [the staff's] concerns have to do with the relationship between socialization and academic learning and the development of individual attitudes and social attitudes.

He talked often about the value of treating people, both teachers and students, as individuals. This he believed should be reflected in one's teaching. The staff were aware of his notions about schooling and engaged in discussions about that vision.

This vision was not static; it changed in the second year as the staff's curriculum implementation focused on theme days in which subjects were integrated throughout the school. Thus, the 'ideal' in the figure should be viewed as a moving target for as one approaches the 'ideal' through one's practice it evolves into something else.

The ideas of leadership, collegiality, and reflection have been added to the figure to illustrate conditions that support the shift of a school staff from the real to the ideal. Self-reflection, is seen as a necessary, but not a sufficient condition to provide a vision of what teaching could be (the ideal). Reflecting upon one's own practice can usually provide a perspective on current practice (the real). The figure also incorporates the concepts of formal knowledge and personal knowledge and practice previously discussed.[5]

Thus, knowledge of different kinds played different roles in helping teachers to bring about a change at Lakeview. The knowledge that came through reading and the workshop activity served as a catalyst, offered a source of new ideas, and provided fuel for a vision of better teaching for the staff. Print materials that presented current practice of schools in a critical light appeared to give the principal and staff permission to challenge the work of the school and change it. It was difficult to distinguish between the influence of formal knowledge and personal and practical knowledge in promoting the change, as over time they blended together. The information-rich environment that we found at Lakeview worked to the advantage of the staff only because certain conditions prevailed. These we discuss below.

Conditions for Change

We bring this chapter to a conclusion by describing three conditions we believe necessary if knowledge is to be used in effective ways by teachers. We present these conditions in the form of three propositional statements. They are derived from our analysis of the Lakeview case study in the light of recent literature.

Teaching Needs to Be Seen as Problematic

This position assumes that most aspects of teaching are problematic in the sense of being open to debate, criticism, and questioning. Curriculum is regarded as providing general guidance for teaching but is limited in its ability to inform the specific context in which any individual teacher finds himself or herself. This stance gives individuals 'permission' to question, challenge, and seek alternative approaches to deal with the task of teaching more effectively. Research findings and policy statements are regarded as starting points for discussion, not propositions to implement. From this perspective, the complexity and the contextually bound nature of a teacher's work does not lend itself readily to the notion of 'fidelity' in which ideas generated in one setting can be directly transferred to another.

This view stands in contrast to the position that many aspects of teaching, such as curriculum content and the way it should be taught, are fixed or given. From this point of view knowledge on teaching presented in the form of papers and workshops may be regarded as sacrosanct suggesting that teachers accept the ideas and wisdom generated by educational researchers and policy-makers.

To illustrate our first proposition, we return to the situation of the staff at Lakeview in the Fall of 1985. A basal reading programme was in place in the school when the new principal and teachers arrived. The programme could have been accepted, adopted, and followed quite routinely as had been done in previous years. However, the new staff elected to question this programme and to seek something that could be used in its place that would, in their view, teach reading better. They did not undertake this step lightly. They engaged in a thoughtful examination of this particular approach to reading to determine if it was appropriate for their students. Having reasoned that it was not, they began to look for alternatives. They searched for, and found, these alternatives in the writing process and whole-language approach. As this new teaching approach became part of their regular practice, it too came to be questioned.

The questioning of this new approach began when the staff invited an expert to examine their changed approach to the writing process and provide some feedback about what they were doing.[6] The writing expert presented what she believed was a balanced critique according to the criteria she posed for the writing process. She pointed out, for example, that she saw a great deal of story writing but not much writing in other subject areas. However, the staff did not respond positively to her comments at first, because they perceived themselves to be 'writing across the curriculum'. Their concerns about her report extended beyond the substance of her review of the writing process. An outside critique was something new to them, and criticism was difficult to take. In time however, they did acknowledge the value in her report and attempted to accommodate her suggestions through discussion and changes in their practice. We cite this incident to illustrate that the staff regarded the curriculum and, indeed, their own evolving practice as problematic which motivated them continually to look for alternatives.

The proposition that teaching needs to be seen as problematic has application beyond classroom practice. This same critical lens can, and indeed should, be used to examine the literature on teaching and school change, as well as the policies and pronouncements that come from policy makers. The literature on teaching and school change as well as policy pronouncements usually have little to say in propositional terms about what teachers should do to improve their practice. However, the Lakeview situation shows that when a critical stance is taken in viewing research and policy, it provides a basis for discussion, debate, and on occasion, inspiration. In addition, such research and policies have value in creating expectations for what schools can be, thereby providing visions for better teaching practices.

Change Efforts Need to Focus on the Substance of Teaching

The work of teachers revolves around the teaching of school subjects such as mathematics, science, and language arts. Yet the literature on school change and the cultures of teaching seldom deal with the substance of teaching. The work of Shulman (1986; 1987) has underlined the critical role of content in the work of teachers. He argues that the basis for reform lies in a better understanding of the knowledge base of teaching. He calls the absence of subject matter in research on teaching the 'missing paradigm'. His comments apply equally well to research on school effectiveness. He had this to say:

> Policy makers read the research on teaching literature and find it replete with references to direct instruction, time on task, wait time, ordered turns, lower-order questions, and the like. They find little or no reference to subject matter, so the resulting standards or mandates lack any reference to content dimensions of teaching. Similarly, even in the research community, the importance of content has been forgotten. (Shulman, 1986, p. 6)

Other researchers have drawn our attention to the importance of the subjects taught in schools. Stodolsky (1988) contends that, 'with respect to classroom activity, the subject matters' (p. 1). From a detailed examination of elementary social studies and mathematics lessons she drew the conclusion that teachers arrange instruction in different ways depending on the subject they are teaching. We have argued that the subject matter itself may well determine the way one thinks about teaching and learning (Mayer-Smith, Moon and Wideen, 1994; Wideen, 1994).

The case study described in this chapter illustrates the need for reformers and researchers to consider carefully what they believe should and can be changed. We argue that teachers are seldom interested in generic issues of school change or school climate (unless that climate becomes unbearable). What motivates them is the content they teach, the day-to-day contact with children concerning mathematics, science, and language arts. The teachers at Lakeview began their change by focusing on an aspect of their work that was very important to them and central to their practice — the teaching of language arts. Although their aspirations moved beyond that, in the early stages, it was their own instructional experiences that provided the focal point. The literature on school change has often ignored this issue of ownership and personal practice, addressing issues removed from class-room events and the substance of teaching (such as school climate, school organization, and an array of other general topics that hold limited interest for those working in schools). We posit that Lakeview was a case of successful change because the teachers had a central role in deciding both what needed to be changed and how that change should occur.

What are the implications of this proposition for knowledge and its use in the context of school change? First, it indicates that if reformers expect significant school change to occur in ways that will improve teaching and learning, they will need to focus on content and curriculum issues that are central to the concerns of teachers. Second, it implies something about the type of knowledge that teachers will value and use during the early stages of change. For the teacher considering a change in practice, information about an alternative reading programme may well be more useful and acceptable than information about creating a learning community within the school. Charismatic outsiders telling such teachers what they need to know and how to change their practice will be less valued. Teachers welcome access to such people and the knowledge they can provide at specific and critical times when they are ready to make changes, only, however, when the control of change is situated with the teachers and the principal not with the policy makers and the outside 'experts'.

Group Norms Must Provide and Support a Climate for Change

This proposition that emerges from the Lakeview experience points to the group setting as a powerful vehicle for processing knowledge and bringing about change. Fullan and Hargreaves (1996) have argued that groups in themselves are neither good nor bad; the value of the group comes from the norms, beliefs, and expectations they hold. We further argue that group norms, beliefs, and expectations provide the capacity for change. These must, however, be situated in the instructional issues and teaching practices that those both inside and outside the group see as important.

Undertaking change is a risky business. Anyone who has tried something new, whether it is a golf swing, a new skiing technique, or a new laboratory procedure, knows that for the first short while (and sometimes for the first long while), one's performance often gets worse. A group that supports the need for change often accepts that the outcomes of innovations may be unpredictable. Such collaboration provides a safe environment in which the inevitable mistakes that occur are accepted, and thus establishes a climate in which risk taking and growth are encouraged. The group setting at Lakeview provided the requisite supportive structure in which newly forming skills could be honed and anxiety about failure could be alleviated.

Conclusion

In this chapter we have proposed that both formal, and personal practical knowledge can inform the work of teachers and provide a basis for change. Both are legitimate components of the professional knowledge of teachers. It follows that both must become part of the school agenda for teacher professionalism, teacher development and educational change. Indeed such was the case at Lakeview. The teachers were immersed in knowledge and information of all kinds. Formal knowledge was introduced by the principal and teachers who routinely circulated papers for reading and discussion. Individual, personal, and practical knowledge was shared and extended through group discourse. This individual and group knowledge, and the resulting socially constructed wisdom about teaching, then became public knowledge as the teachers from Lakeview made presentations in other schools.

The use teachers make of knowledge in their thinking, particularly with respect to changing their practice, is more a function of their own contextual imperatives than it is a function of the knowledge itself. As seen at Lakeview Elementary, very traditional forms of knowledge and very traditional forms of delivery can still be highly productive in terms of changing school practice. This case study showed that if school change is to occur, teachers must process and adapt such formal knowledge and make it part of their own personal and practical understanding of what it means to teach and to change teaching. What matters much less than whether formal knowledge is good knowledge or clear knowledge, is how well the context and culture of teaching may support a process of inquiry and discussion through which the knowledge can be made relevant to the 'place' where it can be used.

Personal and practical knowledge has emerged for many as a new foundation for school reform. In acknowledging the value of these formerly unrecognized and unappreciated kinds of knowledge however, we must not lose sight of the value of more traditional forms. To accept this new perspective uncritically will simply replace one dogma with another, at a time when our understanding of how teachers use knowledge to change their practice is still developing. As Elbaz (1991) noted, teachers are not privileged authors with direct access to the truth. Teachers' voices and the knowledge they express are not the only voices or even always the most authoritative ones. As this case study has shown, educational change remains a complex and unpredictable business which demands both the knowledge and expertise that outsiders can bring, as well as the construction of understandings by those who are close to the action and who best understand the context. Sophisticated approaches to educational change call for more sophisticated understandings of teachers' professional knowledge. Any single paradigm is unlikely to capture the sophistication and complexity that productive change efforts will require. School reform is too difficult and too important to rest within a single paradigm.

Notes

1 The research leading to this chapter was supported by grants No. 410–84–1422 and 410–92–1665 from the Social Sciences and Humanities Research Council.
2 The concept of knowledge utilization is far too complex to be unpacked in this section. What follows are some of the more salient issues surrounding the concept and how it has been used by teachers in their thinking. For a more extensive treatment the reader should consult the reviews by Love, 1985; Lindbloom and Cohen, 1979; Glasser, 1976 and Shulman, 1986, 1987.
3 For a more detailed account of this case study see Wideen (1994).
4 In this chapter we use the term 'change' to refer to the global, summative developments in the school; the term 'innovation' refers to the specific practices that the staff implemented which were new to them. The innovations taken together comprised the change.
5 We recognize that any number of other conditions and concepts could be added to this figure as well.
6 This suggestion was made to the staff by one of the authors of this chapter.

References

BALL, D.L. (1988) 'Prospective teachers' understanding of mathematics: What they do bring with them to teacher education', Paper presented at the meeting of the American Educational Research Association, New Orleans, LA.
BROWN, J., COLLINS, A. and DUGUID, P. (1989) 'Situated cognition and the culture of learning', *Educational Researcher*, **18**, 1, pp. 32–42.
BURDEN, P. (1990) 'Teacher development', in HOUSTON, W.R. (Ed) *Handbook of Research on Teacher Education*, New York, Macmillan, pp. 311–28.
CARTER, K. (1993) 'The place of story in the study of teaching and teacher education', *Educational Researcher*, **22**, 1, pp. 5–12, 18.
CLEMINSON, A. (1990) 'Establishing an epistemological base for science teaching in light of contemporary notions of the nature of science and how children learn science', *Journal of Research in Science Teaching*, **27**, 5, pp. 429–45.
COCHRAN-SMITH, M. and LYTLE, S. (1990) 'Research on teaching and teacher research: The issues that divide', *Educational Researcher*, **19**, 2, pp. 2–11.
CONNELLY, F.M. and CLANDININ, D.J. (1990) 'Stories of experience and narrative inquiry', *Educational Researcher*, **19**, 5, pp. 2–4.
DONMOYER, R. (1990) 'Generalizibility and the single-case study', in EISNER, E.W. and PESHKIN, A. (Eds) *Qualitative Inquiry in Education*, New York, Teachers College Press, pp. 175–200.
DOYLE, W. (1990) 'Themes in teacher education research', in HOUSTON, W.R. (Ed) *Handbook of Research on Teacher Education*, New York, Macmillan, pp. 3–24.
EISNER, E.W. (1983) 'Anastasia might be still alive, but the monarchy is dead', *Educational Researcher*, **12**, 5, pp. 13–14, 23–4.
ELBAZ, F. (1983) *Teacher Thinking: A Study of Practical Knowledge*, London, Croom Helm.
ELBAZ, F. (1991) 'Research on teachers' knowledge: The evolution of a discourse', *Journal of Curriculum Studies*, **23**, pp. 1–19.

ERICKSON, F. (1986) 'Qualitative methods in research on teaching', in WHITTROCK, M. (Ed) *Handbook of Research on Teaching*, 3rd ed., New York, Macmillan, pp. 119–61.

FENSTERMACHER, G.D. (1994) 'The knower and the known: The nature of knowledge in research on teaching', in DARLING-HAMMOND, L. (Ed) *Review of Research in Education*, **20**, pp. 3–56.

FULLAN, M. (1991) *The New Meaning of Educational Change*, Toronto, Ontario, OISE Press.

FULLAN, M. and HARGREAVES, A. (1996) *What's Worth Fighting For in Your School*, Second Edition, Toronto, Ontario, Ontario Public School Teachers' Federation, New York, Teachers College Press, Milton Keynes, Open University Press.

FULLAR, F.F. and BROWN, O.H. (1975) 'Becoming a teacher', in RYAN, K. (Ed) *Teacher Education* (74th Yearbook of the National Society for the Study of Education, Pt. II), Chicago, University of Chicago Press, pp. 25–52.

GLASSER, E.M. (1976) *Putting Knowledge to Use: A Distillation of the Literature Regarding Knowledge Transfer and Change*, Los Angeles, CA, Human Interaction Research Institute.

GOODLAD, J.I. (1984) *A Place Called School: Prospects for the Future*, New York, McGraw-Hill.

GOODLAD, J., VON STEOPHASIUS, R. and KLEIN, M. (1974) *Looking Behind the Classroom Door*, Worthington, ID, Charles A. Jones Publishing Co.

GRIMMETT, P.P. and MACKINNON, A.M. (1992) 'Craft knowledge and the education of teachers', *Review of Research in Education*, **18**, pp. 385–456.

HARGREAVES, A. and DAWE, R. (1990) 'Paths of professional development: Contrived collegiality or collaborative culture and the case of peer coaching', *Teaching and Teacher Education*, **4**.

HAVELOCK, R.G. (1969) *Planning for Innovation through Dissemination and Utilization of Knowledge*, Ann Arbor, MI, Center for Research on Utilization of Scientific Knowledge, University of Michigan.

HAWKINS, D. (1967) 'I, thou, and it', A presentation made to the primary teachers residential group in Loughborough, Leicestershire, England.

HOPKINS, D. and WIDEEN, M. (1984) *Alternative Perspectives on School Improvement*, London, New York and Philadelphia, Falmer Press.

HOUSE, E. (1981) *The Politics of Educational Innovation*, Berkeley, CA, McCutchan.

ILLICH, I.D. (1971) *Deschooling Society*, New York, Harper and Row.

LIEBERMAN, A. (1984) (Ed) *Rethinking School Improvement*, New York, Teachers College Press.

LINDBLOM, C.E. and COHEN, D.K. (1979) *Usable Knowledge: Social Science and Social Problem Solving*, New Haven, CT, Yale University Press.

LOUIS, D. (1981) 'External agents and knowledge utilization: Dimensions for analysis and action', in LEHMAN, R. and KANE, M. (Eds) *Improving Schools: Using What We Know*, Beverly Hills, CA, Sage.

LOVE, J.M. (1985) 'Knowledge transfer and utilization in education', in GORDON, E.W. (Ed) *Review of Research in Education*, Washington, DC, American Educational Research Association.

MACMILLAN, C.J.B. and GARRISON, J.W. (1984) 'Using the "new philosophy of science" in criticizing current research traditions in education', *Educational Researcher*, **13**, 10, pp. 15–21.

MAYER-SMITH, J.A., MOON, B.J. and WIDEEN, M.F. (1994) 'Learning to teach within the two cultures of the humanities and sciences', Paper presented at the annual meeting of the National Association for Research in Science Teaching, New Orleans, LA, April.

MILES, M. and HUBERMAN, A.M. (1984) *Qualitative Methods: A Source Book of Method*, Los Angeles, Sage Publications.

PHILLIPS, D.C. (1983) 'After the wake: Postpositivistic educational thought', *Educational Researcher*, **12**, 5, pp. 4–12.

Marvin F. Wideen, Jolie A. Mayer-Smith and Barbara J. Moon

SCHÖN, D. (1983) *The Reflective Practitioner*, New York, Basic Books.

SHULMAN, L. (1986) 'Those who understand: Knowledge growth in teaching', *Educational Researcher*, **15**, 7, pp. 4–14.

SHULMAN, L. (1987) 'Knowledge and teaching: Foundations of the new reform', *Harvard Educational Review*, **57**, pp. 1–22.

SMITH, J.K. (1983) 'Quantitative versus qualitative research: An attempt to clarify the issue', *Educational Researcher*, **12**, 3, pp. 6–13.

SOLTIS, J.F. (1984) 'On the nature of educational research', *Educational Researcher*, **13**, 10, pp. 5–10.

STENHOUSE, L. (1984) 'Artistry ad teaching: The teacher as focus of research and development', in HOPKINS, D. and WIDEEN, M. *Alternative Perspectives on School Improvement*, London, Falmer Press.

STODOLSKY, S.S. (1988) *The Subject Matters: Classroom Activity in Math and Social Studies*, Chicago, University of Chicago Press.

TOM, A.R. and VALLI, L. (1990) 'Professional knowledge for teachers', in HOUSTON, W.R. (Ed) *Handbook of Research on Teacher Education*, New York, Macmillan, pp. 373–92.

VON GLASERSFELD, E. (1985) 'Constructivism', in *The International Encyclopedia of Education*, Oxford, Pergamon Press.

WIDEEN, M. (1994) *The Struggle for Change: A Case Study of One School*, London, Falmer Press.

ZEICHNER, K.M. and GORE, J.M. (1990) 'Teacher socialization', in HOUSTON, W.R. (Ed) *Handbook of Research on Teacher Education*, New York, Macmillan, pp. 329–48.

Chapter 11

Development and Disenchantment in the Professional Lives of Headteachers

Christopher Day and Aysen Bakioğlu

Research Context

Despite extensive literature searches there appears to be little research which is concerned specifically with secondary-school headteachers' development.[1] Sociological studies have been carried out in other occupational groups (Hall and Schneider, 1972; Berlew and Hall, 1966; Bray, Campbell and Grant, 1974), and life history research in the field of education focuses on the progress of teachers (Sikes *et al.*, 1985; Ball and Goodson, 1985; Elbaz, 1983; Clandinin, 1985; Huberman, 1988, 1993). There are a few studies which focus on the first years of headteachers in their position. Leithwood (1992) pointed to the socialization of newly appointed principals in Canada; Weindling and Earley (1987) recommended that new headteachers need to receive special consideration and support from their peers; and Daresh's (1987) study indicated that the first year of headteachers is typically full of frustration and anxiety. In a longitudinal study of twelve high-school principals, Parkay *et al.* (1992) speculated that principals' expectations about school change become more realistic as their experience increases. However, there are few studies which investigate headteachers' long-term professional development, and the effects of this on their school leadership and management. Yet, arguably, the professional development of headteachers/principals as leaders with responsibility for managing the survival, maintenance, vision and culture of schools is a crucial factor in their successful school development. Within this, opportunities for teacher development, too, will to some extent be dependent upon the quality support of their headteachers. In a seminal research study on the lives of teachers, Huberman identified four necessary conditions leading to professional satisfaction during the lives of teachers:

- an enduring commitment to the profession after being appointed with tenure;
- 'manageable' classes, and where one can maintain good relations with pupils;
- good relationships with colleagues; and
- a balance between school and home life/personal interest.

(Huberman, 1993, p. 249)

In planning for support of headteachers' professional development it is important to ask questions about the degree to which organizational climate, psychological, social and personal histories affect attitude, expectation and behaviour — in short to conceptualize headteachership itself as a developmental process in which the maintenance of commitment, efficacy and motivation is of paramount importance.

It appears, from the limited available literature (Weindling and Earley, 1987) that the level of perceived difficulties differs between newly appointed and more experienced headteachers. In a study of junior schools in England, for example, Mortimore *et al.* (1988) found that new headteachers (less than two years in post) are 'generally associated with less effective schools' and suggests the provision of ongoing support for heads to equip them to meet the needs of a changing society (Mortimore *et al.*, 1988, p. 276). The research thus began by focusing upon headteachers' perceived difficulties, first through questionnaire, and then extensive interviewing. A number of possible hypotheses were linked with the biographic variables during the design of the questionnaire. There appeared to be a correlation between headteachers who perceive they have difficulties and their age, gender, qualifications, length of time in post and size of their school.[2]

Analysis of questionnaire responses revealed that these factors in themselves provided an incomplete, oversimplified and possibly inaccurate map of headteachers' development and that further qualitative work would be necessary in order to understand the interplay between them. It was clear that there are multiple pathways and trajectories through different phases of headteachers' lives, and since 'experience' and 'difficulties' were the main variables which influenced the development and perceived effectiveness of headteachers it was decided to investigate these further.[3] The emerging research questions were:

- What are the detailed difficulties which are experienced by headteachers at different times in their careers?
- If there are significant relationships between perceived difficulties and variables, do headteachers experience identifiable developmental phases during the time they are in post?
- If so, what kind of distinctive characteristics do phases have?
- Is there a most effective phase in headteachers' careers?
- How does each phase influence the development of headteachers' professional lives and their role effectiveness?

The qualitative research centred on investigating headteachers' perceptions of development through interview. In a sense, each headteacher was asked to tell his or her 'story'. The basic assumption derived from the questionnaire results was that headteachers did have difficulties with respect to psychological, social, historical and internal and external environment issues during different phases of their careers. Their stories highlighted, for example, the kinds of difficulties they experienced whilst achieving each new role; how they managed their roles and constraints, and how they were affected by an environment which was subject to accelerating and externally initiated change. Thus, the influences of the Education Act and Teachers' Industrial Action in England of the last decade were inevitably high on the headteachers' agendas during interviews.

Equal emphasis was given to each phase of headteachers' development in this research in order to avoid the overemphasis of 'career stage' theories on the early work years which has been criticized by Osipow (1973); and Hall (1976). Within each phase were a number of variables which related to age, attitude, environment and experience. Headteachers' career planning in the short- and long-term, the effects of personal life on work, such as having children of the same age as the students, losing a member of the family, having a supportive partner, having to look after a sick or disabled elderly relative, were also investigated. Details of their pre-headship post work were also investigated to discover to what extent these related to preparation for headship. For example, it was found that difficulties at the beginning of headship were linked to the limitations of work and responsibilities experienced during the deputy headship period.[4]

Methods

The opinions of 305 headteachers in the Midland Region of England were elicited by questionnaire. In addition documents and materials on schools' management plans, school prospectuses, and other documentations were reviewed. 196 questionnaire responses were received, a response rate of 64.2 per cent. After analysing these, interviews were conducted with an opportunity sample of 34 of these headteachers. Further follow-up interviews were conducted with five of these. Questionnaire and interview-survey methods were used in the research to ensure 'methodological triangulation'. The limitations of each method were offset by combining these methods through triangulation of the data (Bromley, 1986).

In this study, therefore, the term 'phase' was preferred to 'stage'. Stage implies distinct periods of time that differ qualitatively from both the preceding and succeeding stages whereas a phase may include behaviour across several domains (Sheull, 1990). Phases are recurrent in that individuals can pass through the various phases in and between each of many different content domains. Karmiloff-Smith (1984) summarized the difference: 'The phase concept is focused on the underlying similarity of process, whereas the stage concept usually refers to similarity of structure.'

The Four Phases

The questionnaire and interview data revealed that headteachers experienced different developmental phases from taking up the post to their retirement, and that these had distinguishable characteristics. Most of the longest serving headteachers' stories revealed that they had experienced four different phases which could be classified as 'initiation', 'development', 'autonomy' and 'disenchantment'.

A content analysis of the interviews revealed categories *within* each of these phases which illustrated the complexities of, and variables within, individual development. For all but the heads in the fourth phase these categories were:

- confidence (measure of self-belief);
- effectiveness (quality of their work and results);
- ambition (to change, to succeed);
- enthusiasm (willingness to be involved actively);
- management style (as defined by the heads);
- reaction to external demands (as they influence school culture); and
- development of professional expertise (strengths and weaknesses).

As headteachers moved through each phase, their ability to manage the tensions which these produced in a way which was productive both for themselves and the school appeared to become increasingly crucial.

Initiation: Idealism, Uncertainty and Adjustment

The initiation phase was identified by the heads as consisting of two key processes; one of them was learning on the job which might take any length of time depending on the problems that headteachers encountered; another aspect was realizing that although they had new ideas, new hopes and aspirations about what they wanted to do for the school, they had to work to accommodate these within an existing framework and structure. Without taking account of their predecessors' work, new initiatives would not be effective. Two sorts of beginnings were reported; simple, easy beginnings and difficult beginnings (Huberman, 1989). When new headteachers came to a school which had a good reputation and good community relationships, initially they felt comfortable and happy, for there were not so many problems to combat. Positive, innovative, and active staff assisted the new headteachers in putting their ideas into practice more easily. If the previous headteacher had the same management style as the new headteacher, there was no need to spend time on this area. Similarly, if the previous headteacher was not very popular with the staff, again an easy beginning was reported. This was because the staff were willing to have a new headteacher and ready to accept what he or she introduced as change. Difficult beginnings were associated with problems previous headteachers left, such as making decisions about redundancies of the staff, problems of the amalgamation of two schools, a falling rolls position with a difficult budget, no allowances left to allocate to the staff; and coming to the post at a time when many externally imposed changes were being implemented; for example when headteachers arrived just before the implementation of the local management of the school this contributed, not surprisingly, to a difficult beginning. Headteachers who had started their careers in 1985 reported that industrial action created tension between the staff and had an impact on headship:

It was very frustrating because things you wanted to do and get on with, you couldn't do. You could simply try to hold the situation together, you couldn't make progress. You could see things regressing in some ways. It was a very depressing and frustrating time. (Headteacher Q)

In this phase enthusiasm ruled in the early months, and a perceived challenge was to initiate changes immediately, for example in the organization and structure of management regardless, it seemed, of existing cultures. In the very early months headteachers seemed very idealistic and had a strong desire to make their mark on the school as soon as they could. They had preconceptions about the main characteristics of a good headteacher:

One has got to have a good, well-established, well-known formal system of consultation . . . As a head you need a skill to be able to look at the particular innovation, how important it is, then on that basis decide how you are going to introduce it to effect change. I think, to be successful, as a head, you also have to deal with people, you have to be sensitive to little things which tell you people are under stress, are worried . . . you have to be able to recognise it. (Headteacher 2)

All of the newly appointed headteachers disagreed with their predecessor's management style which was identified as autocratic, and introduced a consultative management style. They used consultation as a strategy for staff development. They encouraged their staff to give their ideas for school improvement and expected them to expand their views on negative and positive aspects of the school. After two and a half years, one of the headteachers reported that staff had got used to his style of running the school, as opposed to that of the previous head:

I put things up for discussion, I put out proposals and I expected people to come back and say yes or no, why, in which ways they approved, like at staff meetings for example. At the very first staff meeting I took, the staff didn't want to talk. It's not a staff meeting then is it? It is just the monologue from me. And that's how it used to be. Staff meetings now are discussions, and staff meetings now *are* staff meetings and they can talk back as well as being given information. (Headteacher Z)

Visibility and availability were seen as being important elements of consultation. Through the second and third year they started to realize the gap between their ideals and the limitations imposed by the school context. More realistic planning was considered as they learned the culture and began to manage it. In this phase, although the headteachers' enthusiasm was at its peak uncertainty about the job led them to spend a lot of time learning about each aspect of their role. (New headteachers who had been pastoral deputy headteachers found that deputy headship and headship were similar but that headship was at a more senior level. Because of this similarity, former deputy headteachers responsible for student welfare experienced fewer problems. Newly appointed headteachers seemed to spend the first year finding out about daily routines but even in the third year some of the headteachers admitted that they were still not confident in some tasks they had not experienced before.) On taking up the post, 'first time' headteachers faced a greater amount of uncertainty than they had previously experienced. The variety of new roles created uncertainty, and a vital task in the beginning was to learn quickly about these.

This period was described as the hardest time in headteachers' careers. In retrospect heads saw that progress which they had expected was unrealistic. More experienced headteachers reported that this initial idealism was replaced by realism. There was enormous diversity in the organization which meant that the headteacher had to build a great many relationships, in order to persuade and plan to implement all the changes they wanted to make. Making too many changes in the first year without getting to know the school culture, staff and community was identified by the experienced headteachers as an error. In fact, experienced headteachers suggested that heads needed to be in the job two or three years before they could really say what it was all about. Throughout the initial years, then, they started to identify the needs of their school and claimed to have achieved some small changes concerning the physical plant only. One headteacher who had been in post for two and a half years stated that:

> I have done a lot of sort of superficial things, perhaps not very significant changes, I have not made changes in what for me, are essential aspects of the school, which is in the way children learn ... So from that point of view I am in the phase of seeing what the problem is but not getting close enough to it and solving it. (Headteacher 3)

It was clear that this phase contained within it three subphases or steps. These were: *idealism, uncertainty* and *adjustment*. However, within each of these were individual differences. For example, headteachers' first concern in the initiation phase was to identify and manage the difference between their new tasks as headteachers and their previous tasks as deputy headteachers. In their new role they had greater parental, staff and pupil involvement, a much more social role. The responsibility for other people's career continuity and career development created stress. A second concern focused on how they would respond to a problem which they experienced for the first time. This led to a feeling of inadequacy in some:

> The first year was very much a learning experience for me, I felt a lot happier when the first year was over (...) When I started again on the second year I was much more confident because I knew I had done it all before, not all of it, because there are things that you meet for the first time. But I felt the routine the second time was easier, it felt more relaxing (...) I think you are more confident, you can cope with most of the things. (Headteacher W)

A third pressure point was the longer working hours which they experienced and the greater variety of tasks they had to carry out.

The new headteachers also stated that in the initial year they experienced a kind of cultural shock between being a deputy and being a head:

> I have been a deputy for eleven years in one school and there are a lot of friends there. I was very unsure about leaving all those people that I knew. Coming into a new situation, there was an element of strangeness about it. (Headteacher W)

A further related difficulty was the culture of the existing senior-management team. The school cultures in which new heads find themselves can be intimidating, because of existing disparities between school philosophies and their aims. For example senior-management attitudes and behaviours often reflected the previous head's style and those of new heads who came with their own ideals about what makes an effective school were not always welcomed:

> The difficulty has been in the management team itself where there were some expectations at the start with deputies. For a while people always said 'Mr X always used to do this' or 'He was very good at doing that' and I am thinking I do not want to know that, because I am not a student of his. (Headteacher 3)

Gaining the respect of staff and children and learning every aspect of the work could take almost three years according to the heads who were interviewed.

Distinctive features of the initiation phase, therefore, were feelings of uncertainty and inadequacy:

> You are always uncertain, when you put things out for consultation, whether or not you are going to get the answer back, that actually you would feel comfortable with, so there is uncertainty there. (Headteacher X)

> I took a piece of paper in to my first meeting, I was shaking. I was quite apprehensive about that. I might have done so much better. (Headteacher M)

> My first day I spent waiting for a crisis to happen and wondering how I would manage it when it did. (Headteacher P)

Initial idealism and enthusiasm transferred into realism at the end of the first year:

> I think there was an element of sort of newness and therefore enthusiasm about being new and wanting to make a good job of it, because I was new. I think the enthusiasm that I have got now is still there but tempered more with reality, with realism, with knowing what is possible. (Headteacher W)

The first few months you are extremely enthusiastic, . . . because just the euphoria of getting a job, a new challenge . . . I think it changes, inasmuch that you realize you can't do it all in a day. It takes a little longer and you sit back and think perhaps I have got to manage my time, changes you have got to make, and plan it out a bit more carefully. So I am still enthusiastic but perhaps more realistic. Things take a little longer than you'd hope for. (Headteacher Z)

Development: Consolidation and Extension

Interviews with headteachers of four to eight years of experience revealed features which collectively were distinguishable from those of headteachers in other phases and to which those in later phases referred as applying to them during this phase. Development-phase headteachers still seemed enthusiastic, enjoyed working and wanted to continue, though the level of the enthusiasm changed from time to time depending on the headteachers' self-esteem:

It may have taken a bit of a dip a while ago, when I was beginning to feel 'What was I doing?', 'Was it worth it?', 'Couldn't someone else do the job better?' . . . I still feel the general trend is pretty even, I still feel enthusiastic. (Headteacher P)

This was perceived to be the most active, most satisfactory, most rewarding phase in their careers. During the initiation phase when the achievement (of long-term ambition) was a strong feature of their lives, the main concern had been getting to know the environment, introducing some physical changes and managing changes imposed from outside of the school. Heads had been unable to establish preferred management structures. However, in the development phase, headteachers started to feel at ease with daily routines and began to try to develop their school as much as they could in accordance with their vision. They appeared to be constructively self-questioning, have greater confidence in some areas while being aware of the existence of areas about which they were still uncertain. Initial uncertainty was replaced either by an acceptance (leaving things to happen in the usual way) or continued change and development in pursuit of school improvement. In most cases 'reaching a plateau' was not perceived as acceptable. Being over confident was reported as a danger. One headteacher with six and a half years of experience said that:

I'd hate to believe that one reaches a stage where one's competent in everything that one does. (Headteacher P)

The interview responses supported the analysis of the questionnaire data that headteachers in the development phase reported fewer difficulties than in other phases. Externally imposed changes were implemented with relatively few complaints.

> I call it innovation overload as a whole and (. . .) too much innovation at the same time. I am quite happy to cope with innovation overload, quite excited to some extent by innovation; for example National Curriculum, Local Management (are) quite exciting innovations, all welcome, but also we have Records of Achievement. Appraisal is the next thing and so on . . . You are thinking how can you keep abreast of all these innovations and at the same time, maintain good standards in your school. (Headteacher Q)

> Our real problem is not creating change. It is managing the number of different things that happen all at once in school. (Headteacher P)

However, growing confidence, increased effectiveness and constructive self-examination were the principle characteristics.

> I've always got inside me a question which says 'Am I doing the job as well as I could?' 'What am I doing wrong?' And you sometimes think, when you get something right, you know, it goes down well but you've always got a question about this because you don't have anyone coming and saying, 'We've seen quite a lot of practice around the Authority (School District) and what we see you are doing is great'. You don't get that very often. You don't actually know, so you are uncertain. I am uncertain all the time about how competent I am. Am I doing a good job? And you have these crises that occur when you do feel inadequate from time to time and you think, I am not keeping on top of it, it is too much, I am not coping, I need somebody who's got more capacity than I have, I am burned out. You get these sort of feelings from time to time, but somehow you get over those and you come back again. (Headteacher P)

A feature during this development phase, was the creation of changes in school and staff-development planning, and the enhanced effectiveness of the school and the headteachers themselves. In almost all cases as a result of the retirement of members of the 'inherited' senior-management team, headteachers had opportunities to build new management teams. Indeed, one of the distinctive features of headteachers in this phase was that most of them established various teams for developing a better public image of their school. Most of the headteachers in this phase indicated that their greatest success was in connection with delegating more responsibility, showing the staff that they valued them and involving them in the work of the school:

> I have been trying to find a successful way of involving as many staff as possible in making decisions and in working together because I do believe that team work is important. A cooperative approach, you could

call it. So one of the successes I feel that is not yet fulfilled but it is on the way, is creating teams to manage various areas of school curriculum. (Headteacher P)

In order to involve teachers in management processes, three out of seven heads established, for instance, curriculum-management teams. As a consequence of the team work, these areas were reported to be developing.

Curriculum is better now, because it's being better managed by the people than it was before, with more enthusiasm. (Headteacher P)

Headteachers also tended to give more responsibility to more teachers and less responsibility to teachers who had it before, but were not using it effectively.

When I first came to the school, they had something called faculties in the school. There were only a limited number of those and each head of faculty belonged to a thing called an academic board and I scrapped all that and it only came in after a few years, between two and three years this time, when I had the chance to allocate incentive allowances (. . .) I gave more responsibility to more and less responsibility to one or two that had had it before, but weren't using it. So I changed the responsibilities and gave more staff an incentive to work and as a consequence of that, I think we get better results, more people are involved. (Headteacher P)

Most of the headteachers agreed that they were able to establish their own preferred 'flatter' management structures after the first three years and were able to appoint new staff after the fourth and fifth years. Disagreement with the previous headteachers' allocation of the responsibilities initially created conflict between heads of department and the headteacher. After approximately three years they were able to initiate major changes especially in staff responsibilities and allowances, thus changing the most disliked legacy of their predecessors. Similarly as time went by, staff were appointed who held the values espoused by the headteacher, and this seemed to be a factor which increased the effectiveness of the school. Headteachers visited classrooms to see how the curriculum worked and reported that it was being delivered in a much more effective way than they had previously imagined. It seemed that heads in this phase respected the expertise of colleagues in particular areas and did not interfere. All of the heads reported 'tremendous' development in specific areas, particularly school–community relationships. One headteacher with six and a half years of experience reported that:

Work experience, careers, all that has been tremendous over the last two to three years. It's taken the last three years, six and a half in all. The last three years have seen tremendous changes. The first three years didn't see so many changes, but the last three years have. So, if you draw on your graph that's it going up, it's going up like that, it's getting steeper, not tailing off at the moment, as far as the school is concerned, because of the people in it and what they are doing. (Headteacher P)

Development-phase headteachers appeared to be more confident about the way to deal with staffing relationships, staff discipline and staff competency. They became more effective in handling staff where there had been previously perceived problems. Although ambitions were not entirely fulfilled a relatively comfortable stage was reached relating both to individuals' life-development phases and the school context in which they worked. In this phase there were two alternatives available — either to continue the career in the same school or look for a bigger school and use acquired experience there. A period of secondment was also used by some heads in this phase as an opportunity to develop, and as a 'breathing space' to make up their minds about the rest of their careers.

The development phase was described as being a starting point for effectiveness.

I am older, more experienced, I have got an organization in the school structure that makes managing easier. I have delegated, under the new collegiate system. I delegated more responsibility out. I've given the staff more right to contribute, but I've also given them more responsibility to respond. (Headteacher F)

It was believed by the heads interviewed in the 'autonomy phase' however, that whilst effectiveness increased rapidly during the development phase, it later declined.

Autonomy: Single loop learning

After becoming 'established' a phase was identified in which ambition in terms of career mobility though not contributions to the improvement of the school, was satisfied. Two kinds of response were reported by the headteachers in the autonomy phase. The philosophy underpinning new externally imposed national initiatives (e.g., National Curriculum, school-based financial management, national testing) was criticized and given as a reason for lack of enthusiasm.

The first year or two as a head was a very, very exciting time. That excitement's gone. It wears off fairly quickly in a couple of years. You go from a period of excitement to a period of routines and then of managing the situation that you have got, which comes with experience, so I don't have that sense of excitement about the job any more that I had in the first few years, and that kind of enthusiasm. (Headteacher B)

Yet this third phase was also characterized by continuing self-confidence. Richness of previous experience assisted in the management of complicated and difficult situations and managing the school became easier:

> You (are) getting more and more confident about the job you (are) doing. It is also a case of the more experience you have the more confident you become and when new things crop up, you deal with them. You know how to deal with them in a better way than you did previously. (Headteacher H)

At the beginning of this phase competency was perceived to have increased as a consequence of experience, which provided a databank of alternatives with known advantages and disadvantages. This enriched source of information became a means of reviewing and assessing previous decisions and informing new decisions.

> Effectiveness is increasing gradually. It is hard to see this, but I think I was very active at the very beginning because I was so naive that there is a sort of accidental effectiveness (. . .) I think effectiveness means carrying people with you and means having a creative way of thinking and planning and you gain confidence . . . because in the early years, in the first three years I wasn't carrying staff with me and having to demonstrate and to be a bit of a detached showman in a kind of way, and that wasn't carrying the whole school. (Headteacher I)

Headteachers in this phase identified themselves as experts in educational management:

> I feel at the top of the job, because every year that passes you have more experience. Day by day you are known in the community, you are known in the school. (Headteacher Q)

> I am an expert in broad education and management because I have spent so much time over the past years looking at management, management structures, personal management issues, how you handle staff, things of that nature rather than teaching methodology. (Headteacher O)

> I have more expertise than I had at the beginning. I have less energy now but I am older than eleven years ago. I was stronger physically but I was less wise. But I am more wise now. (Headteacher B)

> I have got lazy with administration because I have got people to do it for me. I had to do it before, myself. I am more interested in the wider, bigger issues now and I can do it, I can give time. (Headteacher F)

> In terms of doing the job I feel fairly relaxed in my capacity to cope with what is going on in school. (Headteacher J)

However, during this phase headteachers perceived that they had less energy, increasing prudence, nostalgia for the past, dissatisfaction with new external initiatives, a greater personal resistance to change, and (among some) a desire for an autocratic management style.

One of the longest serving headteachers pointed out that as a consequence of a participating decision-making style, he felt less effective and less decisive because individual decisions were not appreciated any more:

> I was certainly more decisive and more autocratic earlier on in my career than I am how ... I can still make quick decisions, I think the style has changed, times have changed. There is now a great need to consult, to discuss with others before implementing decisions. That is far more time consuming, therefore decisions from me become less significant ... I am conscious that probably I am not as an effective decision maker now as I was. (Headteacher O)

Here the headteacher seemed to be acting as chief executive of the school, surrounded and supported by a senior-management team, operating in a similar way to Ball's (1987) 'Managerial Style' of management:

> The head may or may not value wide social contacts with the staff, but the accomplishment of managerial headship does not require a close working relationship across the whole staff. The day-to-day running of the school and the ongoing decision-making and policy-making process are focused upon the work of the senior management team. (Ball, 1987, p. 100)

Disagreement with central government's decisions created a feeling of being forced in a certain direction with which they had no sympathy. 'Autonomy' here had both positive and negative effects upon individual development and leadership effectiveness. It was positive in the sense that the headteachers perceived that they were in control of the school by virtue of experience, knowledge, power and influence and vision; but it was negative in that they perceived that their control and vision were under threat. Most of the headteachers in this phase believed that there had been so many government initiatives imposed at the same time that the possibility of achieving all of them successfully was difficult. They seemed to have become overwhelmed and struggled to implement multiple changes, unable to complete one of them before moving to another:

> I wish that Government would stop having good ideas in order that we could actually consolidate the ideas they have already had in the last three years. (Headteacher D)

> 1988 Act brought a lot more administrative duties, a lot of communication and liaison work in various bodies not only in the school. We obviously have governing bodies and committees, I don't reject it all, but a person who used to do his own thing, making decisions in the old style finds it very hard. (Headteacher I)

The obligation to collaborate with governing bodies, with communities, with feeder schools seemed to be a problem in this phase for headteachers who used to work in the old style. Morale of staff and heads themselves was at a low ebb:

There is a lot of government legislation to put pressure on teachers. The government has been kicking teachers around, they have been complaining about all sorts of things. Teachers' morale is very low. The government encouraged parents to have a go at teachers . . . quite enjoy headteachers, threatening them with statements like performance related pay and appraisal, accountability, parents have a right to know this. They put on more and more pressure. (Headteacher B)

Six headteachers in the autonomy phase felt pressured into their old style and all of them stated that they had changed too much by applying a collegial style of management. They believed they still need an autocratic approach:

I have been trying to establish ways of collaboration, which is why the school is built upon teams. Teams are about people, collaborating with one another in the classroom, across the school. Collaboration between the schools, it is nothing more than a big bank, so I suppose it philosophically goes back a long way and I suppose I have a problem actually, because sometimes I think my personality can be that of an autocrat. I am not sure that I am a natural democrat. Perhaps I want to be and I try very hard to be, but my inclination is always to be very democratic and to build teams to work with people, I have always enjoyed it and I think that it promotes a fruitful way of life really. So it goes right back then, but then of course you can see how that affected actually management literature and the idea of the organic organization, mechanical organization. It gives it in all sorts of ways, it has got an expression; management structure. But I couldn't put it into practice because the school wasn't ready for it. Because actually you see I happen to believe the most difficult way of working is in a collaborative way. It is far more difficult, because it is easier to make tight rules and it is easier to make procedure. It is easier for me to give you an order, it is easier for you to take an order. It is easier to take an order than to think yourself. Thinking is painful, it demands responsibility. (Headteacher F)

Despite agreement with the principles of democratic management, these headteachers appeared to be guardians of tradition and found it very difficult to change. Unwillingness in applying a consultative management style did not seem related to staff competency and staff readiness, but directly to the headteachers' preference and professional history. Resistance towards further change appeared to be one of the typical characteristics of the autonomy phase. Energy was channelled into controlling the stability of their school environment rather than its development. One head's comments provide a testament to the complex dynamics of being a head, even in this phase:

Confidence is perhaps like a graph. There are times when you become more confident and then in other situations things go wrong. Your morale and confidence take a dive (. . .). (Headteacher F)

In Argyris and Schön's (1974) terms, many heads began to engage in 'single-loop' learning in which actions were designed to maintain what is rather than develop what might be. As a consequence, the beginnings of disenchantment were identified.

Disenchantment

It was not surprising that declining confidence, enthusiasm and increasing personal 'fatigue' were seen as characteristic features of the disenchantment phase, as a sense of mortality increased. Complaints about the behaviour of the 'new generation' and about innovations were raised in the interviews. Headteachers started either to 'ease off', lost their motivation or their health deteriorated as they approached retirement. This phase might be called 'disenchantment' (see also Huberman, 1989). Here if the individual reached a point where there was no actual development, resulting in a plateau, this was accompanied by increasing work pressure, stress, ageing and emotional or physical sickness and, for the staff, deterioration in morale and motivation:

I think disillusionment is easy . . . It is very difficult to be an officer, carrying out policies with which you not only disagree, but you know are wrong and you can see it. I am worried to death because of this government's legislation and overwork. (Headteacher B)

I have a lot of apprehensions about the future of education, because local and national governments are making some terrible mistakes, in my judgment, and I am right. (Headteacher J)

It is no good coming into education unless you are an optimist. If you are thinking in a pessimistic way you seem to become disillusioned. (Headteacher J)

Headteachers in this phase appeared not only to disagree with the centrally initiated changes, but also to give a freedom of choice to their teachers as to whether or not to implement them:

When there is a new set of regulations I say 'Do not feel you have to do this immediately, let's have a good look at it, let's delay doing something until next year. Let's not, because the government says we have to do this by such a time, let's not feel that we have got to do it now, let's not change the way we do things, the way we teach, let's not jump in too quickly (. . .) There are a number of government restrictions, and I realize I am on record here, that I would ignore. There are two or three things in the Education Act that I have consciously ignored. (Headteacher B)

One of the headteachers managing inner-city schools with eleven years' experience explained his feeling of fatigue as a consequence of the heavy burden of responsibility:

If there is a reason why I am mentally and emotionally, tired, it is an accumulation of carrying those responsibilities which have grown over the last two to three years and I think there is a limit how much longer this can go on. (Headteacher B)

Certainly the last two years I was struggling, then very often simply because of changes from outside. (Headteacher E)

They claimed to resist change of this kind in order to protect their teachers from being overburdened and to respect their views on change. It seems likely also that lack of energy and lack of enthusiasm contributed. When the headteachers who identified themselves as disillusioned were asked to talk about their education philosophy, they centred upon their substantive personal selves:

I don't know. I don't know. I think it is true to say that I have a sort of pragmatic approach to my job. (Headteacher E)

I became a born again Christian. I don't mean just going to church on Sunday morning. My brand of Christianity is based on detailed scriptural reading daily. (Headteacher E)

Education is concerned with the human development and the creation of a new world for the future. (Headteacher Q)

Storr (1988) has noted that this retreat to the self is a characteristic consequence of ageing.

In this phase, many headteachers suffered illness (mental or physical) and afterwards felt they had lost their control over the school. Most of them admitted that when they returned to school after prolonged absence they could not recognize it because of the many changes. All of the headteachers who became ill and disillusioned reported that they used to work eighty to ninety hours per week and in the end they had the pressure of the Education Act forced on them to change their style, to handle huge budgets which they were not trained for, to liaise with governing bodies. As a result they totally lost their enthusiasm.

The feeling of being under the control of governing bodies led to early retirement on the part of some headteachers.

Governing bodies are very powerful in setting policy and discipline, but they said, they only set it, they don't actually make it (. . .) The power of headteachers is less now. I am going at the right time. The new laws about governing bodies have been very confusing and people are just beginning to understand this. (Headteacher M)

The headteachers' feeling of disillusionment is encapsulated in the statement below:

I think one becomes ill and feels less successful and more guilty and worried when you feel you haven't got any control over your destiny. Stress is one thing you can't control. You have no control of what's going on and people don't listen. They don't understand and quickly following on that stress situation, is that you then are overcome by bitterness and I really thought of stress and anxiety and bitterness . . . When you are overwhelmed with so many changes you feel worn out. (Headteacher E)

The pressure led some headteachers to retire earlier than their colleagues used to do pre-legislation. A number of reasons could be suggested for this situation. There was no culture of early retirement and headteachers used to work up until they were 65. Schools were much more stable places and headteachers were supposed to set a daily routine and staff used to know the routine all year round. Headteachers did not have the daily pressure of work suffered by their colleagues in the 1990s. Most of the headteachers who were interviewed stated that they had been planning to retire before their 60s. It seemed a sense of mortality was heightened and this led to the headteachers thinking about earlier retirement and relaxation:

There are other things to do, lives are running out. How much longer am I going to live, ten years? . . . One of my colleagues retired at the age of 62 and had six weeks' retirement before he died. I don't want six weeks' retirement, I'd like ten years. Look at the life expectancy of a head retired after 60, compared to a head retired before 60. It's frightening. I'd like to have a few more years to do things. There are lots of places I haven't been and I'd like to spend time in my garden and get bored. (Headteacher B)

Increasing concern about ageing, about life expectancy and mortality led to them spending more time planning the rest of their lives outside school more realistically. School improvement became less of a consideration as personal-life considerations and concerns increased. Lack of confidence and enthusiasm towards daily routines of the school, towards change, were observed. A general failure in effectiveness of the headteacher, ambiguities in the management style, a feeling of being less skilled in new initiatives and 'frozen' professional expertise and 'single-loop' learning were the characteristic features of headteachers in the disenchantment phase.

Conclusion

The data generated from this study indicate that developments in the thinking and practices of headteachers, like those of other professional groups, are complex and affected by life history, previous role preparation, inherited school culture, external environments and personal-belief factors, and their ability to manage stress. It is clear, however, that in terms of knowledge generated by research into life cycles, headteachers are already entering (or have entered) a phase during which, although there may be a desire to leave their mark upon future generations, they are likely to be primarily concerned with stabilizing (their careers) and maintaining them within an increasing awareness of mortality. In short, many will be in 'mid-life transition' and experiencing some level of personal change related to this. Within the contest of ambitions for effectiveness and success in their work, then, they may well be having to learn to manage personal dilemmas of generativity versus stagnation and ego integrity versus despair, always assuming an awareness of these. Indeed, the interviews of headteachers in different phases revealed that these were indeed central to their management of the initiation, development, autonomy and disenchantment phases of headship.

There are close similarities also between the headteachers' phases of development identified in this research and those identified in research into teachers' career cycles. For example, it is possible to envisage Burke *et al*'s (1984) eight stages as fitting comfortably into these. Induction and competency building (initiation); enthusiasm and growth (development); career frustration and stability and stagnance (autonomy), career wind down, career exit (disenchantment). More significantly, Huberman (1989), Prick (1986) and Newman's (1979) identification of a loss of energy and enthusiasm and an increase in conservatism (which we call autonomy) in those over the age of 50, revealed also through the headteachers in this research, provides cause for concern for all those concerned with the relationship between leadership and school effectiveness. It appears from this research that though the optimum periods in the development of headteachers' thinking and practice are in the first two phases of their careers as heads it is in the third and fourth stages when effectiveness may be declining that review, re-assessment and planned support is crucial.

There are similarities with the five-stage skill-development model proposed by Dreyfus and Dreyfus (1986) though significant differences in interpretation. Headteachers claimed that they moved, from 'novice' to advanced beginner and competence (during the initiation phase), then to proficiency and expertise (during the development phase). Researchers have identified characteristics related to expertise, such as, the ability to make quick, confident judgments under pressure (Johnson, 1988); encoding new information more quickly and completely (Chase and Simon, 1973); displaying a rich repertoire of strategies and appropriate mechanisms for accessing and applying them (Larkin *et al.*, 1980); better conceptual understandings of subject matter (Leinhardt and Smith, 1985); and the ability to take a holistic view of complex situations (Chase and Simon, 1973; Anderson, 1983). By inference, many of the headteachers interviewed in the 'development' phase possessed and applied these qualities and skills. However, whilst those in the 'autonomy' phase also possessed these, there were clear indications that non-rational life factors were affecting their use for development purposes. Indeed, 'being an expert' allowed many of the headteachers to resist change. So it is the use to which expertise is put rather than its simple possession which is significant in judging effectiveness.

Above all one of the distinctive characteristics of heads in this phase was their resistance to the external changes when these did not fit their personal practical knowledge. They sought to be autonomous, that is to be able to determine their own policy for their schools without external influences. They set a value system in their schools and their definition of the 'effective school' was unique and peculiar to each one.

Day *et al.* (1990) claimed that the more heads demonstrate their use of authority the less will be the personal investment of colleagues in the enterprise. Most of the heads in the 'autonomy phase' preferred the above approach and refused to consult or share the decision-making. The 'team' approach was not appreciated by the heads in this phase; and having expertise seemed to be a rationalization for avoiding development.

In terms of learning, heads in the 'disenchantment' phase did not indicate any progress. There was less concern for their own or their teachers' professional development. Headteacher 'B' provided an illustration of this. He was 55, and had been a headteacher for eleven years. He held a BA and Certificate of Education and worked in a small city school. He admitted a feeling of fatigue and anticipated early retirement:

> I've been in this particular post long enough. I think the post and I will be tired of each other and somebody else should be here, somebody with fresher eyes and a bit more physical energy.

He tried to persuade staff to change, rather than encouraging discussions, sharing the decision-making or taking into consideration teacher suggestions:

> I think the trick, the solution, lies in preparing the ground for change, is persuading people that what you have now is not as good as it could be, it isn't right, and then examining ways in which it could be done better ... and then saying this is how we're going to do this then people will get upset.

Leaders who see themselves as organizers and decision-makers experience difficulty because they create dependency and find themselves increasingly isolated (Murgatroyd and Gray, 1989). Headteacher B made decisions and then tried to persuade staff to adopt them in order to avoid their resistance. (He later admitted that communication between himself and his staff was not working very well in his school.) He related to his staff principally through a formal structure of meetings and committees, a form of 'contrived collegiality' (Hargreaves, 1994). As a consequence of this he admitted that he was disenchanted. Perhaps one of the reasons of his disenchantment phase was the approach he had over the years in 'being the manager rather than a leader'. The loss of 'vision' for the future of the school is one of the characteristics of heads in this phase.

A recent large-scale self-report study of occupational stress among 2638 headteachers of primary and secondary schools in the UK, which was carried out at the time that the data for this research was collected, provides further validation for the claims made in this study in relation to the need to provide occupational support for heads in a managed way at particular times in their development. It concluded that in the management of education as a whole, 'work overload' and 'handling relationships with staff' (with ageing the three fundamental difficulties identified by headteachers in this research) are the main categories of job stressors, that the 'training and develop provision for senior managers in education has traditionally been haphazard and thinly spread'; that teachers in all sectors 'seem to be using coping strategies which are counter productive'; and that, 'A continuous process of mid-career development for heads is absolutely fundamental if we are to avoid managerial burnout at a later date' (Cooper and Kelly, 1993, pp. 141–2).

This research provides further information, then, which suggests that potential for learning and development among school headteachers declines after an initial surge over four years within the first eight years of headship; and that the reasons for this decline are connected with life-phase and social-psychological factors. In terms of school effectiveness and potential improvement this is a depressing story; and in terms of the development of headteachers' thinking and practices, it suggests the urgent need for intelligent planned support.

Notes

1 Recent work by Evetts and Smith in UK are exceptions to this, though their research focuses primarily upon career analysis in relation to promotion and gender issues (Evetts, 1992; Smith, 1975).
2 No significant gender differences emerged from the qualitative data. Earlier questionnaire data revealed that female headteachers (18 per cent of the sample) tended to lead smaller schools, and experienced difficulties caused by the practices of the previous (male) headteacher.
3 We must thank Andy Hargreaves for reminding us of this, and the seminal work of Michael Huberman (1988, 1989).
4 Space does not allow a report of these in this chapter. For further details, see Bakioğlu (1993), PhD Thesis, School of Education, University of Nottingham.

References

ANDERSON, J.R. (1982) 'Acquisition of cognitive skill', *Psychological Review*, **89**, pp. 369–406.
ANDERSON, J.R. (1983) *The Architecture of Cognition*, MA, Cambridge, Harvard University Press.

ARGYRIS, C. and SCHÖN, D.A. (1974) *Theory in Practice: Increasing Professional Effectiveness*, San Francisco, Jossey-Bass.

BALL, S.J. (1987) *The Micro-politics of the School*, London, Methuen.

BALL, S.J. and GOODSON, I.F. (1985) *Teachers' Lives and Careers*, London, New York and Philadelphia, Falmer Press.

BAKIOĞLU, A. (1993) 'Headteacher Development: Relations between Role Effectiveness and Headteachers' Career Phases', PhD Dissertation, University of Nottingham.

BERLEW, D.E. and HALL, T. (1964) 'Some determinants of early managerial success', Cambridge, Massachusetts, Sloan School of Management, Massachusetts Institute of Technology.

BIGGE, M.L. and SHERMIS, S.S. (1992) *Learning Theories for Teachers*, New York, Harper Collins.

BRAY, D.W., CAMPBELL, R.J. and GRANT, D.L. (1974) *Working with Organisations and their People: A Guide to Human Resources*, New York, Guildford Press.

BROMLEY, D.B. (1986) *The Case Study Method in Psychology and Related Disciplines*, Chichester, John Wiley and Sons.

BURKE, P.J., CHRISTENSEN, J.C. and FESSLER, R. (1984) 'Teacher career stages: Implication for staff development', *Phi Delta Kappan*, Educational Foundation, Bloomington, Indiana.

CHASE, W.G. and SIMON, H.A. (1973) 'Perception in chess', *Cognitive Psychology*, **4**, pp. 55–81.

CLANDININ, D.J. (1985) *Classroom Practice: Teacher Images in Action*, London, Falmer Press.

COLLIN, A. (1977) 'Mid-life crisis', *Working Paper No. 14*, Department of Management Studies, Loughborough University of Technology.

COOPER, C.L. and KELLY, M. (1993) 'Occupational stress in headteachers: A national UK study', *British Journal of Educational Psychology*, **63**, pp. 130–43.

DARESH, J.C. (1987) 'The highest hurdles for the first year principal', Paper presented at the Annual Meeting of the American Educational Research Association, Washington, DC, April 20–4.

DAY, C., JOHNSON, D. and WHITAKER, P. (1985) *Managing Primary Schools*, London, Harper and Row.

DAY, C., WHITAKER, P. and JOHNSTON, D. (1990) *Managing Primary Schools in the 1990s: A Professional Development Approach*, 2nd ed., London, Paul Chapman.

DREYFUS, H. and DREYFUS, S. (1986) *Mind over Machine: The Power of Human Intuition and Expertise in the Era of the Computer*, New York, The Free Press.

DUIGNAN, P.A. (1990) 'School-based decision making and management: Reprospect and prospect', in CHAPMAN, J.D. *School Based Decision Making and Management*, London, New York and Philadelphia, Falmer Press.

ELBAZ, F. (1983) *Teacher Thinking: A Study of Practical Knowledge*, London, Croom Helm.

ELLIOTT, K.P.J. and WILLIAMS, G. (1981) *Improving Your Professional Effectiveness: A Handbook for Managers in Education*, Sheffield City Polytechnic, Pavis Publications.

ERIKSON, E.H. (1963) *Childhood and Society*, New York, Norton.

EVETTS, J. (1992) 'When promotion ladders seem to end: The career concerns of secondary headteachers', *British Journal of Sociology of Education*, **13**, 1, pp. 37–49.

HALL, D.T. (1976) *Careers in Organisations*, Pacific Palisades, Goodyear.

HALL, D.T. and SCHNEIDER, B. (1972) 'Correlates of organizational identification as a function of career pattern and organisational type', *Administrative Science Quarterly*, **17**, 3, pp. 340–50.

HANDAL, G. (1990) 'Promoting the articulation of tacit knowledge through the counselling of practitioners', Keynote paper at Amsterdam Pedalogisch Centum Conference, Amsterdam, Holland, 6–8 April, in DAY, C. (1993) 'Reflection: A necessary but not sufficient condition for professional development', *British Educational Research Journal*, **19**, 1, pp. 83–93.

HARGREAVES, A. (1994) *Changing Teachers, Changing Times*, London, Cassell, New York, Teachers College Press, Toronto.

HARGREAVES, A. and FULLAN, M.G. (1991) *What's Worth Fighting for?: Working Together for Your School*, Ontario Public School Teachers' Federation.

HUBERMAN, M. (1988) 'Teacher careers and school improvement', *Journal of Curriculum Studies*, **20**, 2, pp. 119–32.

HUBERMAN, M. (1989) 'The professional life cycle of teachers', *Teachers College Record*, **91**, 1, pp. 31–57.

HUBERMAN, M. (1993) *The Lives of Teachers*, London, Cassell.

JAQUES, E. (1965) 'Death and the mid-life crisis', *International Journal of Psychoanalysis*, **46**, pp. 502–14.

JOHNSON, E.J. (1988) 'Expertise and decision under uncertainty: Performance and process', in CHI, H.T.M., GLASER, R. and FARR. M.J. (Eds) *The Nature of Expertise*, NJ, Lawrence Erlbaum Associates Inc/Hillsdale.

JUNG, C.G. (1933) *Modern Men in Search of a Soul*, New York, Harcourt Brace.

KARMILOFF-SMITH, A. (1984) 'Children's problem solving', in LAMB, M.E., BROWN, A.L. and ROGOFF, B. (Eds) *Advances in Developmental Psychology*, **3**, pp. 39–90, Hillsdale, NJ, Lawrence Erlbaum Associates.

KARMILOFF-SMITH, A. (1986) 'Stage/structure versus phase process in modelling linguistic and cognitive development', in LEVIN, I. (Ed) *Stage and Structure: Re-opening the Debate*, Norwood, NJ, Ablex, pp. 164–90.

LARKIN, J., MCDERMOTT, J., SIMON, D.P. and SIMON, H.A. (1980) 'Expert and novice performance in solving physics problems', *Science*, **208**, 4450, 20 June, pp. 1335–242.

LEINHARDT, G. and SMITH, D. (1985) 'Expertise in mathematics instruction: Subject matter knowledge', *Journal of Educational Psychology*, **77**, 3, pp. 247–71.

LEITHWOOD, K.A. (1990) 'The principal's role in teacher development', in BRUCE, J. *Changing School Culture through Staff Development*, 1990 yearbook of the Association for Supervision and Curriculum Development.

LEITHWOOD, K.A., BEGLEY, P.T. and COUSINS, J.B. (1992) *Developing Expert Leadership for Future Schools*, London, New York and Philadelphia, Falmer Press.

LEITHWOOD, K.L., JANTZI, D. and FERNANDEZ, A. (1993) 'Secondary school teachers' commitment to change: The contributions of transformational leadership', Paper Presented at the Annual Meeting of the American Educational Research Association, Atlanta, April.

LEITHWOOD, K.L. and MONTGOMERY, D.J. (1986) *Improving Principal Effectiveness: The Principal Profile*, Toronto, OISE Press.

LEVINSON, D.J., DARROW, C.N., KLEIN, E.B. and MCKEE, B. (1978) *The Season of a Man's Life*, New York, Knopf.

MACMILLAN, R.B. (1993) 'Approaches to leadership success: What comes with experience?', Paper presented at the Annual Conference of the Canadian Society for the Study of Education, Ottawa, Ontario, June.

MARSH, C., DAY, C., HANNAY, L. and MCCUTCHEON, G. (1990) *Reconceptualising School Based Curriculum Development*, London, New York and Philadelphia, Falmer Press.

MORTIMORE, P., SAMMONS, P., STOLL, L., LEWIS, D. and ECOB, R. (1988) *School Matters: The Junior Years*, Somerset, England, Open Books.

MURGATROYD, S. and GRAY, H.G. (1989) 'Leadership and the effective school', in RICHES, C. (Ed) *Human Resources Management in Education*, Milton Keynes, Open University Press.

NEUGARTEN, B.L. (1968) *Middle Age Ageing*, Chicago, University of Chicago Press.

NEWMAN, K. (1979) 'Middle aged, experienced teachers' perceptions of their career development', Paper presented at American Educational Research Association Meeting, San Francisco.

OSIPOW, S.H. (1973) *Theories of Career Development*, New York, Appleton-Century-Crofts.

PARKAY, F.W., CURRIE, G, and RHODES, J.W. (1992) 'Professional socialisation: A longitudinal study of twelve high school principals', *Educational Administration Quarterly*, **28**, 1, pp. 43–75.

PRICK, L. (1986) *Career Development and Satisfaction among Secondary School Teachers*, Amsterdam, Vrije Universiteit.

SCHÖN, D.A. (1992) 'The theory of inquiry: Dewey's legacy to education', *Curriculum Inquiry*, **22**, 2, pp, 119–39, Summer.

SHEULL, T.J. (1990) 'Phases of meaningful learning', *Review of Educational Research*, **60**, 4, pp. 531–47.

SIKES, P.J., MEASOR, L. and WOODS, P. (1985) *Teacher Careers, Crises and Continuities*, London, Falmer Press.

SMITH, D. (1975) 'Career structure of headteachers in a Midlands city', *Educational Review*, **28**, pp. 31–41.

STORR, A. (1988) *Solitude*, London, Flamingo, Harper Collins.

SUPER, D.E. (1957) *The Psychology of Careers*, New York, Harper and Row.

WATTS, A.G. (1981) 'Career patterns', in WATTS, A.G., SUPER, D.E. and KIDD, J.M. (Eds) *Career Development in Britain*, Cambridge, Published for CRAC by Hobsons Press.

WEINDLING, D. and EARLEY, P. (1987) *Secondary Headship: The First Years*, Windsor, NFER-Nelson.

Notes on Contributors

Aysen Bakioğlu is an Assistant Professor in the Department of Education at the University of Marmara, Istanbul, Turkey. Her research interests focus on the effectiveness and professional development of principals, effectiveness in teaching/self evaluation at the university, training and development systems in industry, school based professional development in private schools, students' beliefs and how those influence their learning. She is the country representative of ISATT (The International Study Association on Teacher Thinking).

Miriam Ben-Peretz is a Professor at the School of Education, University of Haifa, Israel, formerly Chair of the Department of Teacher Education and Dean of the School of Education. At present, she is the Academic President of Tel Hai College. Main research interests include curriculum theory, teacher thinking and teacher education. She is the author of many books including *The Teacher Curriculum Encounter — Freeing Teachers from the Tyranny of Texts*, SUNY Press (1990); *Learning from Experience: Memory and the Teacher's Account of Teaching*, SUNY Press (1995). She has published numerous articles in refereed journals in English, German and Hebrew.

Christopher Day is a Professor of Education, Chair of School of Education and Head of Advanced Studies, University of Nottingham. Prior to this he worked as a teacher, lecturer and local education authority adviser. His particular concerns centre upon the continuing professional development of teachers, teachers' thinking, leadership and school cultures. Recent publications include *Insights into Teachers' Thinking and Action* (co-edited with M. Pope and P. Denicolo) (1990) Falmer Press, *Research on Teacher Thinking: Towards Understanding Professional Development* (1993) (co-edited with J. Calderhead and P. Denicolo) Falmer Press, and a series for Open University Press entitled 'Developing Teachers and Teaching' (current). He is Chair of the Continuing Professional Development Committee of the Universities Council for the Education of Teachers, Editor of *Teachers and Teaching: Theory and Practice*, an international journal and Secretary of ISATT (The International Study Associated on Teacher Thinking).

Tomas Englund is a Professor of Education at the Department of Education, Stockholm Institute of Education, Sweden and also at the University of Orebro, Sweden. His research interests centre on curriculum theory/didactics, curriculum history, political socialization/citizenship education and the philosophical aspects of education. Among his publications is *Curriculum as a Political Problem* (Chartwell Bratt) and articles in various journals, e.g., *Journal of Curriculum Studies, Curriculum Studies* and *Scandinavian Journal of Educational Research.*

Andrew Gitlin is a Professor of Educational Studies at the University of Utah. Recent writing projects include: *Teachers Voices for School Change: An Introduction to Educative Research*, Teachers College Press, 1992, *Power and Method: Political Activism and Educational Research*, Routledge, 1994 and *Becoming a Student of Teaching: Methodologies for Exploring Self and School Context*, Garland, 1995 (co-author Robert Bullough).

Ivor F. Goodson is a Professor at the University of Western Ontario; he is a member of the Faculties of Education, Sociology and Graduate Studies and The Centre for Theory and Criticism. He is also the Frederica Warner Scholar at the Margaret Warner Graduate School of Eduction and Human Development, University of Rochester. He is the author of a range of books on curriculum and life history studies. They include *Studying Curriculum: Cases and Methods, School Subjects and Curriculum Change, Biography, Identity and Schooling* (with Rob Walker) and *Studying Teachers' Lives*. He is the Founding Editor and North American Editor of *The Journal of Education Policy* and the National Editor of *Qualitative Studies in Education*.

Andy Hargreaves is Director of the International Centre for Educational Change and Professor of Educational Administration at the Ontario Institute for Studies in Canada and also International Research Professor at the Roehampton Institute in England. He has written and researched widely on teachers' work, teacher cultures and professional development in Europe and North America. Among his recent books are *Changing Teachers, Changing Times* (Cassell, Teachers' College Press and OISE Press, 1994) which received the 1995 Outstanding Writing Award from the American Association of Colleges for Teacher Education; *Schooling for Change* (with Lorna Earl and James Ryan, Falmer Press, 1996), and *What's Worth Fighting For? Working Together for Your School*, second edition (with Michael Fullan, Ontario Public School Teachers' Federation, Open University Press and Teachers College Press, 1996).

Gill Helsby is a Senior Researcher in the Centre for the Study of Education and Training at Lancaster University. Her research interests include the impact of recent curriculum initiatives on teachers' work practices and teachers' professional development. She is co-editor of a forthcoming book on Teachers and the National Curriculum.

David Labaree is an Associate Professor of Teacher Education at Michigan State University (USA). He is author of *The Making of an American High School*. Currently he is doing research on the history of teacher education, educational reform, and teacher professionalization.

Jolie A. Mayer-Smith is an Assistant Professor in the Department of Curriculum Studies in the Faculty of Education at the University of British Columbia, Vancouver Canada. She teaches courses in Curriculum and Instruction and Biology for secondary preservice teachers. Her research interests include preservice teacher education, post secondary science teaching, conceptual understanding in genetics, and collaborative research in education.

Gary McCulloch is a Professor of Education at the University of Sheffield. His recent published work includes *Educational Reconstruction: The 1944 Education Act and the 21st Century* (Woburn, 1994). His current research is on the social history of mass secondary education and on the professional cultures of teaching.

Milbrey Wallin McLaughlin is a Professor of Education and Public Policy at Stanford University. She is Co-Director of the Center for Research on the Context of Teaching and co-principal investigator (with Shirley Brice Heath) of a multi-year project that examines community-based resources for youth in diverse community settings. McLaughlin also directs the Pew Forum on Educational Reform. She is the author or co-author of several books and articles on education policy issues, contexts for teaching and learning, productive environments for youth, and community-based organizations. Her recent books include: *Urban Sanctuaries* (with Merita A. Irby and Juliet Langman; Jossey-Bass, 1994); *Identity and Inner-City Youth: Beyond Ethnicity and Gender* (with Shirley Brice Heath; Teachers College Press, 1993); *Teaching for Understanding: Challenges for Policy and Practice* (with David K. Cohen and Joan E. Talbert; Jossey-Bass, 1993); *Teachers' Work* (with Judith Warren Little; Teachers College Press, 1993).

Claudia Mitchell is a Associate Professor in the Department of Curriculum and Instruction in the Faculty of Education at McGill University. She has written extensively in the areas of literacy, gender studies, literary criticism, popular culture, and teacher education.

Barbara J. Moon is a doctoral student in curriculum at Simon Fraser University, Burnaby, B.C. She teaches undergraduate Biology and Science Education. Her research interests include secondary and post-secondary science education, gender issues in science, sociology of research, and cultural criticism.

Susan Robertson teaches and researches in the areas of educational politics, sociology and policy formation at the University of Auckland, New Zealand. Her particular areas of interest are teachers' work, labour process theory, policy formation and the State, and globalization. She has written and published in these areas in a range of edited collections and journals, including *Discourse, Education Links, Urban Education, Our Schools Ourselves* and the *Australian Journal of Public Administration*. Her book on the changing nature of teachers' work will be released shortly.

Ciaran Sugrue is a Lecturer in Education at St. Patrick's College, Dublin (a college of Dublin City University) where he teaches courses on Teaching and Curriculum to undergraduate student teachers and on qualitative Research Methodology and schools as organizations to post-graduate students. He is a former primary teacher who has worked in the primary schools' inspectorate also. He holds a MA in Philosophy from University College Dublin, a M. Ed from Trinity College Dublin and he completed his doctoral studies at the Ontario Institute for Studies in Education (OISE). He is involved in a number of European Union funded research projects and is particularly interested in issues of change and educational leadership. Other interests include initial teacher education, life long learning for teachers, induction, teacher thinking, school cultures, teacher biography and life history, and teacher education reform in developing countries. He has published articles on many of these issues and his forthcoming book with Falmer Press argues for a more inclusive reconstructed vision of child-centred teaching which is grounded in the multiple realities of classroom life.

Joan E. Talbert is Co-Director of the Center for Research on the Context of Teaching (CRC) at Stanford University. Her current research investigates teachers' professional communities as contexts of teaching and educational reform. She has published articles on teachers' career patterns, school organization, and secondary school teacher communities. Her recent publications include: *Teaching for Understanding: Challenges to Practice, Research, and Policy* (with David K. Cohen and Milbrey W. McLaughlin; Jossey-Bass, 1993).

Sandra Weber is an Associate Professor in the Department of Education at Concordia University, Montreal. She has many publications in the areas of second language teaching, the education professoriate, and teacher education. More recently, her work has focused on the popular culture of childhood and teacher identity.

Marvin F. Wideen is a Professor in the Faculty of Education at Simon Fraser University where he works in the Institute for Studies in Teacher Education. Prior to his becoming involved in teacher education, he worked both as a teacher and as a principal in public schools. He writes and conducts research in the areas of teacher education, science education and school improvement. His recent works include *Staff Development for School Improvement, Becoming a Teacher* and *The Struggle for Change.*

Index